Branson: Behind the Mask

Tom Bower is an investigative historian, broadcaster and journalist. A former producer and reporter for BBC Television, he
is the author of twenty books, including biographies of Robert
Maxwell, Mohamed Fayed, Gordon Brown and Conrad Black.
Broken Dreams, his investigation into corruption in English
football, won the William Hill Sports Book of the Year Award in
2003, and his two most recent biographies – of Bernie Ecclestone
and of Simon Cowell – were *Sunday Times* bestsellers. He lives
in London.

Branson: Behind the Mask

TOM BOWER

FABER & FABER

First published in 2014
by Faber and Faber Ltd
Bloomsbury House
74–77 Great Russell Street
London WC1B 3DA
This export paperback edition first published in 2014

Typeset by Ian Bahrami
Printed in England by CPI Group (UK) Ltd, Croydon CRO 4YY

The right of Tom Bower to be identified as author of this work
has been asserted in accordance with Section 77 of the Copyright,
Designs and Patents Act 1988

A CIP record for this book
is available from the British Library

ISBN 978-0-571-29710-8

FSC
www.fsc.org
MIX
Paper from
responsible sources
FSC® C101712

2 4 6 8 10 9 7 5 3 1

To Sophie

Contents

Plates

Branson with Governor Bill Richardson of New Mexico at Spaceport America, the base for Virgin Galactic, in 2010. © *Bloomberg via Getty Images*

Branson with key allies in America: Bill Clinton and Al Gore, in 2006, and Arnold Schwarzenegger, then governor of California, in 2009. © *Getty Images*

Branson bids for American stardom in the Fox TV series *The Rebel Billionaire: Branson's Quest for the Best.* © *WireImage for Fox Television Network*

Branson's battle to protect Virgin's privileges by preventing collaboration between British Airways and American Airlines in 2008. © *Anthony Devlin/PA Archive/Press Association Images*

Virgin's financial crisis in 2000 was overcome after the company embraced Tom Alexander's idea to launch low-cost mobile phones. © *REX/Stuart Clarke*

Branson's success depended on his close relationships with politicians, not least Tony Blair. © *Mirrorpix*

Branson with Jayne-Anne Gadhia, Virgin Money's chief executive. © *Mirrorpix*

The launch of Virgin Blue in Australia. © *David Gray/Reuters/ Corbis*

Branson with Gordon Brown in 2007 at the launch of a train powered by biodiesel. © *Toby Melville/Reuters/Corbis*

American billionaire Vinod Khosla, whose ideology that businessmen could justifiably profit from ventures favourable to the environment attracted Branson to the 'green' cause.
© *Bloomberg via Getty Images*

Branson with Brawn's winning Formula One team, which he sponsored in 2009. © *Getty Images*

Virgin's longstanding feud with BA: in 1991, Virgin staff re-dress BA's iconic Concorde in Virgin livery, while Branson poses gleefully in the foreground. © *Mirrorpix*

BA chairman Lord King. © *Mirrorpix*

In 2006, Virgin executives admitted involvement in an illegal cartel with BA. Iain Burns and three other BA executives stood trial for price fixing. © *Dominic Lipinski/PA Archive/Press Association Images*

Branson promotes Virgin Media with Olympic sprint champion Usain Bolt. © *REX/Tom Oldham*

Virgin's attempts to profit from privatised NHS services generated protests in 2012. © *Demotix/Press Association Images*

Introduction

The British love chancers. Tilting on the edge, they entertain the public by breaking rules, escaping blame and feeding gossip. Rich or poor, these rare personalities fascinate and excite. Few are more popular in Britain than Richard Branson. Celebrated as the nation's most successful buccaneer, Branson once attracted more Twitter followers than President Obama, and nearly as many fans as David Beckham. Over the past forty-five years, his colourful exploits have earned him adoration as an English rebel entitled to his wealth. He is a self-made and self-deprecating man whose flamboyance endears him to aspiring tycoons, who snap up his books and flock to his lectures to glean the secrets of fortune-hunting. He is an entrepreneur idolised and lauded as a hero by ambitious young men and women.

For others, Richard Branson is a scoundrel, a card player with a weak hand who plays to strength. Those who come off second best scorn the showman as a one-dimensional poseur who manipulates Virgin's image through a wily media machine. For them, the mystery surrounding Branson's businesses and wealth has grown over the past decade, but their criticisms remain ill defined. Branson's contradictions are glaring but confused by a smokescreen.

Just how a school drop-out became a billionaire has become the stuff of legend, repeatedly recounted by Branson but more accurately described by others. His self-portrayal as the defiant tycoon risking danger has generated endless free publicity. His reward is global celebrity.

Inspiration, persistence and shrewdness have contributed to creating the Virgin empire. Plus, by Branson's own admission, breaking the rules. 'If I want to do something worthwhile,' he wrote recently, 'or even just for fun, I won't let silly rules stop me.' Without adequate shame, he has described cheating in his school exams, committing a tax fraud and lying to the police. Less publicised is his attitude towards maximising his wealth.

'As far as I am concerned,' wrote the exhibitionist, '[I] would do anything, however outlandish, that generates media coverage and reinforces my image as a risk taker who challenges the government.' Sex, he continued, was one way 'to promote Virgin's image'. Over the years, Branson has never complained if he is painted as a philanderer. He has even publicly speculated about his son losing his virginity to a well-known singer. In his breathless quest for publicity, he has recycled unprovable stories, including the assertion that a senior French politician asked for a bribe of £1 million in exchange for permission to open the Virgin Megastore on the Champs-Élysées on Sundays. Branson's colourful memories are rarely challenged. Over the decades, the cheers have grown and the doubts have subsided. The mystery is whether his business is still worth billions of pounds; the controversy is whether he deserves accolades for being Britain's most successful businessman.

Around 2011, the then sixty-one-year-old reached a crossroads. At the climax of a 'seven-year journey', he renounced raw capitalism. Branson had converted to green politics tinged with populist socialism. Virgin, he said, was set to undertake 'a sea change on a journey to transform itself into a force for good for people and the planet'. Some speculated that Branson had experienced a hormonal change, while others assumed he was plucking at another opportunity, but insiders recognised that Virgin required rebranding.

'My message', he wrote, 'is a simple one: business as usual

isn't working. In fact it's "business as usual" that's wrecking our planet. We must change the way we do business.' Capitalism, Branson believed, had 'lost its way a bit. The short-term focus on profit has driven most businesses to forget about the long-term role they have in taking care of people and the planet.' His transformation into the caring people's champion of the environment and its population was not pure altruism. Green, the billionaire realised, was a money-making opportunity. To recapture Virgin's appeal, he was reinventing his corporation as a benevolent profiteer blessed with a social conscience.

The 2008 economic crash had damaged Virgin. Although outsiders regarded the empire, ranging over trains, health and finance, as resplendent, his airlines had suffered a financial crisis. The sum of his disparate investments no longer added up to the billions certified by the rich lists published in the *Sunday Times* and *Forbes*. In his secretive world, the financial reality had been concealed. Among his problems was the brand's fading appeal to the youth market. Virgin's attraction was increasingly confined to an ageing generation sceptical of new ideas. In the inevitable momentum – either becoming bigger and more visionary, or smaller and parochial – Virgin no longer offered innovation. Branson presented his personal dilemma as a social and environmental crisis that challenged all financial and political leaders. 'While business has been a great vehicle for growth in the world,' he wrote, 'neither Virgin nor many other businesses have been doing anywhere near enough to stop the downward spiral we all find ourselves in.'

The tycoon offered a solution, summarising his new philosophy in a book, *Screw Business as Usual*, published in 2011. He challenged those who weren't afraid to follow the title's standpoint to show they meant it. His message to corporations was subversive: 'Profit is no longer the only driving force.' Instead, he argued, corporations should be doing good for 'humanity and the environment . . . Business needs a heart. In the past, business has been all about making money, which is fine, but it hasn't been about being a responsible citizen.'

His criticism of profits was matched by a condemnation of environmental vandalism: 'Resources are being used up: the air, the sea, the land – are all heavily polluted. The poor are getting poorer. Many are dying of starvation or because they can't afford a dollar a day for life-saving medication. We have to fix it – and fast.' Even disbelievers, he said, 'admit that people everywhere are mucking up things'.

His best-selling book, a catalogue of Virgin's good deeds and famous names, placed Branson on a pedestal: 'We must change the way we do business. Do good – and the rewards will come.' Part of the cure, he wrote, was to eliminate a 'false dilemma' from business talk. 'It is becoming more and more clear that there is no incompatibility between doing business in an ethical and transparent manner and achieving good financial results.'

His appeal for transparency was written on Necker, his sun-kissed Caribbean island, which he bought for £180,000 in 1978 and which he was to use as his tax haven. Throughout his career, Branson has sought to avoid taxes: first illegally in a purchase-tax fraud, and later legitimately by carefully structured corporate pyramids, which ultimately led to his permanent move to the Virgin Islands as a tax exile from Britain after 2006.

In the opening pages of his book, Branson anticipated the day when 'No governments or businesses will be able to hide behind secrecy and jargon any longer.' Indeed, he urged his readers to appreciate the transparency of his own conduct. In his relations with business and the public, he wrote, 'If you're open and honest with them and if they know there are no secrets, then they trust the brand.'

His advocacy of ethical transparency is shared by campaigners for a fairer world. His obedience to his own sermon can be judged by the ownership of his flagship airline, which runs through eleven companies. Virgin Atlantic Airways (GB) is owned by Virgin Travel Group (GB), which in turn is owned by Virgin Atlantic (GB), which is owned by Bluebottle Investments (UK) Ltd (GB), which is owned by Bluebottle UK Ltd (GB), which is owned by Virgin Holdings Ltd (GB), which is owned by Classboss Ltd (GB), which is owned by Virgin Wings Ltd (GB), which is owned by Bluebottle USA Mobile Inc. (BVI), which is owned by Virgin Group Investments Ltd (BVI), which is finally owned by Virgin Group Holdings Ltd (BVI).

Virgin Group Holdings Ltd, incorporated in the British Virgin Islands, is owned by trusts whose principal beneficiary is Branson and his family. But to prevent any tax charge ever arising against the Bransons, the legal documents make it absolutely clear that trustees and not the Branson family actually control Virgin Group Holdings. As usual in tax havens, the identity of all the trustees is not disclosed.

Running a business from Necker is much easier now than when Branson bought the deserted island. Keeping in touch by telephone, email, Skype and video-conferencing while gazing across a blue ocean is the dream of many people. No one should begrudge Branson the foresight to make a dream come true. But the reason his airline is owned by eleven successive companies, ending in the British Virgin Islands, is not so its owner can enjoy the sunshine. Rather it is to avoid scrutiny and taxes. Or, more bluntly, to achieve the opposite of the transparency that Branson advocates.

Among Virgin's strengths, Branson wrote, is that it 'stands for something beyond making money'. Virgin, he believes, is 'about making a difference in the world', which has been elevated by capturing 'a new level of responsibility'.

The agency for dispensing wisdom and money is Virgin Unite, Branson's charity for transforming the planet. 'Our vision', he wrote, 'is a world where business is a force for good, helping people to thrive in balance with our planet. Our mission is to be a leading catalyst and an incubator for innovative Global Leadership Initiatives.' Every year, the billionaire's charity donates at least £1.5 million in cash to chosen causes.

For the majority, Branson's generosity confirms his heroic status. They are attracted by his fame and undoubted achievements. They do not distinguish celebrity from greatness. The riddle appears contrived. The challenge is to discover the truth behind the mask.

1

Blow-out

The explosion was deafening. Without warning, a thunderous blast flashed across the parched scrub. Over forty engineers, seeking protection behind a chain-link fence, fell like matchsticks on to the dirt. Swirling dust blocked out the Californian sunshine. As the sand drifted away, the silence of the Mojave desert was broken by screams and the grating sound of a hiss. The temperature at 2.34 p.m. on 26 July 2007 was over 100 Fahrenheit – dangerously high, even for an uncomplicated test.

Confused and shocked, Al Cebriain, a mechanical engineer, struggled to stand up, but collapsed back on to the ground. Seventy feet from the detonation, he looked across the scrub at a deep crater where seconds earlier a six-foot metal tank containing compressed nitrous oxide had rested on a concrete block. Shifting his gaze from the debris, he spotted that a jagged hole had been ripped across a steel shipping container and the chain-link fence was bent. Near by was the cause of the persistent hiss: gas was escaping from a toppled cylinder.

Cebriain could see shredded clothing, baseball caps, bandannas and men's glasses, all covered by splinters of metal and concrete carried by the blast. Above that flotsam was a ghastly sight. Arms and legs lay like garbage on tufts of brown grass. The screams of fellow rocket engineers injured by the blast ripped through the dry heat.

There had been no warning. Just minutes earlier, Luke Colby's familiar voice on the loudspeakers had issued the last command from the safety of a control vehicle parked a hundred yards away. Those inside the truck were monitoring the experiment through cameras located around the test site. All the images were being recorded. Most members of the team had preferred to watch the experiment 'live', sitting cross-legged on the sand behind the chain-link fence. They had done so many times, and no one had ever voiced concern for their safety. An engineer had said, 'OK.' But when the gas was released through a valve designed for the rocket engine, the explosion was instant.

Al Cebriain staggered towards the twisted fence. Two colleagues were obviously dead. One was dying. His head was being cradled by a friend staring tearfully at the limbless torso. All three had been sitting in front of the fence, much closer to the test than anyone expected. Later, insiders would acknowledge that the three, intimately involved in the use of nitrous oxide to power the rocket, had darted at the last moment around the fence to get a closer view. Shards of metal from the exploding tanks had ripped through their bodies.

The deaths occurred at an unusual airport. Located on a soundless plateau over 4,000 feet above sea level, the 2.3-mile runway across the Mojave desert is both a parking lot for abandoned jumbo jets, the graveyard of reputations and fortunes, and the home of ambitious private corporations building spaceships, rockets and equipment for futuristic travel. The remoteness added secrecy to the location's advantages. Clustered along the runway's apron, the occupants of the hangars appeared eerily immune to the tragedy unfolding about a mile away. The only visible movement came from the 5,000 wind turbines along the Tehachapi Pass overlooking the airport.

Ten minutes after the explosion, the local sheriff arrived. The medics followed. After making sure that the injured were dispatched to hospital and the corpses and limbs sent to a mortuary in Bakersfield, the sheriff ordered the survivors to move away while he spun tape around a wide area to prevent anyone meddling with a potential crime scene.

News of the catastrophe sparked bewilderment. Insiders knew that the engineers employed by Scaled Composites were pumping nitrous oxide gas through the valve which would be used to propel Virgin Galactic's rocket into space. Until then, progress on Richard Branson's expensive investment appeared to be unproblematic. The 'cold-flow' test had been executed safely many times. No one could explain the cause of the fatal explosion.

Some engineers, however, were not completely surprised. 'Nitrous oxide can be dangerous,' they had warned their colleagues. 'It's cheap, but you've got to be careful with this stuff.' The warning was ignored by Glenn May, one of Scaled's experts, who had just returned from extended leave. May treated nitrous oxide as a harmless plaything, even propelling his bicycle around Mojave using a rocket fuelled with the gas. 'He's comfortable with nitrous oxide,' thought an engineer, dispassionately. During the countdown to the disaster, May had enjoyed the carnival atmosphere around the fence and encouraged his two colleagues to join him and get a closer view. Now, a pathologist was assembling his body parts for examination, and an undertaker had been summoned to deliver three coffins.

Burt Rutan, the Scaled director responsible for developing Virgin Galactic's rocket, was attending a conference in Palm Springs. 'I didn't know that nitrous oxide was that dangerous,' he later said. Taking risks, he added, was normal for pioneers. His British partner was less sanguine. 'It's not considered a hazardous material,' said Richard Branson in a measured statement. 'We just don't know why the explosion occurred.' The owner of 50 per cent of Virgin Galactic did not mention his prediction three years earlier that the rocket would blast into space with six passengers during 2007 itself.

Ever since Branson had bought into the space business in 2004, he had used the rocket to promote the Virgin brand. 'My gut feeling', he explained, 'was that we would get millions and millions of dollars of [free] publicity around the world by being the first people to take tourists into space.' For three years, Branson had been touting $200,000 tickets to the super-rich eager to experience four minutes of weightlessness and a glimpse of the globe before tilting back towards Earth. Virgin's ride into space had glorified the corporation's image. The explosion could endanger the brand, the foundation of Branson's fortunes.

The tycoon depended on his publicists to contradict the cynics. Through a well-tuned network of sympathisers employed by the media, his loyalists smothered those questioning the use of nitrous oxide and defused any doubts about the rocket's safety. The summary of perfunctory media reports delivered the following morning to Necker confirmed their success. No doubts were cast on Virgin's ability to eventually succeed in its ambition to send tourists into space. There was an unfortunate contrast between the pristine sand on his Caribbean island and the desert scrub in Mojave after the explosion, but trust in Branson meant that even the bereaved families uttered no criticism of their employer.

After the explosion, at 5 p.m. Randy Chase arrived at the site to investigate the cause of the incident. Born in 1953 and raised on a small farm, Chase was employed by California's Occupational Safety and Health Administration (OSHA). His task was to decide whether the deaths were caused by accident or possibly criminal negligence. If Chase suspected any misconduct, two reputations – Burt Rutan's and Richard Branson's – might suffer and Virgin Galactic's fate would be jeopardised.

Barred from entering the site by the local sheriff's tape, Chase viewed the devastation in the fading light. Live images had been transmitted from the remote cameras guided by agents employed by Hazmat, the agency responsible for detecting chemical hazards. 'God knows what happened,' he said. He had studied industrial safety at a local college, and thereafter had investigated accidents in mines, factories and oil wells. He knew nothing about 'cold-flow' tests of nitrous oxide through valves. 'No one's to touch anything on the scene until I get back,' he ordered. He would drive through the night back to his home and collect his clothes, ready for what he anticipated would be a long inquiry into 'a high-profile accident'.

In the morning, Chase returned to Mojave. His orders, he discovered, had been disobeyed, and the control truck had been moved from the site. 'We needed to protect the computer hard drive,' he was told. Chase unquestioningly accepted the explanation, unaware that the engineers' visible shock masked fears about the rocket's safety.

For the first time, Chase inspected the area. The isolation was eerie. The hot sun intensified the silence across the scrub. 'There are no blood stains in front of the fence,' he noted. 'All the deaths happened behind the fence.'

None of the engineers corrected Chase's inexplicable error. Chase knew that the explosion had been recorded on video by Scaled and also on eyewitnesses' mobile telephones. But he was unaware of one particular clip showing Glenn May darting in front of the fence with two other engineers just before the explosion. He saw only two videos showing the three men walking towards a gap in the fence but no further. He would be emphatic that any eyewitness who saw the three in front of the fence 'is wrong'.

The approach of the engineers had been to volunteer their co-operation and play on his ignorance. Drinking coffee in the Voyager, the cosy diner underneath Mojave airport's control tower next to the runway, Chase became relaxed among his new friends. The diner's walls were covered with photographs of

Burt Rutan celebrating his triumph in 2004 as the winner of the Ansari X Prize, a competition aimed at encouraging commercial flights into space. The ruddy-faced designer with mutton-chop sideburns had sent one man into space in a cheap rocket, boasting afterwards that 'this rocket is safer than conventional rockets'. While Chase could not be immune to the pioneer's distress over the tragedy, he was at the same time impressed by Rutan's self-confidence. The eccentric designer, living in a half-buried pyramid sticking out of the sand near the airfield, commanded respect among the small community.

Earning profits from space is a big risk. Fortune-hunters would do better drilling for oil, because those gambling on space need to be more stubborn, more creative and more charismatic than other ego-tripping adventurers, if only to attract investors. Ever since the end of the Apollo missions to the moon and the shuttle disasters, space had lost its shine. NASA, the American space agency, generated disillusion and was criticised for being bloated and dishonest. Washington had slashed the agency's funding, especially the budget of the orbiting International Space Station. Each trip to the station by the space shuttle, with seven astronauts aboard, cost about $1 billion. To save money, NASA had paid the Russian government to deliver payloads and astronauts. Now, in a bid to reduce costs permanently, American entrepreneurs were being encouraged to develop cheap rockets to place satellites in orbit for experiments in a gravity-free environment and to deliver payloads and people to the space station. Their profits depended on building a reusable rocket or capsule so that space travel would resemble journeys by conventional aircraft. By adapting proven technology, rockets in the future would repeatedly take off, fly and land back on a runway.

Richard Branson had been following Rutan's progress ever since he had registered Virgin Galactic as a proprietary name in July 2002 – 'several years before I met Rutan', he would say.

The idea had been sown by someone mentioning that 90,000 people had signed up to Pan Am's First Moon Flights Club during the 1960s. The members included Ronald Reagan and Barry Goldwater. For the world's master of publicity, the potential of Virgin Galactic became incalculable.

The idea had been born in 1998. Chatting in a bar in Marrakech with Steve Fossett, his competitor in a round-the-world balloon race, Branson had heard about Rutan's project to launch rockets from an old B-52 bomber. Two years later, Will Whitehorn, Virgin's media-relations supremo, visited Rutan's factory in Mojave and saw SpaceShipOne under construction. The cost – about $26 million – had been financed by Paul Allen, the co-founder of Microsoft. The two men hoped to land the $10 million Ansari X Prize, which would be won by the first team to launch a manned spacecraft twice in two weeks using the same engine and sending it into space 100 kilometres from the Earth before returning.

Whitehorn monitored Rutan's progress. Two tests had been dangerous but successful, and by summer 2004 Whitehorn was sure that Rutan would win the prize. On 21 June, SpaceShipOne had completed an unpublicised piloted flight into space, landing back at Mojave airport. Rutan's first publicised launch was due to take place on 29 September. The cost to buy into his venture, Branson was assured, was low, and considering that in 1986 Rutan had designed the first propeller plane to fly non-stop around the globe, the chances that Branson might be picking a winner were high. The clincher was the name. Virgin Galactic would give him the ultimate marketing image to reinvigorate his brand globally.

On the day, WhiteKnight, a specially built twin-fuselage plane, moved slowly towards the runway. Attached under the fuselage was SpaceShipOne, the manned rocket. Strapped inside was Mike Melvill, the pilot. Just before take-off, a casket was placed alongside Melvill in the cockpit. Inside were the cremated remains of Rutan's mother, who had died four years earlier. WhiteKnight took off and over the next hour climbed to 50,000 feet. Then, SpaceShipOne was dropped into the atmosphere and within seconds was soaring like a corkscrew at three times the speed of sound towards space. Spectators monitoring the flight at Edwards Air Force Base in the Mojave desert gasped as Melvill rolled twenty-nine times before crossing the winning tape sixty-two miles above Earth. After three minutes of weightlessness, he began the glide back to California. All the steering and other functions were performed manually without computers and, because of the low speed, there was no need for any heat-deflecting re-entry technology. Rutan had achieved a remarkable success. The second flight was due within ten days. Branson made the telephone call.

Branson's audacity in business is to bid low in order to try to tilt the deal in his favour from the outset: firstly, because he wants a bargain; and secondly, because he has considerably less money than wealth-watchers assume. His sales patter is consistent: 'We're risking Virgin's invaluable name, and you're getting all the upside.' In 2004, he balanced Rutan and Allen's money and skills against his commitment of the Virgin brand. However, Branson added that if SpaceShipOne returned safely, he would make a serious financial investment to accelerate Rutan's ambitions. In exchange for adding the Virgin Galactic brand name to SpaceShipOne, he offered $1 million to Scaled Composites, Rutan's company. Both Rutan and Allen embraced Branson as a valued partner.

With the deal agreed, on 4 October Branson was standing in front of dozens of cameras in the Mojave desert to watch the launch of Virgin Galactic's SpaceShipOne. He had arrived amid media reports that the intention was for the spacecraft to carry the first tourists into space in 2007. Branson's declaration to the cameras generated euphoria among enthusiasts. Until then, the only journey for tourists to the International Space Station 250 miles above the Earth cost over $20 million aboard a Russian Soyuz rocket. 'We'll be the first in space,' Branson told the crowd.

Standing next to him was Burt Rutan, a remarkable aerospace designer recognised internationally for his achievements. As an adventurer he had much in common with Branson. Dressed in a leather jacket, the sixty-year-old saw himself as a modern version of the Wright brothers. Politically, he and Branson were not soulmates. Rutan was a fierce conservative who derided global warming, opposed liberal causes and loathed political correctness. He did, however, share with Branson a contempt for bureaucratic paper-pushers, who in the context of this operation were the US government's regulators. Success, he hoped, would silence the naysayers. 'We proved it can be done by a small company operating with limited resources and a few dozen dedicated employees,' he pronounced proudly to over fifty journalists. Branson applauded that sentiment and stared like a thrilled schoolboy as WhiteKnight roared down the desert runway and took off, with SpaceShipOne glistening underneath.

As before, SpaceShipOne was dropped from the aircraft at 50,000 feet and, after firing its rocket, soared seconds later past the winning post 69.7 miles above Earth. After two minutes in space, the craft tilted and glided back towards the Mojave. Rutan and Virgin Galactic had won the prize. Media attention was Branson's oxygen, but on this occasion his publicists did not need to contrive any excitement. A genuine frenzy swept through the crowds. They loved Branson's promise of space tourism for everyone within three years. Although Virgin's 'space travel' was a trip that lasted less than five minutes outside the Earth's atmosphere – 'a high-altitude bungee jump', the critics carped – the joyful crowd embraced the company's spectacular achievement. Their cheers were interrupted by a call from the president.

Squeezing into an office with Rutan and Paul Allen, Branson listened to George W. Bush's congratulations over a telephone loudspeaker.

The success of that day in 2004 more than satisfied Branson's requirements. For some years, he had been trying to shift the focus of Virgin's expansion from Britain to America. So far, a commercial breakthrough there had eluded him. Triumph depended on boosting his own and Virgin's image. To be effective, he needed to occupy his favourite place – the spotlight. Staging stunts for free publicity had been Branson's prime weapon over the previous thirty years, and had produced profitable results in Britain. By contrast, his flamboyant feats in America had barely registered with the media and the public. In the past, he had entered New York's Times Square on top of a tank to promote Virgin Cola, and had dangled from a crane apparently in the nude with a cell phone strategically placed to boost the marketing theme that Virgin Mobile's charges were transparent with 'nothing to hide'. On that occasion, the small crowd had failed to notice that Branson was wearing a skin-coloured bodysuit. His gimmicks had produced a scattering of photographs in obscure newspapers. Smudged images were no substitute for a sustained advertising campaign, but the finances of the billionaire had deteriorated after the 9/11 attacks. Unable to afford a multimillion-dollar advertising budget, Virgin Atlantic struggled. Virgin Galactic, Branson hoped, would change everything.

Virgin's publicists instinctively presented Virgin Galactic as the underdog and a poke in the eye for NASA. Their script was quickly abandoned. NASA, Branson realised, would be the source of future contracts. This was no time to be making new enemies, especially as his $1 million investment had produced an unexpected bonus. Within days of the launch, SpaceShipOne received an official blessing. The prestigious Smithsonian Museum in Washington had agreed to exhibit the rocket in its permanent collection of milestones in aviation history. Daily, thousands of visitors would gaze at the craft's gleaming shell with the iconic logo – 'Virgin Galactic' – emblazoned on the tail fin. The catalogue entry was priceless: 'Private enterprise crossed the threshold into human spaceflight, previously the domain of government programs.' For just $1 million, Virgin was set to become firmly established in America. Virgin Galactic would be developed by The Spaceship Company, jointly owned by Virgin and Rutan's Scaled Composites. Under contract to The Spaceship Company, Scaled would develop the motor and obtain the safety licence from the Federal Aviation Administration (FAA) allowing them to carry tourists into space. Reassuringly, Northrop Grumman, the aerospace giant, would soon after buy a 40 per cent stake in Scaled.

Four days after the Mojave triumph, Branson embellished his success. Seven thousand people, he said during a newspaper interview, had already registered to make a paid flight in 2007. 'A tremendous take-up,' said Branson, mentioning that Virgin Galactic would carry at least 50,000 people over ten years. Those who paid the full fare immediately, he added, would be at the front of the queue of the 500 passengers who would fly in the first year. 'We are extremely pleased because it just means that the gamble we took seems to have paid off.' His commitment to spend $110 million, he continued, would earn $100 million from passengers in the first year.

Rutan was unfazed by his partner's certainty. The designer uttered optimistic assurances about the problem-free process of scaling up the spaceship and its engine. There were no doubts about converting his crude two-man rocket into a sleek craft capable of carrying two pilots and six passengers up into space in a non-orbital flight, meaning that after a few minutes they would be heading straight back to Earth. Branson might have asked questions, but he was driven by marketing rather than engineering. His comprehension of the problems was best assessed by the appointment of Will Whitehorn, Virgin's media specialist, as the rocket supremo. Whitehorn's lack of engineering qualifications was concealed by his thrill at having found a Virgin winner – an aspiration held by all Branson's outriders.

Branson's own enthusiasm was shared by Stu Witt, the chief executive of Mojave airport. Surrounded on one wall of his office by the memorabilia of twenty years' service as a US Navy fighter pilot and at the opposite end by elk skins collected from afternoon hunting trips in north California's mountains, the former Top Gun welcomed Branson for bringing glamour and money to the shabby desert outpost. 'He's a neat guy,' Witt told everyone in the Voyager diner. Branson had reignited the executive's ambition to transform Mojave into the Silicon Valley of the space business.

Witt's military charm flattered the billionaire. Joining Rutan's exploratory venture, he told Branson, could be compared to the pioneering voyages of Christopher Columbus and Ferdinand Magellan. 'State-sponsored exploration is over,' Witt told Branson. 'It's back to low-cost private enterprise.' Witt's enticing imagery predicted that millionaires would commute by helicopter from Beverly Hills to Mojave and, one hour after leaving their mansions, would be blasting off into space for a day trip to the Middle East or Australia. 'You're a pioneer,' Witt had told his visitor. 'Planes are the safest travel ever. Now make space the same.'

Witt may not have warned Branson sufficiently that Rutan's plan to scale SpaceShipOne up to SpaceShipTwo was risky. 'It's like going in one step from a Kitty Hawk to a DC3,' Witt would later say. At the time, no one told Branson that Rutan knew how to expand his spaceship but seemed to know little about the technology involved in developing a bigger reusable rocket motor. By his own admission, Branson struggled to understand a corporate balance sheet, so engineering technology was a challenge. Usually, he relied on others to worry about the detail.

Delegation was his management style, but in reality his lack of expertise allowed no alternative. Outsiders had the impression that his unique ability was to perceive advantages invisible to others. In the past, that instinct had rewarded him with great wealth, but on this occasion he appears to have failed to understand the fundamental principle of designing a rocket: the motor must be perfected before building the spaceship. By nature, Branson prided himself on breaking conventions and doing the opposite. 'The rich think they'll be successful with everything they touch,' Witt would tell friends. 'Their planning is essential, but their plans are worthless. Pushing at the frontiers is their forte, but they're working in a hostile atmosphere.'

Branson was uneducated about science. In search of a PR coup, he wanted to believe Rutan's assurances that expanding SpaceShipOne would be achievable. Since Scaled was an accomplished aircraft company, he assumed that building a bigger rocket motor would be no different than swapping the engine in a Boeing 747. Branson did not appreciate the consequence of his innocence as he embarked on his final attempt to become a major player in America.

2

Rebel Billionaire

Expanding Virgin's operations into America had been Richard Branson's plan ever since he had rescued his business from the financial difficulties that began in 1999, and which were compounded in the aftermath of the 2001 terrorist attacks on America. Starved of cash, he had survived by selling a house in London, a hotel in Majorca, shares in an Oxfordshire restaurant and nearly half of Virgin Atlantic. To break out of the straitjacket, he needed to expand. Australia was one target, but success on the other side of the Atlantic was his dream.

Naturally, he chose not to highlight those problems when he met a group of journalists for breakfast in Los Angeles in October 2002. To relaunch himself and Virgin, he wanted positive profiles describing his genius. Size mattered in America, and in anticipation of the meeting, his publicists had briefed each journalist that the 'Virgin Group comprises 350 companies with an annual revenue of $8.1 billion'. What appeared to be a repeated exaggeration was never challenged. No journalist who was minded to doubt the publicists' hyperbole would be allowed near their employer. 'Richard Branson', the publicists continued, 'is head of the privately held Virgin Group, which oversees a vast empire which includes Virgin Mobile, Virgin Atlantic, Virgin Blue, Virgin Express, Virgin Megastores, V2, Virgin and Radio Free Virgin.' Not mentioned was the fact that seven out of those eight companies were at the time losing money, and three were on the verge of closure. And beyond those eight, Virgin did not have complete ownership of any profitable major trading company.

Branson's supreme confidence was built on his conviction that his ambitions would always become reality. During the breakfast, he regaled his guests with his plans to expand Virgin's empire across America – on land, in the air and on the internet. In particular, he described his plan to launch Virgin America, a cut-price airline based in California. The journalists appeared to be impressed, but the publicity after the meeting barely justified the effort. In his attempt to attract attention among serious American players, he had made no further progress than his disclosure six months earlier to another group of journalists that he intended to raise £2 billion ($2.9 billion) by selling or floating Virgin Blue, Virgin Mobile, Virgin Entertainment, Virgin Atlantic, Thetrainline.com, Virgin Active, Virgin Rail and Virgin Money over the next eight years. The only objective conclusion was that Branson needed cash.

Two years later, in 2004, his finances had been restored by Virgin Mobile's success, but progress in America had stalled. Buying into Virgin Galactic was one solution, although it did not satisfy his appetite for instant fame.

Ever since he prematurely left Stowe, a private boarding school, in 1967 aged seventeen to produce a magazine called *Student* from a London basement, Branson had sought recognition. Even as a wayward teenager, his gift was to attract talented people to join his easy 'family' lifestyle and develop ideas. 'He plucks what he wants out of you,' disclosed Eve Branson, his influential mother, about her protégé's star quality. Unlike his friends raging against the Vietnam war, Branson was a putative trader in search of ideas that would earn him money. One friend suggested selling records, and another mentioned a recording studio. Although he knew nothing about music, Branson snapped up his pal John Varnom's suggestion to call the new business Virgin Records. The first record which, fearing failure, he reluctantly supported was Mike Oldfield's

Tubular Bells. The album's phenomenal success made Branson a millionaire at twenty-three. Skilfully, he had retained all the rights, leaving Oldfield with a comparative pittance. Flush with money deposited in the Channel Islands, he banked on outrage to expand his business aggressively. Notoriously, he promoted himself by gambling on the Sex Pistols, an anarchic punk band, and Boy George, before expanding into property and clubs. Along the way, many erstwhile friends became outraged at his reluctance to meet their expectations of a proper reward and his readiness to use the courts to enforce his wishes. 'You don't have to be a complete shit to be a success,' he said. His growing number of enemies were not convinced. They noticed that by the late 1970s, the rebellious youth had been transformed into a rebel tycoon with a mercenary attitude towards keeping the 'family' fortune for himself and a hardening disposition towards his partners.

That trait burst into public after he accepted a proposition in 1984 from Randolph Fields, an American lawyer, to launch Virgin Atlantic, an airline catering to the hip and the hot. To succeed, Branson campaigned against BA, characterising the airline as an old-fashioned monopoly and caricaturing Lord King, the airline's chairman, as a blimpish toff. King had lost the bitter battle, and Branson, already famous for daredevil stunts in speedboats, was hailed as a public hero. In 1992, he became one of Britain's richest businessmen by selling Virgin Music to EMI for a record £560 million – a sale that was directed through the Channel Islands to avoid £84 million in taxes. To his associates' fury, he shared the windfall with only two friends, creating yet more enemies among those who felt betrayed after working for nineteen years to build up the company. To placate them, Branson pleaded that he personally had received no money, but in his subsequent autobiography he wrote: 'For the first time in my life I had enough money to fulfil my wildest dreams.'

With his financial credibility enhanced, Branson searched frenetically for new ventures, becoming an accomplished deal-maker and a global celebrity. In America, his entrepreneurship was hailed in Congress and the White House. He boosted his fame by taking more risks in round-the-world balloon trips. His celebrity flourished until 1998, when the public became outraged by the shocking service on Virgin Trains. His famous publicity machine failed to suffocate the criticism. The halo had slipped, and some City players spoke fearfully about associating with Branson. As his businesses languished, his reputation began to slide. He needed money to survive, but his opportunities in Britain appeared to be exhausted. America was his best chance. The possibility of featuring in an American reality-TV show to promote himself would, he hoped, be the beginning of a rebirth.

For years, Branson had snapped up offers to make cameo appearances in TV series such as *Friends* and *Baywatch*. In 2004, he planned fleeting appearances in Hollywood films including *Superman* and *Casino Royale*. The publicity excited curiosity but not the same wild excitement as Donald Trump, the then fifty-eight-year-old New York property developer, was generating on television.

Prior to 2004, Trump had played himself in eighteen different movies and sitcoms. He had featured on endless magazine front covers, authored five best-selling books – including, most recently, *Trump: How to Get Rich* – and anointed several sky-scrapers 'Trump Towers'. In 2004, his fame was confirmed by *The Apprentice*, America's third most popular TV show, which revolved around the tycoon's hunt for a nascent successor. Huge audiences awaited Trump's trademark finale, as he mercilessly pointed his finger at that week's loser and declared, 'You're fired!' The drama transformed the programme into a cultural touchstone and confirmed Trump as an icon, with 500,000 people applying to star in his second series in 2005.

Every reality-TV hit breeds attempts to reproduce its success. During Branson's career, his fortune had been earned and lost by copying incumbents. In seeking publicity, he did the same. The potential show was pitched by Branson to Mike Darnell, Fox TV's zany head of alternative entertainment. Branson's idea was a contest between aspiring tycoons vying for his job as president of the Virgin global empire. Fox, the producers of *American Idol*, the season's runaway success featuring Simon Cowell, believed that Trump, whose show was on a rival station, could be toppled by another vain Englishman.

Darnell and Branson had much in common. Although the four-foot-eight-inch TV producer was normally dressed as a cowboy, in torn jeans and snakeskin high-heeled boots, he was, as the *New York Times* told its readers, 'always racing to one-up his rivals with over-the-top imitations and bizarre send-ups'. Darnell, a former child actor, boasted about how he hunted for 'visceral emotions' by producing reality shows about aliens, a beauty show in a women's jail and a quiz featuring adopted children picking out their biological fathers from a line-up. Fortunately for him, the failures had been outweighed by the hits. Embarrassed about his initial rejection of Simon Cowell's offer to broadcast *American Idol*, which turned out to be such a sensation, Darnell became enamoured of Branson. Finding that 'one extraordinary individual who has the right stuff to follow in his footsteps', said Darnell, would grip America. The winner would receive a $1 million prize and the position of president of the Virgin empire.

Darnell handed the production to Jonathan Murray, based in Los Angeles. From the outset, Murray had no doubt that the purpose was to 'familiarise Americans with the Virgin brand'. At his first meeting with Branson in London, Murray understood that he was to use shots of Virgin Atlantic planes whenever possible, in a programme showing 'how Branson leads and what his process is'. In Darnell's description, Branson was taking 'a select group of America's best and brightest around the world to relive his experiences and dilemmas'. Darnell spoke of contestants being pitted against each other in a series of death-defying stunts filmed in exotic locations in ten countries on five continents. 'Each week,' he chortled, 'one will be left behind.' Originally called *Branson's Big Adventure*, Darnell renamed it *The Rebel Billionaire*, with the subtitle *Branson's Quest for the Best*.

Twenty-five thousand applied to appear in Branson's show, just 5 per cent of Trump's wannabe list. The competitors would be flown around the world on Virgin planes, alongside a crew of 135 technicians, with the climax of each programme featuring video shots of the loser at the side of the runway as the plane took off with Branson inside. Unlike Trump's competition, Branson's contestants were not tasked with proving any business acumen. Instead, their skills were judged by having them walk a tightrope between two hot-air balloons apparently one mile in the air, dance naked in front of a crowd or go over an African waterfall in a barrel. On paper, the competition appeared visually exciting, but its success depended on the chemistry injected by Branson's personality. During the death-defying antics, Branson was filmed sipping tea from a silver service. 'To be honest,' he would typically say, 'I'm worried that Sarah may not make it.' Branson's expression was as flat as his words. Unlike Trump, he lacked the aggressive flamboyance to outrage the audience.

Darnell doubted that the winner would be appointed Virgin's president for more than a brief moment. His prime interest was to crush *The Apprentice*. Branson's principal aim was to exploit the unlimited opportunities to promote himself. 'If *Rebel Billionaire* is a success,' he told the *New York Times*, 'Virgin will be almost as well known in America as it is in England.' His message to the *Los Angeles Times* was similar: 'In one fell swoop we should get Virgin completely well-known in the States.'

'The show', praised one newspaper, 'reflects the Virgin way of doing things.'

Branson's intentions passed unnoticed among the American public. Few realised that his ambition went beyond self-promotion: his competitive urge was equally important. While playing the underdog to win sympathy, Branson often genuinely disliked those he challenged.

Donald Trump was described by many as an egotist decorated with a pompadour hairstyle. But despite the occasional financial crisis, his business triumphs were genuine. Branson's image as a hippy thrill-seeker contravening conventions to help mankind disguised the same lust for profits that galvanised Trump. Although there was room for both men in the world, Branson was intolerant of co-existing with opponents. During an interview with the *New York Times*, he derided Trump: 'His show is based in an office. I never spend any time in an office. And none of my businesses have ever gone bankrupt.' That last assertion was open to question. His shops, clothing and cosmetics businesses had all withered amid debt. And his next assertion was plainly wrong: 'We are building five spacecraft right now in the Mojave desert. They will take people into space starting in 2006. Already some 6,000 people', he added, 'have indicated they want to fly.' Branson's exaggerations were rewarded. The previews for *Rebel Billionaire* enthusiastically favoured him. 'Trump may already know that nothing succeeds like success but here comes Sir Richard to remind him that what goes up must come down,' chirruped a Chicago newspaper. The honeymoon ended after the first show was broadcast. Instead of excitement, there was a yawn.

In the nature of show business, the blowback was vicious. *Rebel Billionaire*, wrote a *Washington Post* reviewer, joins the genre of reality shows 'that are sillier, stupider and more ridiculous all the time'. He continued, 'This show doesn't just feature hot-air balloons. It *is* a hot-air balloon. It could drift out to sea and never be missed.' Another, parodying Branson's description of 'a search for excellence', wrote, 'Bored rich guy dangling money for the common rabble, then sitting back to watch the rats grovel, cringe, connive and betray for a bite of the cheese.' The universally scathing reviews were matched by low audiences. Only 4.85 million Americans watched the first programme. 'Fox executives', reported the *Los Angeles Times*, 'who heavily promoted *Rebel Billionaire* were stunned when the two-hour premiere bombed last week.' Others reported that Branson's show 'flopped', and while 'contestants leap over a 350-foot gorge, Richard Branson continues to seem creepy'. Another wrote that the programme had 'Nothing to do with business acumen . . . [it] just shows the impulse to lick the boots that kick you is not limited to dogs.' Two weeks later, the reaction was worse. 'The show is going over with viewers like a lead balloon,' reported Reuters. 'It started with dismal ratings three weeks ago and declined nearly 20 per cent in average audience.' While Branson's audience fell below four million, Trump was attracting sixteen million viewers.

'Richard was very disappointed that the show didn't get a bigger number,' admitted Jonathan Murray, recalling that Branson repeatedly telephoned to seek commiseration about the bad ratings. 'It was hard for him for the show not to be a success.' Mike Darnell denied responsibility for the series.

Trump chortled at the challenger's humiliation. 'I love to beat my opponents,' he told reporters after the first programme. 'I think his show is nothing to do with business. I mean, I'm not going to hire a guy based on the fact he's going to climb on top of a hot-air balloon. Branson even failed at the balloon business. The guy has spent his whole life trying to circle the world in a balloon and then some guy comes out of nowhere and beats him to it.' Trump could not resist telling the *New York Daily News*,

'I thought the show was terrible. And I thought he was terribly miscast. He's a lot of hot air, like his balloons.' He even wrote to Branson, saying, 'You have no television persona,' and then told newspapers the same: 'I don't know the guy but I think he's got zero personality and zero television persona.' Finally, his researchers rumbled the truth about Branson's commercial career. In a letter to the *New York Times*, Trump commented on their original effusive description of Branson, which had been based on information distributed by Virgin's publicists. 'Your article about Richard Branson failed to mention any of his numerous failures, including cola and cell phones. Also I find it hard to believe that anybody in the airline business is in fact a billionaire.'

Trump had no doubt discovered that virtually all of Branson's flotations of his companies had flopped, at the investors' expense. Shares in Victory Corp., a clothing and cosmetic retailer, were down 95 per cent; shares in Virgin Express, a cut-price airline based in Brussels, had fallen 93 per cent; Australian airline Virgin Blue's shares were down 10 per cent; while the shareholders in Virgin Music, his original success, had not earned any profits, but would discover that Branson had secretly profited by reselling the shares he had bought back from them. His suspicious transaction was referred to the Department of Trade and Industry for investigation but was ruled to have happened too long ago to merit any action. Companies that had invested in Virgin's assets had also lost money. Singapore Airlines, which bought 49 per cent of Virgin Atlantic for £630 million in 1999, had written off its entire investment; EMI, which eventually bought Virgin Music, had lost 30 per cent of its value; and the value of Stagecoach's 49 per cent stake in Virgin Trains was down 60 per cent.

The Rebel Billionaire was won by Shawn Nelson. The wild-haired twenty-six-year-old founder of the LoveSac Corporation, a manufacturer of bean bags which he claimed operated through a network of seventy-eight shops with 400 employees, was, like all the contestants, a genial self-publicist. Branson handed Nelson, whom he had blessed as a 'Mini-Me', Fox's cheque for $1 million and offered him a three-month stint as president of Virgin Worldwide. Shortly after, Nelson's business stumbled and he was accused by critics of indulging in a 'complicated shell-game' to strip the company of its assets. He denied the complaints, and although his three-month spell as president of a Virgin company was not a meaningful experience, Virgin said that he had enjoyed the competition despite the setbacks. All the contestants, however, were constrained from speaking to the media by stiff non-disclosure agreements.

Humiliation in the TV ratings did not disturb Branson's public image. Entrepreneurs, he stoically repeated, prospered by learning from failure. Nevertheless, unlike Trump's show, Branson's was not recommissioned. The finale was played out in September 2005. Coincidentally, Branson appeared at a fashion show in New York's Bryant Park to hear Trump loudly condemn Branson's show as 'bombing'. In retaliation, Branson predicted to their audience that SpaceShipTwo would be taking off with passengers in just two years' time. 'My aeronautical engineers', chirruped Branson in front of Trump, 'are designing a Virgin hotel to be built on the moon, or perhaps orbit around it, with glass-encased sleeping areas. You could be making love in these see-through domes and looking at Earth.'

Branson's fantasy was enhanced by finding an ally – Governor Bill Richardson of New Mexico. The politician had long lamented New Mexico's failure to attract any futuristic industries since the atomic bomb had been developed in the state during the 1940s. Searching for ideas to reverse the decline in the state's population and generate hope among the young, befitting his campaign slogan 'Run with Richard', he pondered a suggestion by Rick Homans, his secretary for economic development.

Homans had become a Branson zealot. After reading about the rocket's success in the Mojave and watching Branson's video promotion of Virgin Galactic, Homans had found a hero. 'New Mexico', he had told Richardson in 2004, 'should aim for the gold standard of the commercial space industry – and that's Richard Branson.' Listing the names of other states that had been enriched by the space and aviation industries, Homans described Branson's space venture as New Mexico's 'biggest economic opportunity for decades. We can't afford to pass it up.' If Virgin Galactic moved to New Mexico, Homans told Richardson, he would create over 3,000 new jobs and, according to one study, earn the state about $750 million by 2020. Richardson soon shared Homans's idolatry of Branson. The visionary, they agreed, should be lured to their desolate state.

Like dozens of ideas that arrived at Virgin's headquarters in Hammersmith, west London, the message from Rick Homans was discarded with little thought. Ignoring the rebuff, Homans flew to London to meet Will Whitehorn. Instead, he was greeted by Alex Tai, a Virgin Atlantic pilot who ranked among the headquarters' gofers. 'Will's not available,' Tai told Homans. 'They're not taking me seriously,' Homans realised. Ninety minutes later, Tai understood what Homans was offering: nothing less than an airport dedicated to Virgin Galactic. The mood changed. 'Hang on a moment,' said Tai. Ten minutes later, he reappeared with Whitehorn.

Whitehorn knew that SpaceShipTwo could easily take off from Mojave, but the desert runway lacked glamour. Branson wanted a prestigious structure to entice more punters to buy a $200,000 ticket. At the end of two hours' conversation, Whitehorn declared, 'New Mexico is where Virgin was always destined to be.' Homans returned to Santa Fe with a two-page memorandum of understanding outlining New Mexico's agreement to build an airport for Virgin's exclusive use.

Naturally, Branson sought a better offer. Early in 2005, along with Burt Rutan and Stu Witt, he visited Arnold Schwarzenegger in his office in Sacramento. The three asked California's governor to finance the construction of a special facility in Mojave. Branson's request was not unusual. His philosophy was clear: others always paid. Stu Witt was shocked by the negative reception: 'We were met with, "Hey, what brings you guys here?" It was cold. Incentives, we were told, are a race to the bottom. Branson wanted to bring $300 million to the state, and he was greeted with such arrogance.' Rutan agreed: 'California lost an incredible opportunity. The governor didn't understand it. And they let that opportunity get away with a smile on their faces.'

Soon after, Whitehorn called Homans. 'Richard's on. He wants to seal the deal with Governor Richardson.' Branson was a master of identifying men with either hope or money. Governor Richardson had both. 'Yeah!' exclaimed the governor in November, blessing Branson's generosity for planting the Virgin flag in the desert, forty-five miles north-east of Las Cruces, the nearest town. 'Richard is tying his brand to New Mexico's promises,' cheered Homans, echoing Virgin-speak.

Two weeks later, in December 2005, Homans flew to London to unveil their agreement – by then over 400 pages long – in front of an audience at London's Science Museum. The New Mexican government, Homans revealed, would sign a twenty-year lease with Virgin Galactic to use the airport. Three thousand eight hundred people from 126 countries, he repeated from Virgin's script, had paid a deposit for a seat on the spaceship. One hundred, he continued, with Whitehorn's nodding agreement, had paid the full $200,000 for flights beginning in 2008 or early 2009. No one seemed to notice that the take-off date had slipped, or at least no one appeared to care. And no one questioned the exaggerated statistics about the rocket's abilities and timetable. The unpublished detail of the contract reflected Branson's tough negotiation and his optimism. Once the runway and the terminals were completed, Virgin would pay only $1.63 million in rent annually, plus a sliding scale of fees for each take-off.

Virgin Galactic had committed itself to launching a minimum of 104 flights in 2010 – two a week – carrying a minimum of 592 passengers annually. By 2015, Virgin assumed there would be at least 720 flights per year – two every day – carrying 4,104 passengers. The company would employ at least 174 local staff. Other clauses minimised Virgin's liability if the rocket did not use the new airport.

Homans flew from London to Los Angeles to meet Branson. The tycoon arrived from Australia and then crossed the city to an airport used by executive planes. Homans was waiting there with the governor's jet and the actress Victoria Principal, Branson's mascot for Virgin Galactic. Branson himself was in 'ensnaring mode'. He intended to effusively lard his commitment to Richardson with praise, making it nearly impossible for the politician to abandon the $200 million project. Not that Richardson had any doubts. On the flight south, Homans wrote Branson's speech, filling it with flattery for Richardson.

'Where is this place we're heading to?' asked Branson.

'Nearest small settlement is Truth or Consequences,' replied Homans, referring to a godforsaken strip named after a 1950s TV game show.

After they had transferred to a helicopter in Santa Fe, Homans told Branson through the headphones they were all wearing, 'We need a name for the airport.' Branson gazed wearily out of the window as Homans thought, 'This is the world's best marketing and branding man. He'll have the best idea.'

'Spaceport America,' said Branson.

'Great,' gushed Homans.

At that moment, Branson leant against the helicopter's door to catch some sleep. The door flew open. Amid shrieks and shock, and with Branson held by the straps in his seat, the door was hauled back into place.

The sight after landing in the desert satisfied Branson's expectations. On a dry plateau 4,300 feet above sea level, not far from where the first atomic bomb had been tested, the governor was waiting to be wooed. Behind him were thirty-five journalists who had been bussed to an obscure exit on the Upham highway. Branson's appearance in the wilderness was embellished by his opening comment: 'We're going where no one has gone before. There's no model to follow, nothing to copy.' Richardson looked grateful to be hooked. He would immediately ask the state legislature, he said, for $100 million. The spaceport with launch pads and a giant runway would cover 1,800 acres. 'We're expecting 50,000 customers in the first ten years,' chipped in Branson. Each passenger, he said, would experience a unique view of Earth during six minutes of weightlessness (the media's reports of the duration always changed). Upping the ante, the governor outlined his bolder ambition: 'We'll have a cargo service from New Mexico to Paris taking a couple of hours and there'll be flights to and from orbital hotels where space fliers could take vacations of cosmic dimensions.' No one questioned which industries would ship their cargo to New Mexico or which rocket Richardson was speaking about. SpaceShipTwo was not designed to fly through space, and Branson could not afford the billions of dollars it would require to develop such a craft. Those details were irrelevant. All that mattered was Richardson's timetable dovetailing with Branson's certainty. After the first flights started in 2007, said Branson, 'Virgin expects to launch three flights a day from the spaceport by 2010. Each flight will carry six passengers.' The spaceport terminal, he said, would be designed by Lord Rogers, the famous British architect. He was mistaken. Lord Foster, another well-known British designer, was appointed.

After the ceremony, there was a celebration at a steak house in Santa Fe. 'Our first job', Richardson told Branson, 'is building the road across the desert. Ten miles long.' Branson smiled. He enjoyed benefiting at other people's expense. The governor agreed that Branson could fly back to Necker on the state's jet. 'I'll pay for the fuel,' offered Branson. He was accompanied by Homans, who, after spending the night in Branson's house, flew back to New Mexico. Not many people, he reflected, enjoyed such intimate moments with the great man and played Scrabble with him and his wife Joan after dinner.

In Mojave, Stu Witt was irritated. He could not see why anyone would want to take off from New Mexico rather than taking a helicopter ride from Los Angeles to Mojave airport. But he consoled himself: 'Branson hasn't invested a dime in New Mexico, and people will want destinations. They'll want to go somewhere, not return to the same point.'

Branson had a spaceport and ticket-holding passengers. He now needed more money to develop the spaceship. Boosted by Burt Rutan's encouraging reports, he flew in March 2006 to Dubai, a haven of cash-rich sheikhs. Amid the publicity for the start of Virgin Atlantic's daily flights to the Gulf state, he hoped to persuade the Maktoums, the ruling family, to invest in Virgin Galactic. 'A number of companies around the world are offering space travel,' he said, 'but they haven't tested and built any spaceships. They certainly haven't had any test flights into space. Virgin is the only company in the world that has achieved that.' To embellish Virgin's victory in space, Branson described his discussions with Robert Bigelow, an American aerospace entrepreneur, about developing inflatable pods so Virgin's space tourists could stay in 'a space hotel by the end of the decade'. During the visit to Dubai, he said that Virgin had registered 'seventy-five fully paid bookings'. The sceptics were dismissed. 'Personally,' said Branson, 'I think there's a demand for space hotels.'

One year later, in March 2007, the tempo increased. Selling tickets and rooms in space hotels needed agents, so forty-seven 'space agents' associated with the Virtuoso travel network were invited by Virgin to a two-day training course at the Kennedy Space Center in Cape Canaveral. The session started with a slick film. 'It blew me away,' Mike Melvill, the pilot, told the viewers as he stepped out of SpaceShipOne. 'It really did. You really do feel you can reach out and touch the face of God.' Melvill was followed by George Whitesides, the executive director of the National Space Society. 'Stephen Hawking plans to hop a flight on Virgin Galactic,' he said. 'Virgin Galactic is the private company with the only reusable manned spacecraft that has successfully flown to space and back.' Virgin Galactic, the travel agents were told, would be taking off on schedule from the spaceport. The agents departed as enthusiasts. They were convinced there were many Americans eager to spend their pocket money on a unique thrill.

In New Mexico, not everyone was convinced by Governor Richardson's 'pay to play' spaceport or Branson's promises. 'This is your classic Old West story of your snake-oil salesman', scoffed John Grubesic, a member of the New Mexico senate, 'who comes to the dying town promising to revitalise it. Unfortunately people have bought it, hook, line and sinker.' But no one had any reason to assume that Branson did not sincerely believe that Scaled could deliver the rocket as promised.

Soon after, Grubesic resigned from politics in disgust. His isolated protest was ignored. Branson's trumpeting of Virgin Galactic had forced America's power brokers finally to recognise the tycoon's importance.

3

The Club

Al Gore, the former American vice-president, flew to London in his private jet in April 2006 to meet Richard Branson at his home in Holland Park, west London.

Long before he entered politics, Gore had campaigned about climate change. *An Inconvenient Truth*, his documentary film warning about the imminent catastrophe of global warming, was due to be released the following month. To mount a popular crusade, Gore needed support from influential businessmen, and was persuaded by environmentalists that Branson embodied the 'can-do' dream. His newfound celebrity in America had magnified his global fame.

Until then, Branson had played at the periphery of the green movement. Invited in 2004 to sponsor the launch of the Climate Group at a celebration at the Banqueting House, in London's Whitehall, attended by Tony Blair, bankers and industrialists, Branson had declined to donate any money and paid only lip service to those classified as 'mission driven'. In the following two years, the Climate Group had attracted support from HSBC, Starbucks, Google and other global brands. Virgin could no longer afford to ignore the environment.

'This is a wake-up call,' Gore told Branson during the three hours he spent with him at his Holland Park home, which adjoined another house that served as his office. 'I've got a plan for you. You're a well-known business leader and you could make more of a difference than almost any other business leader if you do something dramatic and try and get people to pay attention.' An aviation company, said Gore, needed to be seen as caring for the environment.

Branson was conscious of his personal vulnerability. In 2002, Virgin Atlantic had rejected the option of two-engined jets, leasing instead four-engined Airbuses, with Branson promoting Virgin's 'safe' planes for transatlantic flights through advertisements on his aircrafts' fuselages stating, '4 Engines 4 Long Haul'. Four years later, Branson recognised his mistake. Four-engined planes polluted more and were not safer. His awakening coincided with the environmental movement focusing on aviation's greater responsibility for pollution compared to power stations and ground transport. Within thirty years, the campaigners argued, 50 per cent more aircraft would be in the air, yet aviation's carbon emissions were being reduced by only 1 per cent a year. Many supported taxation and strict carbon allowances on air travel. Banning aircraft was not an option for those environmentalists wary of alienating the public who were keen to holiday in foreign countries. Until Gore arrived, Branson had not addressed the conundrum of profiting from a business that polluted the environment. The question, suggested Gore, was how Branson could pose as the 'responsible face of aviation on emissions'. Environmentalists, he said, could embrace aircraft and simultaneously campaign for them to reduce their emissions. In a nutshell, continued Gore, Branson's airline should abandon its boast that 'Virgin produces less ice cubes' and show instead how its core decisions were driven by 'green' credentials. The latest fashion of corporate self-cleansing had been labelled as 'greenwashing'.

Branson found Gore irresistible. Attractive, popular, rich and famous, the politician embodied the qualities Branson admired. He was also offering a solution to a problem. By joining Gore's campaign, Branson would be introduced into the elite of America's Democrats, chief among them Bill Clinton. Over the previous year, the former president had positioned himself as an environmental evangelist. Branson spotted an unusual opportunity: by embracing the cause, he could glow and at the same time earn serious money. He was following a recently established path.

As a normal consequence of the personal relationships between those with political power, in 2004 the Climate Group's leaders had been introduced by Tony Blair to Clinton and his staff at the Clinton Institute. With Gore's help, the group had supplied Clinton, a voracious reader, with documentary evidence for the possible ways of avoiding the 'inevitable' environmental catastrophe. Once immersed, Clinton developed a passion for 'green', combined with a desire to curtail America's dependence on foreign oil supplies. Global warming, he believed, could be stopped without threatening the American way of life.

In *My Life*, the book he published in 2005, Clinton highlighted the importance of billionaires embracing philanthropy. One of the more virtuous ways in which the rich could improve the world, he wrote, was to combat global warming and the constant rise in oil prices by investing in renewable energy. The ideal investment was ethanol manufactured from corn, which, when mixed with petrol, could power cars. The biofuel, wrote Clinton, was a win–win: a tick for American farmers profiting by selling corn to American biofuel manufacturers, and a tick for reducing carbon emissions. Above all, political resistance would be minimal because Americans could still drive their big cars.

Clinton's advocacy of ethanol was not entirely philanthropic. 'Clean technology' and 'green' politics provided a profitable answer to those preaching about 'peak oil'. In their scenario, the world's oil supplies were in permanent decline, leading to a future shortage and an irreversible rise in prices. Clinton's contribution to the debate was called 'big-footing'. His commitment tilted more to mythology than reality – but he intended to profit from the vogue.

Since 2002, Clinton had been a paid adviser to Ron Burkle, a Californian who had earned at least $3 billion from supermarkets and was now seeking other investments and political leverage. At Clinton's behest, Burkle's company, Yucaipa, had invested in a manufacturer of ethanol from sugar cane. The company's owner was Vinod Khosla, who co-founded Sun Microsystems in Silicon Valley before selling it for over $1 billion. He was also an early investor in Amazon and Google. Like many other dotcom billionaires, Khosla foresaw renewable fuels as the next multi-billion fortune-maker. 'We need to declare war on oil,' he said, advocating renewables as the 'mainstream solution' to replace 80 per cent of oil-based energy. If the world failed to heed his prediction, he warned, 'the planet is history the way we know it today'. Powered by his convincing salesmanship, Khosla had become a friend, political ally and commercial partner of Burkle, Gore and Clinton. Together, the 'ethanolites' were promoting the 'drop-in solution' to potential investors: ethanol was easy to produce, easy to mix with petrol and, with generous government subsidies, delivered guaranteed profits.

Branson was introduced to Khosla by the organisers of the Climate Group. Branson's endorsement of ethanol, the campaigners calculated, would electrify their cause. 'We need to dispel the notion that we must make a choice between saving the planet and saving money,' Khosla told him. 'We must find solutions which are good for the environment and also profitable.' For Branson, focused on money since his late teens – as he admitted, his agenda 'was always 99.5 per cent business' – 'green' was an ideal vehicle for new profits. His introduction to Khosla would work out better than the Climate Group had expected.

The celebrities' endorsement of ethanol aroused Branson's curiosity. His interest was further bumped up by Governor Schwarzenegger's decree that 20 per cent of all ethanol consumed in California should, by 2010, be produced in the state itself. Khosla was happy to oblige. Cilion, his new corporation, planned to build nine factories to produce ethanol from corn. The first three would be built in California. 'I am confident', said Khosla, 'that Cilion will be able to produce all of the ethanol that the Governor has ordered for 2010.' Aggrieved at having missed out on the internet billions, Branson was impressed by Khosla's record. His success echoed that of Bill Gates, who had already invested $78 million in an ethanol company, albeit by buying preference shares, which minimised his risk. Persuaded by Khosla and by the same bankers who had profited from the dotcom era that ethanol was a safe bet, Branson's reservations about risking his own money gradually receded. Mixing in the firmament of political superstars and billionaires such as Clinton, Schwarzenegger, Gore, Burkle and Khosla was hooking him. He trusted that Khosla's record as a venture capitalist would help earn huge profits for Virgin from green technology, and relied on Clinton as the promoter.

He was invited to join the Green Rush, financed by businesses known as 'watermelons' – green on the outside and red capitalist within. He could not join on the favourable terms he normally extracted – offering the Virgin brand instead of hard cash – but caught up in the philosophy of Khosla and others, he finally decided not to be left behind. Then, his publicists revealed that Branson and media mogul Ted Turner had discussed ethanol over dinner. Turner had signalled his interest in the environment by contributing $1 billion to the United Nations Foundation and creating the Energy Future Coalition. Once the tabloid newspapers heard that Branson and Turner had discussed rescuing the planet, biofuels were blessed by the media as potential saviours and Branson was hailed as a hero for being appointed by Turner to the Energy Future Coalition's steering committee, of which Khosla was also a member. One of the committee's priorities was to lobby the US government to grant bigger subsidies for developing renewable and alternative fuels from crops. The 'ethanolites' wanted their profits to be guaranteed.

In early 2006, Branson announced that Virgin Fuels would invest $60 million in Cilion. For him, that was an unusually large commitment in a project over which he lacked even limited influence. He was gripped, and in April increased Virgin's commitment to invest in the 'world's biggest' factories, which would produce 100 million gallons of bioethanol a year, to $230 million. The company by then held a majority stake in factories in Indiana and Tennessee.

The following month, his enthusiasm appeared to be justified. Senator Hillary Clinton introduced a bill in Congress to create a $50 billion 'strategic energy fund' to expand the use of ethanol. Her support was a surprise. Previously, she had opposed subsidies for ethanol but, without explanation, she switched, and Khosla received approval for the Mascoma Corporation in Rochester, New York, to convert forest products into cellulosic ethanol. The Greater Rochester Enterprise group published their thanks to Mrs Clinton for her efforts in also obtaining permits for Cilion's two ethanol plants. Those had been negotiated by Yucaipa, who in turn were advised by Bill Clinton. The project, Jerry Wilhelm of the Greater Rochester Enterprise group volunteered in a seventeen-page report, 'would not have happened without the senator'. One month later, Khosla repeated his commitment to build nine bioethanol corn refineries in America, using government subsidies for the $160 million programme. The first three factories in California, he confirmed, would be operational by 2008. Branson appeared to have bet on a winner.

Gripped by what he referred to as a 'golden opportunity' for the Virgin brand and his business, Branson stepped up his commitment. In June, he won approval from the British government to use a mixture of bioethanol and diesel on Virgin's cross-country rail routes and was granted a tax reduction. A month later, he said that Virgin's investment in renewable fuels would increase to $1 billion over the next four years.

Shai Weiss, his adviser and representative on Cilion's board, was a former banker with the gift of being able to talk a good story. With Weiss's help, Branson intended to combine Virgin's commercial investment with a political campaign to promote his environmental convictions. 'We plan to move into this sector in a big way,' said Branson. Calling his plan the Gaia Capitalism Project after a theory developed by his favourite scientist, James Lovelock, Branson mentioned that his future investments would include wind turbines and nuclear power. 'In a few years it will be a major field for us,' he said. 'Nothing is off the agenda.' To boost his cause, he began repeating the mantra, 'The world is fast running out of oil and minerals.'

Flying in his Falcon at 38,000 feet over the Andes or across Africa's bush, he had clearly not understood that the mines below could produce sufficient copper, iron, sulphur and other minerals to sustain the world's industries for hundreds of years. Similarly, he seemed unaware that peak oil was an illusion advocated by prejudiced lobby groups who dismissed the importance of the constant technological advancements which were spurring the extraction of additional oil. He appeared equally unaware of the political manipulation by many oil-producing nations to deny the major oil-exploration corporations access to their vast untapped reserves. To some, his ingenuity reflected his eye for another commercial opportunity. Others believed that for once he had failed to balance the financial risk against his customary self-promotion.

The immediate consequence of the biofuel producers' demand for corn was a dramatic increase in prices for the crop. The cost of grain for animals and poultry rose, and food prices in supermarkets followed. The IMF estimated that the increase in ethanol production in America raised the price of maize across the world by 60 per cent and threatened to cause starvation in the poorest countries. Paradoxically, producing more corn for ethanol generated additional greenhouse gases, undermining the environmentalists' arguments. American motorists also complained: cars which drove sixteen miles on a gallon of petrol could cover only twelve on the ethanol mixture. The environmentalists' enthusiasm was defied by another statistic: filling a car's tank with bioethanol required 250 kilogrammes (550 lbs) of corn – the amount consumed by a single family in a year.

Branson seemed oblivious to those ambiguities. He rarely read scientific briefs and appeared not to fully understand the science of producing ethanol from corn. His staff also disliked delivering bad news. Like his sidekick Weiss, he did not question why George Soros and Bill Gates were producing ethanol from sugar cane in Brazil rather than investing in Khosla's factories in America.

Branson had relied on Khosla's assumption that producing ethanol would be uncomplicated. Khosla had purchased the equipment for his factories from India and hired experienced engineers formerly employed by BP. Among them was Lawrence Peck, an American chemical engineer. Peck soon realised that 'Khosla was just throwing darts at the dartboard to see which would stick. His group seemed to have little idea how to produce ethanol. He wasn't impressive.' Branson discounted the problems. His millions of dollars had bought a ticket to the top table with Clinton and Gore, and proximity to Governor Schwarzenegger, who had assumed importance in his ambitions in the US, especially to launch his new airline.

Since 2003, Branson had been battling to create Virgin America, a new airline based in California. To successfully break into the world's biggest airline market would, he hoped, secure huge profits. However, vested interests were frustrating his efforts: in particular, the established airlines opposed the entry of a new competitor. His would-be rivals complained to the Department of Transportation in Washington DC that Branson was breaking American laws. As a foreigner, he could own a maximum of 49 per cent of an American airline but control only 25 per cent of the votes. The majority of Virgin America's shares, Branson was told, must be owned by American citizens. To obey, Branson sold 77 per cent of the airline to two American investors, Mark Lanigan of Black Canyon Capital in Los Angeles and Nicholas Singer of Cyrus Capital Partners in New York. Both received lawful guarantees from Branson that they would recover their whole investment plus 8 per cent profit. The US government could only acknowledge that Branson's choice of financiers complied with the statutory requirement, but he was compelled to dismiss his American chief executive as one more condition for allowing the airline to take off. The executive was criticised for being too close to Branson.

To finally succeed, Branson needed Schwarzenegger's support, and that materialised in 2006, during the governor's re-election campaign. One of the themes was climate change. Schwarzenegger was posing as 'The Emissions Terminator', focused on the passage through California's legislature of his Global Warming Solutions Bill, known locally as AB32. If the bill was approved, California would be the first state in America to compulsorily reduce carbon emissions, encourage solar and wind power and stimulate the production of alternative fuels. Inevitably, the bill met with vocal opposition. To prove he enjoyed the support of business leaders for his green agenda, Schwarzenegger needed a high-profile event to outflank his political opponents and the pro-carbon lobby. 'If we focus on the leaders, the rest of the world will follow,' counselled Terry Tamminen, Schwarzenegger's environmental adviser. Tamminen asked Stephen Howard of the Climate Group for help. The Englishman suggested convening a round table of chief executives to pledge their support for Schwarzenegger. Branson was on the list.

Tamminen first called John Browne, BP's chief executive. As the head of the world's second-largest oil corporation, Browne had successfully rebranded BP in America as Beyond Petroleum, an environmentally friendly energy producer. His success owed much to his relationship with an egregious network of international power brokers, including Tony Blair. The British prime minister agreed to be the guest of honour and endorse Schwarzenegger.

At BP's expense, a gleaming white tent was erected at the company's terminal on Long Beach's dockside, adjacent to a new BP tanker. Among those who arrived for the reception on 31 July 2006 were the chief executives of DuPont, Timberland, Goldman Sachs, Swiss Re and American Electric Power, James Murdoch of News International – who had left his company's annual gathering at Pebble Beach to support Schwarzenegger – and two hippy billionaires, Sergey Brin, the co-founder of Google, and Branson. Dressed casually, they sat together, casting themselves as ambassadors of the new business chic. 'Branson arrived obsessed by biofuels,' observed one of the participants. 'He spoke of little else.' As they waited for Tony Blair – delayed on his flight from Washington – an organiser calculated that those gathered around the table managed companies that earned half a trillion dollars a year and employed over 300,000 workers. Two years after paying $1 million to brand a rocket Virgin Galactic, Branson enjoyed a secure seat at the top table.

Amid dust and flying gravel, Blair's motorcade roared into the compound. The warmth with which the politician greeted Branson was not lost on Schwarzenegger. The closeness of Branson's relationship with Blair had been witnessed at a reception for the travel industry in Downing Street on 5 April 2000, when Cherie Blair was overheard saying to him, 'I've been talking to Tony, and we agree that we must do something for you.' Soon after, the businessman had received a knighthood, and even Schwarzenegger was impressed when he saw 'Sir Richard Branson' on the guest list. Following his re-election, the governor noted, Branson's interests would deserve support. For the moment, though, the stilted conversation inside the marquee served his purpose. The media's descriptions of Schwarzenegger's 'Big Tent' – including Branson – helped propel AB32 through the legislature and would see Schwarzenegger achieve a 20 per cent lead in the run-up to the election. 'We're going to a baseball match,' Schwarzenegger told Blair at the end of the reception. Both politicians bid Branson a warm farewell.

Now inside the tent, Branson wanted his reward. His competitors and the Californian trade unions were still arguing that Virgin, as a foreign corporation, should be barred from launching Virgin America, despite owning only a minority stake. The solution, he was advised, was to show commitment to America. The combination of Clinton, Schwarzenegger and 'green' was helpful but, to grab attention, he had been told by a leading environmentalist, 'we need grand statements'.

The appropriate forum was the Clinton Global Initiative, a brash annual event held in New York where only those prepared to commit huge sums towards Clinton's favourite causes were invited. Branson had agreed to join Vinod Khosla and Ron Burkle on 21 September 2006 at the celebrity networking party, which would boost the value of their investment in ethanol. Senator Hillary Clinton would also be attending, exciting gossip about her sponsorship of subsidies to an industry favoured by her husband and his friends. By then, Khosla's ambitions for corn ethanol were frequently articulated. 'Twenty per cent of America's farmland', he told Terry Tamminen, 'can produce 100 per cent of America's energy.' Khosla's imagination encouraged Branson in his search for a public-relations coup. To win support in America, he needed not only to be known but loved by the public. He needed a publicity spike to boost the country's perception of a British tycoon.

Rising oil prices were a constant worry for Branson. Over one-third of all airlines' costs were fuel charges, but his airline's financial fate was particularly precarious. Renewable energy was his solution to the problem. Any doubts about his investment had been swept away by the British government's recent publication of a widely praised report about the economics of climate change written by Nicholas Stern, a senior civil servant. One premise of Stern's report excited Branson. The official confidently predicted an irreversible reduction in the world's oil supplies after production hit its peak in 2012. Thereafter, asserted Stern, fuel prices would increase relentlessly. Branson was hooked. The combination of self-interest and his membership of Ted Turner's Energy Future Coalition stimulated his orchestration of a unique gesture at Clinton's blockbuster.

As so often, Branson came up with the idea at the last moment. On this occasion, the wheeze occurred while he was being driven to the hotel in Manhattan. Later, to conceal the spontaneity around his announcement, he would say, 'Some time after meeting Al Gore I was lying in the bath and I thought, "We make a lot of money out of the airline business and the train business. Let's just tie all that money for the next ten years into trying to develop fuels that don't damage the environment."' Whether the idea came to him in the bath or the car was irrelevant to those greeting Branson as he entered the hall dressed in a jersey and jeans. Standing casually among journalists waiting for Clinton to make his opening speech, he mentioned his intention to donate $3 billion over ten years to the Initiative. The news reached Clinton. Instead of making the announcement himself, he pulled Branson on to the stage. This was, Clinton and Branson knew, the largest individual commitment of money to combat climate change – three times more than Ted Turner's contribution. Branson had bought himself prime-time attention. He was given the appropriate words to say by an associate: 'We must not be the generation responsible for irreversibly damaging the environment. We must hand it over to our children in as near pristine condition as we were lent it from our parents.' The $3 billion, he explained, would be sourced from all the profits of his transport corporations. The money would be used to develop biofuels, especially from algae and sugar. 'The world is awash with sugar,' he said, 'and sugar is bad for you, so let's put it in planes.' Below the podium, his staff were shedding joyful tears.

There was, Branson ought to have realised, little chance of Virgin's trains and planes generating $3 billion worth of profits over the next ten years. Their combined proceeds might be at best $1 billion. However, he was obliged to share those profits with his partners – half of Virgin Trains belonged to Stagecoach, and half of Virgin Atlantic was owned by Singapore Airlines. Neither partner would agree to contribute to Branson's plan. Beyond that, the potential profits were further reduced by the earlier announcement that both the airline and train companies were to be sold to the public. Contradictions and inconsistencies had never troubled Branson. In his bid to win recognition in America, he gave the impression he was making extravagant assertions in the hope that they would become true in the future. Amid the thrill of Branson's breathtaking commitment, those complications were irrelevant to Clinton.

As he stepped down from the podium, Branson was surrounded by journalists. $3 billion, he knew, would play big in the media for twenty-four hours. Previous American media profiles of Branson described him as the promoter of the Sex Pistols, the first man to cross the Atlantic in a hot-air balloon and the first provider of manicures on transatlantic jets. This time, to quash the cynics, the Virgin publicity machine pushed their employer as a seriously rich player.

Inevitably, after his announcement Branson was asked by a few sceptical journalists in the audience to reconcile his pledge with Virgin's income. Branson was unfazed. If his transport companies failed to produce $3 billion in profits, he replied, 'I will most likely make up the difference with the profits from other parts of Virgin.' He mentioned Virgin Mobile, the Virgin health clubs and other businesses as contributors. Those doubts were irrelevant pinpricks.

The sympathetic editors at the *New York Times* and *Washington Post* instantly agreed to publish lengthy profiles of Branson that included the accolades he sought. Although failures like Virgin Cola were mentioned, the *Times* highlighted his successes, including Virgin Mobile, which had already earned Branson over £700 million in cash and stock. 'Sir Richard usually owns a big chunk of most of these new companies,' reported the *New York Times*. Only the *Wall Street Journal* reported that Branson refused to reveal the profits from his transport businesses. Will Whitehorn was allowed to predict that the Virgin companies' projected revenues in 2006 would be $14.6 billion, of which $8 billion would come from transport, but that failed to address the actual profit. Branson was untroubled when asked whether he could fulfil his promise: 'They'll be more than welcome to see my books,' he assured inquirers. More important than any audit, he continued, was his reputation: 'If you're hoping to stand up on stage with Clinton and Gore and pledge something, you have got to do it.' Those who still doubted whether Branson could produce $3 billion were assured that the 'commitment' team attached to the Clinton Global Initiative regularly met donors to review the progress of their pledges. Americans were unaware that Branson's finances had been shrouded in offshore mystery since 1973, with only a handful of highly paid advisers allowed to manage his secret accounts for over forty years. Although the public could read what Virgin's corporations did disclose, the limitations of that information prevented any outsider from fully understanding the nature of Branson's and Virgin's finances.

The commitments made that day totalled $5.7 billion, but Branson was the star. The *Wall Street Journal* concluded after hearing about his earlier pledge to invest $400 million over the following three years in Virgin Fuels, 'At least he puts his money where his mouth is . . . Now that Sir Richard has put his brand on it, everyone says it's cool. Well, fine. We wish him well, er, good.' His earlier pledge of committing $1 billion, as reported by the BBC, appeared to have been forgotten.

Branson enjoyed embellishing the circumstances leading up to his headline-catching $3 billion donation. Speaking three weeks later at a celebrity dinner at the Ritz-Carlton in New York, he joked, 'It was actually quite painful when it got down to adding those last few zeros.' To reflect America's expectation that billionaires were philanthropists, Branson would later explain, 'With extreme wealth comes extreme responsibility.'

Intent on capitalising on his new popularity, he sought another headline-grabbing initiative. During a conversation with Gore, they came up with the Virgin Earth Challenge. Branson would offer $25 million to the inventor of a commercially viable process to remove greenhouse gases from the atmosphere. To win, the 'design' would need to remove at least a billion tons of carbon from the atmosphere per year and would be tested over ten years. The winner, said Branson, would receive $5 million immediately and the remaining $20 million at the end of the decade.

Al Gore shared the platform in Kensington, London, in February 2007 to announce the competition and endorse Branson's boast that 'This is the largest ever science and technology prize to be offered in history.' The reason for his initiative, explained Branson, was the threat of the world being overwhelmed by an unprecedented crisis if his Challenge did not deliver the answer: 'We will lose half of all species on Earth, 100 million people will be displaced, farmlands will become deserts and rainforests will become wasteland.' Branson's championing of climate geo-engineering was shared by other billionaires, including Bill Gates. A fortune would be earned by the entrepreneur who backed the best scientists and produced a solution that 'offset' carbon emissions.

Branson was riding a populist wave, although there were some who doubted the accuracy of Gore's award-winning documentary. A number of respected scientists acknowledged the need to cut carbon emissions but accused the politician of exaggeration and even falsification. The Intergovernmental Panel on Climate Change disparaged the imminence of the scenarios which Gore portrayed – of gigantic ice sheets melting fast, seas rising twenty feet to swamp vast areas of land, hurricanes battering coastlines, and the end of the Gulf Stream, causing Europe to plunge into an ice age. Even if Gore's predictions were correct, said his critics, they would be manifested only in many thousands of years. Similarly, some experts criticised Stern's prediction of certain environmental catastrophe as 'tendentious' and 'propagandist'. He was guilty, wrote one analyst, of 'statistical sophistry' by quoting inaccurate mathematical models and peddling bogus science. Branson ignored these opponents. 'Man created the problem,' he told his guests in Kensington, 'and therefore man should solve the problem.' His fame guaranteed worldwide coverage of his competition. Hundreds of submissions began arriving at Virgin's headquarters to be scrutinised by Branson's experts, who included Crispin Tickell, a former Foreign Office ambassador, and Tim Flannery, an eminent Australian environmentalist. Both had been invited to Necker to brief Branson, and both bestowed upon the tycoon credibility as a global champion.

Placing himself at the forefront of encouraging the use of

renewable energy, in 2007 Branson agreed to testify in Congress. He enjoyed annoying rivals by sermonising that aviation was a dirty business ripe for anti-carbon taxes and criticising those in the airline industry who were unwilling to limit carbon emissions. 'If I ground my fleet,' he replied to those who accused him of hypocrisy, 'another company will just step in to meet the inevitable consumer and business demand.' He laughed at Jeff Gazzard of the Aviation Environment Federation, who accused him of advocating bogus green initiatives to make passengers feel guilty. Beyond his exhortations, his practical contribution so far had been to persuade the management of Heathrow and Los Angeles International airports to convert their municipal waste to fuel. 'You've got to start somewhere,' his supporters admonished the cynics. His more serious purpose was to profit from green investments.

In 2007, Virgin Atlantic failed to protect itself against rising oil prices and suffered losses. High oil prices had, in Branson's opinion, become linked with climate change. 'Thank God it's happened,' he said. 'A high oil price is what we needed to actually wake up the world to deal with climate change.' Convinced he could earn millions of pounds by producing a substitute for jet fuel, he adopted Vinod Khosla's ideology that businessmen could justifiably profit from ventures favourable to the environment. Accordingly, Virgin Fuels metamorphosed into the Virgin Green Fund. Investors were invited to pledge £300 million to 'harness entrepreneurship to achieve market-driven solutions to climate change'. Convinced by Khosla that cellulosic ethanol would be commercially viable by 2009, Virgin Green's principal investment was in renewable fuels. The fund's authenticity was partially dependent on Senator Hillary Clinton's new sponsorship of government subsidies for producing biofuels from cellulose derived from woodchips, grass and other organic materials. Khosla, like Clinton and Branson, still ignored critics who blamed ethanol production from corn for damaging the environment.

However, the opponents, including Biofuel Watch, had persuaded the United Nations to commission a Special Rapporteur on the Right to Food to investigate the consequences of the billionaires' investment. The rush for biofuels, the expert reported, was 'a crime against humanity'. To satisfy the increased demand for corn, American farmers were ploughing up pasture and had stopped growing soya beans. As soya prices rose, peasants in the Amazonian rainforests were being evicted from their land, trees felled and synthetic fertilisers spread to grow soya. With less forest, the carbon in the atmosphere would increase and the biodiversity of the soil would be weakened. In America, the fertilisers used to grow the extra corn were emitting huge amounts of additional nitrous oxide, a more poisonous gas than the carbons produced from conventional petrol.

The billionaires dismissed the critics, and by summer 2007 Branson's strategy in America was beginning to succeed. Governor Schwarzenegger offered $15 million in assistance to base Virgin America in San Francisco rather than Los Angeles and, with official approval, the glitzy airline was finally launched. Combined with his environmental business, his plan to spread Virgin Hotels across the country and, above all, Virgin Galactic, Branson had won the recognition he sought. Then suddenly his success was threatened.

4

Knife Edge

Randy Chase's inquiry into the explosion of Virgin Galactic's rocket in Mojave in July 2007 gave Branson good reason to be concerned. Sending famous multimillionaires into space was the lynchpin of his plan for self-enrichment through self-promotion in America. 'A little information in the hands of the less educated people', a Scaled Composites executive had warned, 'could be dangerous to our survival. Some hostile people would want to close the operation down.'

One of the least scientifically educated people in Mojave was Randy Chase himself. Ignorant about rocket motors and nitrous oxide, he was cast into a scientific wilderness among engineers keen to steer the investigator away from any conclusion which might damage Mojave's most prominent customer. Virgin Galactic's fate, everyone knew, rested on Chase's decision. Was the explosion an accident, or was it caused by the conduct of Burt Rutan's team, or was the Virgin Galactic motor inherently defective or even dangerous? At the end of his investigation, would Chase recommend that Scaled be prosecuted for a crime?

Sitting in the Voyager diner by Mojave airport's runway, Chase heard the party line from Rutan's employees.

'We want to put eight men into space,' he was told. 'You don't want to stop that, do you?'

'I don't,' agreed Chase.

During other conversations, Chase sensed the jealousy among Rutan's rivals vying for the same prize as Branson. Rutan's glory excited suspicion along the runway. 'It's like an arms race,' Chase concluded. 'It's all about money and prestige.'

During his first hours in Mojave, he had spurned the offer of help from George Whittinghill, one of Scaled's experts. 'He called about nitrous oxide. He seemed to be chasing money,' Chase claimed, believing Whittinghill wanted to be hired by the government. Chase accepted the judgement of others that 'Whittinghill is a horse's arse who doesn't listen to anyone else.' Some believed this was grossly unfair on Whittinghill, but Chase decided that he would rely on Scaled's other engineers. 'I'm getting good co-operation,' he reported to his headquarters, 'so I've decided not to call in outside experts.' The engineers potentially responsible for the explosion had sought to secure Chase's trust. Their expertise would guide the investigator through the evidence as he judged their own conduct.

'Why did the explosion happen?' someone asked Chase. 'Did someone fire a bullet through the chamber?' Chase mocked the fantasy, but he did grasp that there were suspicions about the safety of the fuel and distrust among some of Scaled's consultants in Virgin Galactic's rocket.

The motor used by Virgin Galactic was called a 'hybrid'. In simple terms, nitrous oxide, commonly called 'laughing gas', was pumped into a metal cylinder lined with rubber and ignited. The burning rubber created the high pressure that propelled the spaceship towards the stars. Rutan had chosen the hybrid motor because it was cheap and simple. There was no throttle. After just a twenty-second burst the rocket would be speeding at 2,000 mph – three times the speed of sound – taking a further forty-five seconds to reach space. Since Virgin Galactic was not going into orbit – which would require the spaceship to fly at seven times the speed of sound – a hybrid motor was suitably cheap for tourism.

The complication was the craft's size and weight. Rutan's expertise was in designing aircraft, not rockets. He assumed that he could stretch his original spaceship and increase the rocket motor's size in order for SpaceShipTwo to carry eight people rather than two. Lengthening it was easy, but no one had ever used such a big hybrid motor. His engineers were working in the unknown, especially when it came to keeping the weight down. Achieving the right balance between creating sufficient room for passengers and using the smallest possible motor requiring less fuel was complicated.

To reduce Virgin Galactic's weight, Rutan was using composites rather than metal for the motor's enlarged tank. 'You need to take great care with composites,' an expert had told him. The engineer voiced his scepticism about the glue Scaled was using, but Rutan's response was defensive. He was a fast-paced man who disliked being questioned about what were later referred to as 'the deficiencies in the long process'. The consultant engineer's concerns ranged from 'poor cleaning' to 'no precision in the measurement of the connections'. Rutan, the engineer noted, had a 'blurry overall vision' about burning rubber.

Rutan had no fears about hybrid engines. The safety of using nitrous oxide to burn rubber was endorsed by the US government's guidelines. There was no need, he decided, to question the science, although the law-makers had not anticipated applying their rules to an enlarged hybrid motor. Critically, Randy Chase was similarly reassured after he was shown the official rules issued by the Federal Aviation Administration and an implied waiver allowing Virgin Galactic to fly.

Without any technical advice, Chase did not examine what Rutan's critics before the accident had called 'an aggressive schedule'. One engineer raised questions as to whether Scaled's staff were sufficiently experienced and properly paid. 'They've got inadequate supervision,' he said, believing that aircraft designers like Rutan did not properly understand rocket motors. 'Burt Rutan is driving his staff with a mandate for speed.' After the explosion, many had become angry. Scaled, the engineers claimed, was a corporation in a hurry. Chase ignored those observations. All he wanted was an uncomplicated explanation for the explosion.

Following standard procedure, he relied on individual interviews with the engineers. One by one during August 2007 they arrived, accompanied by Scaled's lawyers, at an office in Mojave. Despite his technical ignorance, Chase felt he had detected a smokescreen. 'They're scared about losing their jobs,' he concluded. 'All the witnesses are concerned not to say the wrong thing. They're not talking straight. They don't want to cause their employer any problems, especially a potential law suit for damages.' The same reticence embraced the families of the three dead engineers. In return for compensation, all had signed confidentiality agreements. Even Al Cebriain, the consultant engineer, was inhibited about revealing what he saw before the explosion.

'We don't want you talking,' the lawyers acting for Scaled had told Cebriain.

'You're imposing damage control over the investigation,' Cebriain replied. Scaled, it had been announced just six days before the accident, was to be sold in its entirety to Northrop Grumman, the aerospace giant, and Rutan understandably wanted no problems. Scaled's lawyers were acting accordingly.

'They're all cautious,' Chase reported to his chief in Fresno. 'They're telling me what they want me to know, and that's limited.' On reflection, Chase interpreted their caution as personal and not professional evasion. 'They're scoffing at me,' he sighed. 'They think that I'm an idiot because I was born and raised on a farm.'

The danger for Branson and Rutan would be if Chase judged Scaled's negligence to be criminal. That conclusion would trigger a more comprehensive investigation by Bakersfield's sheriff and the local district attorney. A forensic examination of the hybrid motor, Scaled's directors feared, might undermine Virgin Galactic's reputation. Their good fortune was Chase's limitations. After clocking up nearly a thousand hours at Mojave, the inspector surrendered. He would not pursue his effort to understand the scientific causes of the explosion, excluding any investigation into Scaled's use of nitrous oxide to burn rubber. Questions about the integrity of the rocket's motor, he decided, were irrelevant. 'Finding out whether a hybrid rocket is safe doesn't matter,' he reported to his chief. 'All that matters is if Scaled took the proper precautions to protect its employees or if their carelessness caused the deaths.'

His conclusion was guided by Scaled's engineers. On several occasions he heard an expert say that 'the fuel was contaminated'. To Chase, contamination meant that Scaled's employees had allowed desert dust to mix with the gas or enter the equipment. 'Their leather gloves are dirty,' he noticed, believing that the cause of the explosion was 'a mundane thing of life'.

Some of the experts, including Cebriain, believed that contamination had somehow subverted the rocket's reliability, but not through dirty gloves. Chase could have properly understood the cause if he had scrutinised a video in slow motion, but he missed that opportunity. The recording of the test showed flames bursting through the top of the tank of nitrous oxide gas. In a cold-flow test, there should have been no fire. The question posed by Scaled's critics was why one had erupted. In the post-mortem completed after Chase had submitted his report, Rutan's engineers would discover that the composite liner inside the tank – made of a petroleum glue – had dissolved and contaminated the vapours and nitrous oxide. As the contaminated vapour and gas passed through the valve, there was friction. Friction causes heat, and that heat triggered the gas to explode. The tank was found 800 feet from the explosion site, while the valve was found 300 feet away in the opposite direction.

Scaled's engineers were shocked by their discovery. None could understand why a similar explosion had not occurred earlier. If the public became aware that errors in the design and manufacture may have caused the explosion, confidence in Virgin Galactic might collapse. Public debate about Virgin Galactic's safety was prevented because Rutan and Branson's executives declined to discuss the incident with critics in the space community. The public were unaware that the composite liners inside the tank would later be replaced with metal. With the slow-motion evidence yet to be minutely scrutinised by Scaled's engineers, Chase was deflected from doubting the stability of the hybrid, and his primitive opinion that dirty gloves had contaminated the nitrous oxide was reinforced.

In Chase's opinion, the negligence was compounded by Scaled's failure to prevent their employees standing so close to the test site. Pertinently, he was not told that an eyewitness's mobile telephone had recorded Glenn May and two others darting in front of the fence just before the test started. Since they were so much closer to the explosion, they died. For his own unexplained reasons, Chase firmly believed that all the casualties – the dead as well as the survivors – had been behind the fence. 'Really, it made no difference,' he later said. 'The fence couldn't protect anyone.' He failed to take the self-evident truth of his observation to its conclusion: namely, that the co-operation he received from some engineers had been limited.

His report was delivered in October 2007 to OSHA's enforcement agency. No one was surprised that Chase blamed the deaths on Scaled's careless safety procedures and nothing more. Over the previous twenty-eight years, despite hundreds of deaths of workers in the oil, mining and other industries, OSHA had not mounted a single criminal prosecution in the county. Since Chase did not highlight any suspicions, his report went no further. Accordingly, there was no reason for the county sheriff, Donny Youngblood, to launch an investigation or even to hold a coroner's inquest to publicly ascertain the cause of the explosion. The district attorney was also excluded from any involvement.

Conveniently for Rutan, OSHA's decision automatically prevented the publication of Chase's report. 'It's just another accident,' Sheriff Youngblood concluded. He felt no reason to cause Rutan more embarrassment.

The suppression of a public debate sparked criticism among a group of British and American engineers. Led by Geoff Daly, a British rocket engineer, and supported by Carolynne Campbell, a designer of small rocket motors, they voiced their worries about a possible cover-up. Since Scaled refused to engage in any debate with their critics, their comments became strident. Sharing a keen interest in the use of nitrous oxide, both Campbell and Daly were alarmed by the description on Virgin Galactic's website that the combination of the gas and rubber is 'benign, stable as well as containing none of the toxins found in solid rocket motors'. In their opinion, that description was inaccurate. 'Nitrous oxide can explode on its own,' said Campbell. 'Unlike oxygen, it's an explosive. And rockets blow up because that's their nature.' Virgin Galactic's motor, she continued, could be toxic. 'There's so much soot coming out the back. That's burning rubber. That could be carcinogenic.'

In a letter to California's district attorney, the two Britons described the dangers Virgin's space tourists would face because of Rutan's reliance on nitrous oxide and burning rubber. Had, they asked, consideration been given to prosecuting Scaled for criminal negligence or even manslaughter? The engineers were ignored. The fine imposed by OSHA on Scaled, based on a fixed tariff determined by the number of employees and not the fatalities, was $25,000. The company's appeal was dismissed. 'A speeding ticket,' concluded Stu Witt. 'Not a corporation-closing penalty.'

Rutan must have been delighted. None of the injured complained. The disaster was forgotten even among those who had bought $200,000 tickets. 'I'll be on the first flight with my parents and family in 2009,' promised Branson, expressing certainty about the timetable. 'Tests', he was later told by Witt, 'should be like sex – behind closed doors with a minimum number of participants.'

In the weeks after the funerals of the three engineers, the deaths were compared to the fate of the doomed Apollo 1 astronauts in 1967. To re-energise Scaled's employees, Rutan's executives appealed to their can-do spirit. Branson was reassured that the rocket motor's safety was not in doubt. As an insurance, Scaled's engineers reduced the temperature of the nitrous oxide. However, at lower temperatures the rocket produced less power and the thrust was less smooth. 'The hybrid could be doomed,' predicted Campbell and others.

Branson needed to reassure the ticket-holders that his timetable was infallible. Virgin's flawless publicity machine, primed to spread confidence and fun, invited Virgin Galactic's passengers to a party in mid-January 2008 at the planetarium in New York's Museum of Natural History. Nearly a hundred ticket-holders arrived. Some had paid a $20,000 deposit; others had paid the full $200,000. '2008 will be the year of the spaceship,' said Branson on the soundtrack of an animated film showing SpaceShipTwo blasting into space. Take-off, he said with certainty, would be late the following year or definitely in 2010. After that, said the commentator with conviction, the reusable rocket would be taking off twice every day from the spaceport. The film's description of the split-second acceleration as the rocket roared into space gripped the audience. Within a minute, pushed deep into their seats by the G force, they would be soaring at 3,000 mph (Virgin's publicity was never consistent about the speed). About twenty seconds later, the rocket motor would stop and the passengers could enjoy four minutes of weightlessness as the craft glided through space before beginning its descent.

The party served another serious purpose. Over the previous months, Branson had been under pressure to prove Virgin Galactic's financial benefits and that it would be environmentally neutral. Virgin's publicists categorised the six millionaire passengers on each trip as 'eco-tourists', but a *Washington Post* writer had described the venture as an example of when 'narcissism trumps common sense and pollutes the fragile atmosphere the rest of us must breathe'. The comment, the publicists realised, attacked Branson's repositioning as a campaigning environmentalist who used his airline's profits to save mankind. Branson's reply to his guests was reassuring: 'James Lovelock has told me that he thinks that what we're doing is one of the most important industrial projects of the twenty-first century. I consider space to be the final frontier that is so essential to the future of civilisation on this planet.' The future of industry, communications, energy and even food, continued Branson, depended on man conquering space. The world's 9 billion population – 'three times more than when I was born' – could be sustained only by developments in space. 'With the end of the oil era and climate change progressing faster than most models predict,' he emphasised, 'the utilisation of space is essential to the logistics of our survival.' Space, he repeated, was the only remedy to the world's overpopulation and the rapid depletion of oil and minerals. Virgin Galactic would save mankind from starvation.

Branson's speech ended in a mumbled anticlimax. Despite his popularity as a speaker, his set-piece public addresses usually lacked fluency or flourish. Hovering behind him was Princess Beatrice, the Queen's granddaughter. Her presence was assumed to be connected to Branson's friendship with Sarah Ferguson, the Duchess of York, but it was also linked to Beatrice's association with Dave Clark, a salesman for Virgin Galactic. Just as Burt Rutan was about to speak, Beatrice and Clark were spotted arguing and then disappearing.

Branson often feared what Rutan might say, but even he could not have foreseen his partner's warning. 'Our goal', Rutan told his audience, 'is making spaceships at least as safe as the early commercial airliners which were introduced in the late 1920s . . . Don't believe anybody who tells you the entry level of the new spacecraft will be as safe as the modern airliner.' The warning could have alarmed the audience, but looking around Rutan could see that no one took his pessimism seriously. The only handicap was the timetable. Every deadline Branson had mentioned since 2004 had been missed. In future, to give the impression that Virgin Galactic's safe launch was on course, he planned to stage regular 'unveilings'.

One year after the explosion, on 24 July 2008, a memorial service was held outside the Voyager diner in Mojave for the three dead engineers. In a sheltered space near a model of SpaceShipOne, a motley plaque was unveiled for an event which remained unexplained to the public. Branson's absence guaranteed the deaths would remain forgotten outside the space community. Four days later, he landed in Mojave in his personal Falcon 900EX jet, called *Galactic Girl*, with his eighty-four-year-old mother, Eve. The Falcon's tail fin was decorated with Virgin Galactic's livery. With a top speed of 662 mph, the private jet carrying fourteen passengers appeared to contradict Branson's environmental credentials. 'Richard lives a certain lifestyle,' explained his aide, ambiguously.

Virgin Galactic was emerging as a godsend in Branson's campaign to elevate the Virgin brand in America. Virgin America's flights between San Francisco and New York had started. To create publicity, Branson arranged for 150 journalists to be flown from San Francisco and Los Angeles to Mojave on the new airline. They would witness the roll-out of WhiteKnightTwo, the specially built plane which would carry the Virgin Galactic rocket to 50,000 feet. Attracting such a remarkable number of journalists guaranteed global attention.

Burt Rutan led the visitors along the tarmac to Scaled's hangar, where he revealed a large shape draped with a white sheet. 'SpaceShipTwo,' confided Virgin's publicists, playing the first of several favourite lines. 'The rocket will be ready for testing and flying next year.' Their assertion proved to be untrue, but since, according to the same publicists, 100 people had paid the full $200,000 for a ride and 175 had paid a $20,000 deposit, the promise needed to be kept alive. 'We've already had a number of inquiries', Will Whitehorn told journalists, 'from people about whether they could be the first to have sex in space. But we haven't accepted their bookings.'

Accompanied by music and melodrama, WhiteKnightTwo was unveiled on the tarmac. 'One of the most beautiful and extraordinary aviation vehicles ever developed,' Branson told his guests, all gazing at the twin-fuselaged plane with a 140-foot single wing, powered by four Pratt & Whitney engines. No one doubted the grandeur of the moment. Rutan's catamaran was three times bigger than WhiteKnightOne, the plane used for the original flight.

Amid the emotion, the visiting journalists did not notice a small hangar adjacent to Scaled's rented by XCOR, a rival space-flight developer managed by Andrew Nelson. Unlike Virgin Galactic, XCOR's Lynx rocket motor had been successfully tested thousands of times. And unlike Rutan's hybrid engine, which needed to be dismantled and refitted to the spaceship after each flight, XCOR used a fill-up-and-go rocket powered by kerosene ignited by liquid oxygen which could be reused hundreds of times, saving money and time. While Virgin Galactic would be launched from WhiteKnightTwo after an hour's flight and would take about an hour to return to a runway, XCOR's cheaper rocket would, according to its designers, reach space from Mojave in just thirty minutes. Unlike Branson's fascination for space tourism, XCOR aimed to deliver payloads into space and carry a single passenger for $100,000. Some of Virgin Galactic's customers had also reserved places on XCOR's rocket. Branson was not unaware of XCOR's advantages. As he openly confessed, he was wholly uneducated about space technology, so he was equally unaware that Virgin had rejected the offer of a stake in Reaction Engines, a more advanced British rocket venture based in Oxfordshire. 'We don't finance the development of new ideas,' Virgin had explained.

On the same day as Branson's party in Mojave, XCOR's executives had headed to the annual aviation exhibition in Oshkosh, Wisconsin. Alongside their Lynx spacecraft was the Dragon, made by SpaceX, Virgin Galactic's biggest competitor. The brainchild of Elon Musk, the billionaire inventor of PayPal, SpaceX was negotiating substantial contracts with the American government for delivering payloads to the space shuttle.

Branson and Rutan appeared oblivious to their competitors when they belatedly arrived in Oshkosh. Amid laughter and applause, they pushed through the crowds in Pavilion 7 describing the previous day's excitement. 'The signal that we wanted to get across', said Branson, 'is that we are getting ready for business.' To his audience of believers, he described a new industry and a new way of life – something nearly beyond the imagination. 'You'll soon be flying with Virgin around the moon and to a Virgin resort hotel in space,' said Rutan. 'Today, I think that can happen in my lifetime.' Take-off, added Branson, could be the following year – 2009. No one mentioned that Virgin Galactic still lacked a viable rocket motor. And even when it was fully developed, it might never be capable of flying in space.

Branson had arrived in Oshkosh in *Galactic Girl*. For a few, the sight of an environmental crusader jetting around in a Falcon promoting his space business was jarring. But the majority applauded the unconventional maverick. Unlike the attitude of American billionaires, his rejection of the vulgar excesses normally associated with vast wealth encouraged confidence. His appearance – modest and genial – during his planned exposure in America would mask the reality of a tough British businessman intent on sealing profitable deals.

Since 1967, when he was seventeen, Branson had concealed his single-minded pursuit of money behind successive charades. Using seduction and salesmanship, he had charmed countless talented musicians, journalists, engineers, inventors, financiers, businessmen and women of all backgrounds. From student publisher to shopkeeper to music producer to airline owner and then simultaneously to investor in dozens of different ventures, his unthreatening manner rarely ceased to win his admirers' trust and their sacrifice. Few remained unimpressed by his successful sale of Virgin Music and the launch of Virgin Atlantic, combined with his dazzling feats in speedboats and hot-air balloons. His victories and glory attracted universal worship – except from his victims. Many former friends, partners and advisers resented the small reward for their contribution to Branson's ventures, especially those in the music business. Few properly understood his instinct to spot their personal weaknesses and his skill at concealing his own. None had grasped that the embrace of the Virgin family implied ownership by the proprietor. Enthusiastically, each offered unqualified loyalty to Virgin executives acting as creative catalysts. Then, the relationships soured. Collaboration meant subservience, not equality. Occasionally, their joint businesses crashed. The consequence of their misjudgement was debilitating. Talented men complained that their trust had been abused. They had flocked to team up with a famous hero only to be disappointed. Betrayal left a sour taste. While telling their stories, grown men became tearful. They slunk silently away, bruised and defeated. Scattered across the world, they blamed misplaced faith in Branson for signing contracts tilted in his favour. They were bewildered by their misjudgement, and their self-esteem had plummeted. In public, nothing was said; confessions of failure were not a good advertisement for future business projects. Any reservations they dared to utter about the global hero were invariably swept aside by a man who, even when defeated, elicited sympathy rather than rebuke.

In 1999, Branson's financial crisis and his failure the following year to land the national-lottery licence could have provoked carping. Instead, he was praised for selling a 49 per cent stake in Virgin Atlantic to Singapore Airlines in a turbulent market; and in 2002, he was admired for pocketing a huge profit from Virgin Blue, a new Australian airline. Overlooked was Virgin Atlantic's weak management, lumbered by rising costs and falling revenue. After 2004, his airline's finances were again threatened. Taking risks to survive was Branson's gospel but, to save Virgin Atlantic, the corporation's cure had been perfidious: Virgin executives broke the law. And the fuse of their criminality had been lit, the British government's prosecutors would claim, with Branson's knowledge.

5

Virgin's Crime

Seven months before Branson stood on the podium in Manhattan with Bill Clinton to pledge $3 billion to the environment, senior executives employed by the world's major airlines were enjoying a gala dinner in Hong Kong as guests of IATA, the industry's global representative. Gradually, conversations on every table were interrupted as the executives – one by one – answered incoming calls or read messages on their mobile telephones. Dark-suited men paled, stood up and left the atrium with phones still clasped to their ears. Their reaction was replicated across the world.

At 6 a.m. New York time on St Valentine's Day 2006, police in America, Europe and Asia had waved search warrants and entered airline offices, seizing records and computers. Shortly after, lawyers arrived to serve subpoenas demanding that the airlines' executives answer questions regarding an illegal cartel. According to the subpoenas, since the late 1980s the airlines had secretly fixed the price of cargo shipped across the world. By removing competition, the airlines had profited at the public's expense.

The tip-off about the crime had been passed to the Department of Justice in Washington DC by lawyers representing Lufthansa, the German airline. By confessing, the company hoped to avoid a massive fine. At the direction of the department's lawyers, over one hundred FBI agents in New York had raided offices at Kennedy airport, including those of British Airways and Virgin Atlantic. Simultaneously, buildings were raided in other countries, including BA's offices at Heathrow. In every country, the police departed with files, computers and downloads of emails.

Sifting through the evidence, the US Department of Justice's lawyers found proof implicating BA and Virgin Atlantic in the cargo cartel. With limited resources, the lawyers decided to focus on twenty airlines, including BA. By virtue of its size, Virgin was classified as a fringe participant and excluded from the investigation.

Unaware of their client's escape, Virgin's lawyers continued to scrutinise the information submitted by the department about the conspiracy. The potential penalty for each guilty airline was 10 per cent of their annual revenue: BA was facing a fine of £850 million; Virgin's fine would be £180 million. For BA, buffeted by a pension-fund deficit, rising oil prices and industrial problems, the financial penalty was crippling. For Virgin, it could be fatal.

In June 2006, the department's lawyers asked each airline: 'Was the same price-fixing happening on the other side of the house – on the passengers' side of the business?' Unanimously, the airlines replied, 'No.' Cargo, the airlines including BA explained, was a self-contained village on the far side of airports staffed by different people. The Department of Justice accepted those denials, without specifically noting that the only airline failing to deny the suggestion was Virgin.

Virgin Atlantic's lawyers in America had asked the company's executives whether other types of price-fixing had been discussed with any rival airline. In reply, Willy Boulter, the director of sales, admitted a secret relationship with Alan Burnett, BA's sales director. Starting in 2004, explained Boulter, directors at Virgin and BA had discussed the Passenger Fuel Surcharge – an additional fee each passenger paid to cover rising fuel prices. Both airlines, according to Boulter, had secretly agreed to avoid mutually damaging competition by imposing the identical surcharge on passengers on the same date. The arrangement, said Boulter, had ended in early 2006. Virgin's lawyers concluded that the discussions amounted to a criminal conspiracy to fix prices.

Considering the appalling relationship between the airlines since Virgin Atlantic's creation in 1984, few would have imagined that the two corporations might have conspired together. But the information the lawyers received was unambiguous. Steve Ridgway, Virgin Atlantic's chief executive since 2001, had approved the secret discussions with BA's executives and, according to the prosecution in the subsequent trial, 'Ridgway did reveal to Sir Richard Branson at some stage that he had some sort of contact at British Airways.' That allegation would be repeated by a defence lawyer, who would tell the jury that while Branson's ethos for his airline was 'fierce competition', Branson 'knew about' the secret discussions with BA about fixing the surcharge. As the prosecutor would tell the jury in 2010, 'You may conclude as you look at the documents and you hear from the witnesses that he [Branson] certainly had an interest in the pricing policy of the airline, Virgin.' Or, as another defence lawyer alleged, 'Sir Richard Branson was kept informed of any information or discussion regarding the Passenger Fuel Surcharge. He knew about it.'

Four years earlier, in 2006, Branson was told by his lawyers, who were still unaware that the airline had been excluded from the US Department of Justice's investigation, that discovery of the discussions about the fuel surcharge with BA could trigger a second ruinous fine. Escape was possible, his lawyers advised. Under American law, the whistleblower of a crime received immunity from prosecution. If Virgin was the first to confess to the Department of Justice, the airline and its executives could avoid fines and imprisonment. The lawyers recorded interviews with three Virgin directors. All three admitted discussions with BA's executives but denied knowing that their conversations and agreements were criminal. Soon after, with Branson's approval, Virgin's lawyer approached the Department of Justice.

Scott Hammond, the department's liaison officer, had not expected the lawyer's telephone call. Until that moment, investigators were unaware of any conversations between Virgin and BA about the surcharge. Nor, they subsequently admitted, would they ever have found any trace of that secret. If Virgin's executives, with Branson's agreement, had not initiated the confession, their agreements with BA would not have been exposed.

'Virgin wants to put down a marker about fixing the Passenger Fuel Surcharge with British Airways,' said the Virgin lawyer. 'Are we the first?'

'Yes', replied Hammond, disguising his surprise.

'I want you to hold our place in the amnesty,' said the lawyer.

'You're the first. You've got thirty days to perfect your marker and tell us if you've got something or not.'

Before the end of that period, Virgin Atlantic and its three senior executives formally confessed to the crime, and in exchange were granted immunity from prosecution and any punishment. The agreement was kept secret until, on 10 March 2007, Virgin's lawyers approached the Office of Fair Trading (OFT) in London to admit the company's involvement in a criminal cartel with BA and again ask for immunity from prosecution.

According to Virgin's confession, the conspiracy with BA had started with a telephone call in August 2004 between Paul Moore, Virgin Atlantic's director of communications, and Iain Burns, his counterpart at BA. Who initiated the call was disputed, but the content of the conversation was agreed. The two men discussed the time and date both airlines would announce the increase of a Passenger Fuel Surcharge to £6. After both referred their discussion to their superiors, the first of several secret agreements was implemented: both airlines would announce their own surcharge on the same day. The background to that first conversation reflected Branson's financial problems over the previous years.

The terrorist attacks on New York and Washington in September 2001 had cost Virgin Atlantic about £100 million over the following year. Despite Branson's confident prediction that his airline would recover within three years, he had postponed the delivery of the new Airbus A380 double-deckers, saying some airports were not ready for the planes. The excuse was denied by Airbus's spokesman, who added that no other airline had delayed delivery. To protect Branson from embarrassment, nothing more was said, but Virgin abruptly terminated publicity of Branson's colourful promises about parties in the sky in the new plane's bars and mile-high sex in its double beds. To conceal Virgin's financial reality – and the airline is still not flying an A380 – Branson resorted to gimmicks to embarrass BA.

His first machination followed Concorde's crash in Paris in 2000, which killed 113 people. In the aftermath, Air France and BA decided, on the manufacturer's recommendation, to abandon the loss-making and unserviceable supersonic plane. Branson criticised that decision. Virgin Atlantic, he said, wanted to buy and fly Concorde. In 2003, he offered BA £1 for the aircraft, the price he said the airline had originally paid. When BA refused, Branson demanded that they should repay £600 million to the government in compensation for what Branson called the 'hoodwink' in the early 1980s. Next, he demanded that Tony Blair, the prime minister, save Concorde. Many were puzzled by his sustained attack. Concorde usually flew half full, lacked spare parts, cost a fortune in fuel and damaged the environment. Yet Branson, despite his financial problems, insisted that Virgin wanted to inherit the plane. The government refused. 'Branson's just looking for publicity,' was BA's comment.

His next wheeze occurred during Virgin Atlantic's inaugural flight to Australia. Branson offered his passengers sick bags decorated with the ill-fated ethnic designs which BA had painted on the tails of its aircraft. BA had discarded the designs amid ridicule.

The third ploy reflected Branson's habit of enjoying a competitor's discomfort. In the aftermath of 9/11, Branson pointedly mentioned BA's financial difficulties, especially as a result of rising fuel prices. Most dismissed his jibes as irrelevant. Virgin Atlantic was a minnow, ranking tenth in terms of passengers carried on the transatlantic routes, and his airline was weakened by his refusal to join a code-sharing alliance with other airlines. But his biting comments did affect BA's struggle to survive.

To compete against the two major alliances created by other European airlines with two American giants – Delta and United – BA wanted to forge an alliance with American Airlines. Branson deemed BA's survival plan a threat to Virgin Atlantic's independent existence, and in 1996 he had orchestrated a blockbuster campaign in London and Washington to persuade the two governments to prevent BA's alliance with AA. In 2004, the circumstances changed, when the EU and the US government annulled all restrictions on transatlantic travel. Among the casualties was the Bermuda Agreement of 1976, which had limited access for flights from America to Heathrow to two American and two British airlines, one of which became Virgin. Overnight, Virgin's lucrative protection at Heathrow disappeared. Branson, as the champion of competition, should have welcomed the benefits to travellers but, since his profits were threatened, he protested.

He railed against BA's new bid for an alliance with AA, yet approached Sheikh Ahmed Al Maktoum of Dubai to discuss co-operation between Virgin Atlantic and Emirates airways. Branson's good fortune was that the public ignored his contradictions. Few ever quite understood his undisguised fears about fuel prices. In public speeches, he often mentioned that 'I am building bioethanol factories to get an alternative to oil and cut

Virgin Atlantic's fuel bill.' He would even repeat his mantra during a visit to Dubai while opening a Megastore.

In early August 2004, alarmed that Virgin Atlantic's finances were being jeopardised by rising fuel prices, Branson began speculating with his executives about BA's reaction to the increases. Would BA levy a higher fuel surcharge? For Branson, BA was the elephant threatening his survival, but his obsession was not reciprocated. BA regarded Virgin Atlantic as one of many small competitors, albeit an unreliable irritant. Considering the historic enmity between Virgin and BA, the likelihood of BA executives inviting Branson to join a conspiracy to fix the surcharge was low. But the evidence presented by the prosecutors in Washington and later London, based on the information supplied by Virgin, suggested the opposite.

In the first days of August, Virgin executives decided to increase the fuel surcharge by £5. Soon after the decision was taken, Branson asked Paul Moore to discover from journalists whether BA intended to levy a higher surcharge than Virgin. Moore reported to Branson that BA was briefing selected journalists that their surcharge would increase.

Soon after, Branson telephoned David Parsley, a sympathetic financial journalist employed by Express Newspapers. 'British Airways', said Branson, 'are going to increase their surcharge.' Branson was hoping that Parsley would discover the amount. After thanking Branson for the tip, Parsley called Iain Burns, who confirmed that BA's surcharge would increase from £2.50 to £6, or possibly £8. The newspaper would publish Parsley's discovery three days later. According to the defence lawyers in the subsequent trial, the timetable laid suspicion at Branson's door. After speaking to Parsley, stated BA's lawyers, Branson told Moore to call Burns. Branson, it was alleged, did not want Virgin to take the lead and make the announcement alone.

If that scenario was true, then Moore would appear to have

made the first call. However, supported by Virgin's executives, Moore emphatically denied taking the initiative and starting the conspiracy. After all, that admission would have cast Virgin as the architect of the crime. The obfuscation benefited Virgin because, from the outset of the Department of Justice's investigation, the American lawyers appeared not to have sought evidence to contradict Moore's version of how the subsequent discussions between Virgin and BA about further increases in the fuel surcharge occurred.

'This is a conversation we're not having,' were the undisputed opening words of the telephone conversation on 6 August 2004 between Moore and Iain Burns. To establish BA as the villain behind the alleged conspiracy, the prosecutors in America and Britain relied on statements signed by Moore alleging that Burns had called him first, thus casting Burns and BA as responsible for initiating the conspiracy. Burns would deny the accusation. His lawyers would say that Virgin's attempt to incriminate BA was a distortion of the truth.

The two men did, however, agree about the content of the first telephone call: Burns revealed that BA was planning to impose a surcharge of £6, while Moore disclosed Virgin Atlantic's agreement to impose a £5 surcharge on long-distance flights. Moore's testimony about the events that followed was critical to the prosecution. He would say that after Burns called him 'out of the blue', he went immediately to see Steve Ridgway, who in turn summoned Willy Boulter, Virgin Atlantic's commercial director. Moore told them, 'You won't believe the call I've just had from British Airways,' and then read his recollection of the exchange from his notebook. Virgin's two executives decided that the airline should agree with BA on the timing of the announcement and match the amount of the surcharge.

The economics of pricing airline tickets is complex. Airlines continuously change their prices without notice. Passengers in any Boeing 777 would be paying about sixty different fares, based on constant recalculations by sophisticated computer programs. A conspiracy between airlines to fix all those prices would be difficult. Fuel surcharges, however, have always been publicly announced. Ridgway knew that Branson was nervous about the mechanics of publicising a surcharge. Some inside Virgin would even say that Branson was 'obsessed' by the actual words used in Virgin's announcement. In particular, he wanted the context of the surcharge – the rising oil prices – to be properly explained.

On 6 August, Branson was satisfied by the statement drafted by Moore, and Moore was told to confirm his agreement about the timing of the announcement with Burns. BA, everyone agreed, would make the first announcement of a £6 increase, and Virgin would follow hours later. This was the conspiracy to which Virgin pleaded guilty, wilfully incriminating BA. There was, however, another version.

Weeks after the £6 surcharge was announced, Branson, according to prosecutors, 'emailed Boulter and suggested that Virgin should consider again increasing its Passenger Fuel Surcharge'. The following day, Boulter discussed a further increase with Alan Burnett, BA's sales director. Boulter reported his agreement with Burnett to Ridgway, and two months after agreeing the £6 surcharge, BA and Virgin Atlantic simultaneously announced that their respective Passenger Fuel Surcharges would go up to £10.

Over the following months, oil prices continued to rise and Virgin's finances were squeezed. In March 2005, after intense discussions within BA and by Virgin's executives, Moore and Burns spoke again. Acting as messengers, they agreed about the timing of their respective announcements that the surcharge would be raised by a further £6, to £16 each way. On 24 June, after more discussions between Boulter and Burnett, both airlines increased their surcharge to £24. In anticipation of the announcement, Moore sent Burns a copy of Virgin's press release. On the same day, Branson appeared on TV to say that he was opposed to fuel surcharges. No one at BA's headquarters was surprised by Branson's inconsistency, but everyone knew that Virgin Atlantic's finances had deteriorated. They would get worse after Hurricane Katrina hit the US. In the aftermath, oil prices soared, almost doubling in one year.

On 1 September, Steve Ridgway told Paul Moore, 'I want you to have another of your conversations with British Airways.' Moore called Branson, and immediately afterwards rang Burns. The two men were messengers of a further increase in the surcharge, but with a twist. Branson had discussed imposing a higher surcharge on first-class passengers with Ridgway, and Moore mentioned that possibility to Burns.

Pertinently, the senior executives of the two airlines were due to meet on Sunday 4 September at Branson's Oxfordshire home. Branson was hosting a cricket match to mark the retirement of Rod Eddington, BA's chief executive, and to celebrate their improved relationship. To repair the damage of the airlines' vicious war, a prosecutor would say, Eddington had 'not so much offered an olive branch; more like an olive tree'.

In the subsequent trial of Burns and three other BA executives, Richard Latham QC, the prosecutor, described events leading up to the cricket match. Branson, said Latham, had told Boulter to 'sound out his contact at British Airways about a potential surcharge increase'. Branson wanted to know BA's reaction if Virgin increased the surcharge again. In particular, Branson wanted Boulter to check with his BA contact 'to see if they would follow if Virgin was to lead with a variable Passenger Fuel Surcharge'. Latham based his allegation on Boulter's own admission to the Department of Justice. Initially, Boulter explained, he was 'reluctant' to fall in with Branson's suggestion because the conversation needed to be 'more sophisticated' and, around the time of the cricket match, several parallel discussions between Virgin and

BA were under way. Nevertheless, before the game, Boulter did speak to Alan Burnett, apparently laying the ground for a conversation between Branson and Eddington when they met.

During that hot Sunday, the two men were seen to be engaged in a lengthy conversation, in which they agreed that surviving in the airline business was tough. Neither could recall, when subsequently questioned, whether the surcharge had been mentioned. They parted on good terms, although BA won the cricket match. Two days later, Virgin increased its one-way surcharge across the Atlantic from £24 to £30/$55. In an email sent to Virgin Atlantic staff on the same day as he announced the surcharge, in a statement vetted by Branson, Paul Moore warned that any photographs of the match should be kept private. 'Please don't put anything up on the intranet [*sic*]!!!!!!!!' he wrote. 'If British Airways follow our surcharge it might not look too clever to show us fraternising two days before.' Two days later, BA imposed the same surcharge. Pertinently, the prosecution would decide not to mention the conversation between Branson and Eddington.

Five months later, the US Department of Justice launched its St Valentine's Day raids to find evidence of a cartel fixing cargo prices. Despite the turmoil, in April 2006 Moore and Burns spoke once more about surcharges, but their relationship ended abruptly once Virgin's lawyers became involved.

Virgin's immunity agreement with the Department of Justice and the OFT included an obligation to hand over all the relevant documents, emails and telephone records to the investigators. To comply, Virgin's lawyers commissioned experts to download data from the company's computers. At the same time, Ridgway and two other executives gave formal interviews and statements to the Department of Justice. Those early declarations described their discussions with BA, but they professed ignorance that they could be criminal. Moore, for example, while implicating

Branson in the discussions within Virgin, told the lawyers, 'We all felt that however dodgy the conversations might have felt, they weren't price-fixing . . . The surcharge was different to the price.' In his early statements, he always referred to 'price-matching' rather than 'price-fixing'. Those statements were unhelpful to the prosecution: the immunity agreement had been granted only in exchange for Virgin's confession to a crime. 'Other interests', a Department of Justice lawyer sighed, 'are coming into play' – not least, the lawyers suspected, to protect Branson's reputation.

Branson, while still uncertain about the outcome, accepted an invitation to an interview at the Department of Justice's office on 14th Street in Washington. He was shown emails sent to himself by Ridgway and others referring to the discussions with BA and asked to comment. To each question he replied, 'I can't remember this.'

'He's not going to get his hands dirty,' concluded an investigator. 'He's saying that he wasn't at the sharp end.'

'You know, Mr Branson,' said an official, 'you're co-operating with the US government because you want us to win. You're here because you want the British Airways folk convicted.'

Branson did not reply. Snitching on BA, he must have appreciated, would have consequences, but if Virgin failed to co-operate, the prosecutors would withdraw the immunity agreement. The airline's owner, the lawyers realised, was reluctant to testify for the prosecution. His priority, they believed, was to exclude himself from any criminal trial. Once in the witness box, he would be vulnerable to a damaging attack on his motives. The defence lawyers representing BA's executives could recite Branson's long campaign against his rival. He might be accused of entrapping their clients in another chapter of their historic enmity. His dilemma presented the department with a problem. Although Ridgway admitted that Branson was made aware of the discussions with BA, the Department of Justice could not prove that

Branson had read the emails addressed to him. Since Branson said that he could not recall any of the discussions, the lawyers in Washington and London decided that his poor memory barred him as a potential witness for the prosecution. He escaped the spotlight. The remaining Virgin executives could not prevaricate. To retain their immunity, they were obliged to provide testimony that persuaded a jury that the BA executives were, like themselves, criminals.

The investigators focused first on Paul Moore, who had been Virgin's contact with Iain Burns. Moore's initial statement had been woolly. He described a close relationship with Burns, but his recollection of their first conversation was vague. In subsequent statements, prompted by the prosecutors, Moore's memory became sharper. Burns would identify two mistakes. Firstly, he did not have a close relationship with Moore. They had first met at a peace-making lunch hosted by Will Whitehorn, and once again at a trade conference. That did not amount to a 'close relationship'. And Burns insisted that Moore had telephoned him first.

Over the following months, the three Virgin executives – Paul Moore, Willy Boulter and Steve Ridgway – each made eight separate statements to the Department of Justice. Increasingly, each man shifted from professions of innocence to outright confessions of guilt and the direct implication of four BA executives in an illegal conspiracy. Thereafter, Virgin's lawyers produced three binders drawn from the company's records to support their admission of a conspiracy. 'A silver-platter approach,' concluded a prosecutor. Virgin Atlantic avoided a £180 million fine.

Willie Walsh, the new chief executive of BA, was unaware of those shifts. He cursed his poisoned inheritance from Eddington's era of the cargo cartel. After lengthy negotiations, in June 2007 BA pleaded guilty in Washington to price-fixing for that cartel and began negotiating the fine. After BA's plea, the Virgin executives could be satisfied that their airline had escaped any sanction.

In London, the OFT's legal team, first led by Simon Williams, grasped the guilty plea as an opportunity to prosecute BA's executives for the fuel surcharge, relying on Virgin's executives as the key witnesses. Ali Nikpay, the OFT director who inherited the case, was particularly keen to pursue BA because no individual had yet been prosecuted under a new anti-cartel law. If convicted, the four faced five years' imprisonment and unlimited fines amid a deluge of media attention.

The OFT's raid on BA's headquarters near Heathrow in July 2007 stunned Willie Walsh. Within the building, his outrage over Branson's betrayal was loud. Many BA executives had always blamed Branson for contriving the 'dirty tricks' litigation in the late 1980s to publicly humiliate their company. They were unforgiving about his successful defeat of BA in 1993 over alleged libels by the airline's former chairman, and now they believed his aggression was being revived, despite the truce initiated by Sir Rod Eddington. Branson, the BA executives raged, had betrayed their trust. One indignant executive even ordered that Branson's cameo appearance in *Casino Royale*, the James Bond film, be edited out of the version shown on BA aircraft. One day, he pledged, there would be retaliation. Another dreamt of repeating an American politician's defiance: 'I'm going to give you a three-minute lesson in integrity. Then I'm going to ruin you.' The reality was, however, indisputable. Ever since Will Whitehorn had invited Iain Burns and Paul Moore for lunch, BA's executives had dropped their guard and trusted Branson.

The OFT's formal indictments shocked the four executives. Instantly, they proclaimed their innocence. Like Willie Walsh, none doubted that Branson had, in his own words, 'screwed us'.

6

Virgin's Saviour

Occasionally, Branson was beaten by competitors, but he rarely suffered the bitter taste of being 'screwed'. He enjoyed a scrap and he fought to win. Opponents could expect no mercy, as BA's Lord King discovered, after he injudiciously cast doubt on Branson's veracity and was compelled to make a humiliating apology about BA's so-called 'dirty tricks'. Branson had enjoyed trashing King's reputation.

Losing no longer bore the same horror for Branson after the rejection in 2000 of his bid to run Britain's national lottery. The first defeat in 1994 had provoked tears, but he had also scored revenge against the winner, Guy Snowden, the chairman of Camelot. In a successful libel action, Branson had shattered Snowden, a decent man. In a BBC TV programme broadcast a year after losing the bid for the lottery, he described how Snowden had offered him a bribe at the end of a lunch in his home. Snowden publicly denied the allegation, and Branson sued for defamation. Branson claimed that Snowden's denial of a bribe implied that Branson was a liar. Branson's victory reinforced his pristine image, but many pertinent questions were left dangling.

In Britain, those sensational triumphs divided sentiment about Branson, but he was more loved than loathed. The majority enjoyed his cheeky taunts, admired his daredevil risks and supported his championing of underdogs. Whether Virgin's publicity machine presented him as the victor or the victim, the company emerged successful.

The Virgin brand had become Branson's cash card. Aspiring businessmen regularly offered him ideas to make their fortune, and the few he accepted agreed to his terms, which tilted the financial odds overwhelmingly in his favour. Robustly, he squeezed suitors to his own advantage.

Tom Alexander's arrival at Branson's London home in 1998 had been no different from that of dozens of predecessors offering joint ventures. Alexander had spent eighteen years in the telecommunications industry, most recently developing BT's mobile-telephone operations at Cellnet.

Alexander's idea was shrewd. After billions of pounds had been invested in building a network of masts and computers to provide a nationwide mobile-telephone service, he had spotted that BT, Orange and T-Mobile owned a considerable amount of spare capacity. He had proposed that Cellnet should create a new network based on renting that spare capacity. It would offer low call rates to owners of pay-as-you-go mobile telephones, especially during the night and at weekends. However, BT's executives were uninterested. The company was focused on developing the new 3G spectrum rather than seeking bottom-end subscribers.

After that rejection, Alexander could either let the idea die and remain at Cellnet, or else find a backer for a private venture. Virgin was his obvious destination. Branson was known as a risk-taker, and the brand was a Mecca for start-ups. The Virgin label appeared to win any product the consumers' recognition. Alexander approached Gordon McCallum, Branson's chief executive. In turn, McCallum persuaded Branson to consider a classic Virgin venture – challenging Vodafone and BT, the established players. Branson made the call as Alexander was driving home at night: 'I love the idea. Give me an outline of the concept and come with your team to Holland Park.'

Alexander arrived with three Cellnet associates. Branson's

visitors soon realised that the tycoon did not understand the telephone business or the technology. But he did agree to support the development of Virgin Mobile.

'I'll give you the money to get it up and running,' said Branson.

The four left Holland Park dreaming about the fortunes they would make from an eventual flotation. Branson's energy and promises, they agreed, were 'empowering'. Virgin was 'a uniquely exciting environment, unseen in any other business'.

After resigning from BT, Alexander called a Virgin executive to inquire where his new offices were located. Before the end of the first week, there had been a 'rude awakening'. There was no Virgin 'hothouse of help' to develop the business's infrastructure. Virgin, he also discovered, had no money to spare, and Branson's assurance of financial support did not materialise. 'I'm surprised', Alexander told his friends, 'that Virgin has no financial resources.' There was neither cash nor any relationship with banks to borrow any money. From the outset, Alexander would need to raise bank loans himself. Effectively on their own, the four rented an office in Euston, with Alexander wandering down Tottenham Court Road to buy coffee mugs, pens and paper.

During those months of struggle, Alexander often despaired. His lifebelt was Branson's occasional telephone calls at 6 a.m. on Sunday mornings. 'What's happening?' asked the voice, just before he went to sleep in Necker. Alexander's self-doubt was dismissed. 'Of course you can do it, Tom,' soothed Branson. To Alexander, Branson's praise was gold dust.

In return, Alexander was offering Branson a potential gold mine. For some years, Branson had not found a lucrative business to exploit his brand. The deal junkie with a weakness for profitable new ideas was often tempted by the offer of a free business in exchange for the brand, but his opportunities were diminishing. He was also restrained by the conservatism of Stephen Murphy, the group's financial chief, and Gordon McCallum, whose focus was increasingly on tax planning and extracting better returns rather than engaging in new businesses. Mobile telephones were the exception, however. Unusually, McCallum said 'yes' rather than 'no'.

After several months, Alexander succeeded in negotiating an agreement to buy network space from T-Mobile, which was owned by Deutsche Telekom. In exchange, the Germans would own half of Virgin Mobile. He now needed over £100 million to rent premises, hire and train the staff, and launch a marketing campaign to persuade Vodafone and BT customers to switch to a new network. On the basis of Alexander's proposal, without any material help from Virgin, J. P. Morgan offered a £126 million loan. 'I took leave of my marbles,' one banker who negotiated the loan would later say. 'I took the risk without any collateral.' The moneyman trusted Virgin's brand. He also anticipated Branson's technique of taking maximum benefit with minimal investment to avoid any financial risk.

With everything in place, Alexander arrived in Holland Park to negotiate with Branson and McCallum the ownership of the remaining half of the shares in Virgin Mobile. Ever since 1967, Branson's balancing of upsides and downsides were Oscar-winning performances. Fixing deals on his way to mutating from a school drop-out into a billionaire had required steely charm to disguise his exploitation of a vulnerable target. The casualties of his empire-building were legion. Mike Oldfield had been persuaded to sell the rights of *Tubular Bells* for a pittance; Randolph Fields, the co-founder of Virgin Atlantic, had been cajoled into relinquishing his financial rights in exchange for a few free transatlantic tickets; most of those involved with Virgin Music – the original creators and the public shareholders – had departed without a substantial reward; and brothers Tim and Rory McCarthy had lost their entire £80 million fortune backing V2, a dud music company established by Branson. Like many others, they had succumbed to skills honed to capture prizes. Occasionally, Branson was rebuffed by tougher combatants, but Tom Alexander was ill prepared for the well-rehearsed performance – not least because the inventor of Virgin Mobile felt indebted to Branson for realising his ambition.

Alexander emerged from Holland Park grateful that his work had been rewarded with about 6 per cent of the shares, to be divided between the four men. Virgin took 44 per cent of the business in return for a minuscule investment, as was Branson's custom. He took few risks and grabbed any profits. Ever since Virgin's failed investments in clothes, cola, cosmetics, cars, cinema and energy, his search for another success similar to Virgin Music and Virgin Atlantic had proved elusive. Unknown to Alexander, Branson desperately needed a commercial windfall. The Virgin Atlantic sale had been just the headline act in a slew of disposals to rescue his fragile finances. Virgin Mobile was a punt with a difference: J. P. Morgan's loan bestowed credibility on the risk.

In the course of over one year, Alexander and his team worked on organising the virtual telephone network's sales and administration. After endless testing, he was satisfied that his invention was ready for sale.

Among Branson's talents was organising spectacular launches. To promote Virgin Mobile he appeared on a float in Leicester Square, surrounded by topless models. He posed just long enough for dozens of photographers to record his illegal stunt before the police arrived and he disappeared. The sexy spectacle was successful. Within two years, the network had signed up 1.6 million subscribers, including many fans of Virgin Music and the Megastores. By 2002, 2.1 million customers were making Virgin Mobile profitable. Instinctively aggressive, Branson could not resist gloating: 'Since our launch in November 1999, billions of pounds have been wiped off the value of our competitors and many established names in telecoms have collapsed.' He anticipated earning over £1 billion personally when the company was floated in the near future. His financial problems were solved – for the time being.

The bonanza, he hoped, would be doubled by launching Virgin Mobile in America. John Tantum, a thirty-two-year-old Californian, had proposed the idea to Gordon McCallum in 1999. After an interview in his Holland Park home, Branson agreed that Virgin would invest a limited amount of money in Tantum's scheme in return for a 90 per cent stake in the American company. Like so many seeking a partnership with Branson, Tantum accepted the lopsided deal. Pertinently, Branson did not offer Tom Alexander a share of the potential profits in America, nor would J. P. Morgan earn any additional revenue. Branson kept the gold for himself. He also excluded Tantum and the American staff in San Francisco from converting without risk any shares into cash.

After two years' work, Tantum was fired. A year later, his replacement was struggling. The sheer scale of the American market made Virgin's attempts appear puny. Lacking money for a sustained promotion campaign, Virgin Mobile USA claimed to have 500,000 subscribers – just 1 per cent of the market – against Verizon's thirty-three million, but many of Virgin's turned out to be illusory. Branson was targeting young people with a pre-pay package that included a telephone sold at a loss. Many customers modified their handsets for use on other networks, or abandoned Virgin without paying the full value for the telephone. The ill-fated American venture was mirrored in Australia. There, Virgin Mobile was reported to have been prosecuted with its partner Optus (owned by SingTel) by the Competition and Consumer Commission for engaging in 'false, misleading and deceptive conduct'. Virgin Mobile's adverts had allegedly failed to reveal the full cash price of the packages and the real cost of terminating the contracts.

The minor disappointments did not hinder Branson's search for cash. The obvious source was selling Virgin Mobile shares to the public through the City of London. His hurdle was a legacy of disappointed shareholders. Ever since Virgin Music's unprofitable flotation in 1988 and the unethical treatment of its shareholders, many City financiers had lost confidence in Branson. His criticism of analysts for scrutinising his businesses had been accompanied by his vow never to seek public shareholders again, but the financial crisis he suffered in 1999 prompted an about-turn. Now, in 2004, Branson needed cash for new ventures, including Virgin America. His overture to the City was brash: 'I'm back. I'm successful. This time you're going to like me.' The five-year-old Virgin Mobile, he told bankers and investors, was worth £1.3 billion ($2.4 billion), and he was selling 25 per cent to personally pocket £279 million after debts had been paid off. He would also charge the new shareholders £311 million, which, according to the accounts, was the debt owed to the Virgin Group.

To many, Virgin's projections about future profits aroused suspicion. Potential investors could not value a telephone company that lacked its own network but simply relied on an advantageous contract with T-Mobile. Virgin's claim to earn 65 per cent gross profit on every call seemed doubtful. Sceptics focused on Branson's assertion that another million customers had been added over the past year, contradicting his own executives' admission that the numbers were unknown. The disbelievers scorned Branson's valuation and ridiculed his price of 285 pence per share. 'There are no plans to change the price range whatsoever,' a Virgin spokeswoman asserted defiantly.

The fight was waged on Branson's behalf by Gordon McCallum and Stephen Murphy. Their adversary was Scott Bruckner, the banker responsible for the flotation. Branson's representatives gave no quarter to get the maximum price. 'They're masters of posturing about the value of the brand and don't want to compromise,' observed an eyewitness. 'They don't show their cards, even to their advisers, until they've extracted every possible concession.' McCallum and Murphy failed to convert the disbelievers. The City's wariness bred tension, and the valuation fell. 'Find out who's to blame,' Branson ordered, convinced there was a conspiracy to denigrate him.

But the City did not deliver the hammer blow that jeopardised the flotation. The fatal threat was delivered by T-Mobile, Virgin's partner. Convinced that Virgin did not have the stomach for an expensive fight, the German company denied the existence of a contract with Virgin Mobile to supply network space for ten years. Deutsche Telekom's assertion horrified Tom Alexander and enraged Branson. Both believed that the Germans had decided to risk an expensive legal fight to neutralise the financial advantage Alexander had negotiated. Branson was the wrong person to choose; litigation was his oxygen. At the end of a tense trial, the judge denounced T-Mobile's witnesses as unreliable and found entirely in Virgin's favour. The victor took the spoils. T-Mobile sold its 50 per cent stake to Branson for about £100 million, giving Branson ownership of about 94 per cent of the company for a comparative pittance.

On the opening day of the flotation in July 2006, the shares were priced at 200 pence, but, fuelled by Branson's critics, they fell to 190 pence. Branson was bruised. His hype had failed – for the time being. The company was valued at £502 million ($925 million), less than half of what he wanted. The £120 million he received immediately was, nevertheless, a lifebelt.

'We must have a party to celebrate,' Branson had ordered, but on the night he did not appear at the venue in east London. He stayed in Necker.

Tom Alexander was celebrating. His shares were now worth about £20 million. Although his reward was a fraction of Branson's profit, he told his friends that he was not upset.

Without the Virgin brand, he explained, the business would not have existed. 'With hindsight, I should have been more worldly-wise. We should have got more, but I had no experience of how share mechanisms worked. We were naive, but it was not just about the money.'

Initially, the doubters were justified. Virgin Mobile gradually lost thousands of customers, and those who remained spent less than Branson had predicted. Virgin Mobile's position deteriorated after the regulator ordered prices to be reduced by 34 per cent.

Despite problems in America and Australia, Branson planned other Virgin Mobile networks across the world. His first stop in April 2005 was India. 'We are planning to do a lot in India,' he announced confidently. Virgin Mobile, he told the local media, would be set up 'in weeks', followed by Virgin Mobile's flotation in America 'this year' for $3 billion (£1.62 billion). Virgin would earn, he predicted, 'about $1 billion'. The only mystery was the identity of the Indian partner who would agree to Virgin 'piggy-backing on his infrastructure' in exchange for the brand but no money. By the time he left India, Branson had still not found a partner, but nonetheless he announced that his $300 million war chest would create networks in China, Mexico, Nigeria and South Africa. After that, he said, his brand would launch in Italy, Spain and France. Operators in those countries, he claimed, were 'ripping off' customers. No one mentioned that Virgin's bid to establish a mobile network in Singapore had just failed. Virgin had been shunned and few gave him much chance of success elsewhere.

And then came a lucky break, the prerequisite for any entrepreneur's success, and the reward for persistence after failure.

Up till now, all Branson's investments in the media had been disappointing. In Britain, he had failed to buy Channel 5 and several ITV franchises. He had sold his stake in British Satellite

Broadcasting (BSB) at a loss after Rupert Murdoch had established Sky. Within eighteen months, Sky had crushed BSB and had grown into a £10 billion Goliath. Branson hankered to find another way into the media. The Virgin brand attracted young buyers, but in 2007 he was flummoxed by how to exploit the buzz, because Virgin Mobile in Britain was no longer struggling. With a large number of subscribers and low costs, the profits had pushed the share price up by 80 per cent since the flotation, but in isolation the network's fate was uncertain. Then Simon Duffy called.

Duffy had recently been appointed the chief executive of NTL, a major American cable company which had bought Telewest, an insolvent British cable network. Duffy was troubled. The original cable companies in Britain and America had been ravaged by bankruptcy. The cost of laying a fibre-optic network under the roads had wrecked the pioneers' finances, and their problems were compounded by government regulations. Among the profiteers from the wreckage was Bill Huff, an American investor. Huff took control of NTL, which had debts of £5.9 billion, in 2003, and later rebranded Telewest as NTL. British customers cursed 'NTHell' for patchy infrastructure, inadequate customer service, indifferent content and confused billing, but Duffy planned to reinvent the network to provide broadband, cable television and telephones. Rebranding NTL, he calculated, would cost over £50 million. The better solution, he decided, was to forge a deal with Virgin. 'We'll call it Virgin Media,' Duffy told Branson, describing how the merged company would challenge BSkyB and British Telecom. 'You can do your normal thing taking on the big boys. Rattle their cage.' Branson was noticeably excited. Ownership of media companies in Britain conferred exceptional status.

Underlying that scenario was a more serious proposition. Duffy knew that Branson wanted a profitable exit from Virgin

Mobile, with cash deposited in his offshore bank accounts. Until Branson could find a buyer, his profits were frozen. His business had always been to earn on the turn – he was a deal-maker, not a company manager. By merging with NTL, explained Duffy, Branson could 'monetise' his shares.

The temptation to grasp NTL's offer and secure cash intensified after Duffy returned to Holland Park accompanied by Jim Mooney, the American chairman of NTL. 'You can get in and out,' said Mooney. 'You'll earn on top-line growth,' he added, implying that the combined revenue would explode. The beauty of the cable business, Branson knew, was the cash regularly paid by subscribers. Every month, 3.3 million NTL customers paid about £43 each, and the potential for growth was huge. Although BSkyB had 8.3 million subscribers, half of British households were still not connected to pay TV, and NTL's advertising income was low.

'We could do great things,' Branson agreed. There was, he convinced himself, no downside.

Negotiating the deal was excruciating. Both sides haggled over their own value. Eventually, it was agreed that Branson would receive £120 million in cash and 10.7 per cent of the new Virgin Media company, worth about £962.4 million ($1.67 billion). Virgin would receive 0.25 per cent of revenue for licensing the brand – £9 million in 2005. Virgin's accounts that year would show an 'exceptional item': a profit of £746.7 million from the sale of 184 million shares in Virgin Mobile. Branson had earned over £1 billion from the British mobile company, and he hoped to earn millions more elsewhere. Tom Alexander's reward had increased slightly.

Shortly after the deal was finalised, Branson heard bad news. Disillusioned by his American employers, Simon Duffy had resigned and had been replaced by Steve Burch, who failed to live up to expectations. 'Where's Steve?' was frequently asked at NTL's headquarters in London about an executive unable to stem 10,000 customers cancelling their subscriptions every month. Resolving Burch's fate and the increasing debts required negotiation, but in the meantime Branson hoped to capitalise on his elevation to media grandee.

In 2006, Branson had described anyone taking on Rupert Murdoch as 'mad', but that was his plan. 'I love a challenge,' he volunteered. No Briton had ever beaten Murdoch outright. 'BSkyB is dominant,' admitted Branson. 'It really is a good company but being dominant is not necessarily good for anyone.' He was gearing up to repeat his familiar dare against a Goliath. He equated the media mogul to Lord King and cast himself as the people's champion. 'BSkyB', he announced, 'is as dominant as British Airways was twenty-one years ago. It is perfect territory for Virgin to move into.' The prize was beyond calculation. 'BSkyB does not like competition,' Branson reassured himself. Without football, BSkyB's profitability was limited, and the recent award of some Premier League games to Setanta Sports, an Irish group, appeared to expose Murdoch's vulnerability. Virgin Media's offer of telephones and broadband would, Branson believed, 'scare' BSkyB's executives.

There was a familiarity to Branson's tactics. In every new business he entered, he played the victim of an 'uncompetitive' monopoly. In the public interest, Branson reasoned, the incumbents ought to step aside to facilitate Virgin's success. Although indebted and stumbling, he forecast that Virgin Media would transform cable TV in a similar manner to his performance in aviation, trains and mobile telephones. A £20 million advertising campaign, he believed, would 'hit BSkyB's soft underbelly' in movies and sport and offer 'better value'. His fellow executives joined his chorus. 'We think that's a weakness we can exploit,' they chimed.

To challenge BSkyB, Branson wanted to buy ITV. If successful,

Virgin Media would not only have a better TV channel than Sky and an outstanding library of old programmes, but could also bid for Premier League football. Although Virgin Media's debt would soar, the interest payments could be covered by ITV's cash flow. There would undoubtedly be a fight, but that was precisely what Branson loved. The prize was Virgin's elevation to media giant and Branson's eventual exit with more money.

The beginning was not encouraging. Branson's call to Sir Peter Burt, ITV's golf-loving chairman, on 8 November 2006 to outline the £4.7 billion ($8.9 billion) offer ended frostily. Although ITV's audiences and profits were declining, Burt was unconvinced by Branson, who in turn was unwilling to back off. Speaking from Necker, he described Burt's reaction to the call as 'very, very warm'. Divorced from the sentiment in London, Branson was unaware of the unease aroused by his bid to control ITV, which was strikingly similar to his offer in 1999 to run the 'People's Lottery' for no profit. In that campaign, many had assumed that Branson's 'charity' was a neat way to endlessly promote himself on TV by offering £1 million prizes to 'Virgin Winners'. His potential ownership of ITV raised similar suspicions.

Branson failed to anticipate the Murdoch family's reaction. James Murdoch, the scion's son, was twenty-one years younger than Branson and keen to establish his own credibility. Nurtured on his father's invasions of competitors' territory, Murdoch retaliated by making a pre-emptive bid for ITV. Just before 6 p.m. on Friday 17 November, Murdoch's bankers announced that his company had paid £940 million for 17.9 per cent of ITV's shares. At 135 pence, Murdoch had paid 20 pence over ITV's closing price and 13 pence more than Branson's offer. Sky's domination was consolidated. Destabilised by the coup, Branson was shocked.

'The Murdoch empire is a threat to democracy,' he raged. The government and the regulators, his publicists repeated, should stop 'Murdoch's cynical and reckless' move and his 'blatant attempt to distort competition'. Branson's mood was not helped by ITV's formal rejection on 21 November of Virgin's offer. He had lost the battle but he would not surrender without harming Murdoch. Branson knew all about protecting and challenging monopolies by securing government support.

James Murdoch announced that BSkyB would not seek a seat on ITV's board or use its stake to exercise 'a material influence' on the broadcaster. Clearly, Murdoch calculated that Labour ministers, keen to retain the support of News International, would not interfere. He was less concerned by Branson's sentiments. 'Sir Richard', quipped Murdoch, 'seems to believe that he and his partners in NTL-Telewest have a unique right to acquire ITV.' British broadcasting, he said, was the 'cosy' victim of the 'dead hand of history' protecting the BBC.

'All of us know that governments are scared stiff of Murdoch,' Branson retorted. 'If the *Sun*, the *Sunday Times*, *The Times*, BSkyB, the *News of the World*, just to name a few of the things Murdoch owns, come out in favour of a particular political party, the election is likely to be won by that particular party . . . If you tag on ITV to that as well, basically we've got rid of democracy in this country and we might as well just let Murdoch decide who is going to be our prime minister.' He urged the government to intervene. 'There comes a time when governments have got to draw a line in the sand. Every single time the Murdoch empire makes a move on more and more of the British media, governments don't have the courage to stand up to them.' The solution, he insisted, was for the regulator to investigate BSkyB and order the sale of the shares. 'A businessman's job', Branson admitted, 'is to try and dominate, but the government's job is to make sure monopolies do not come about and if they do, break them up.' There was truth in Branson's outburst. Rupert Murdoch did enjoy considerable influence. In a recent interview, he had moaned that whenever he visited London, both Gordon Brown and Tony Blair issued competing invitations for breakfast. In private, Branson urged ministers to order an inquiry. Murdoch's power, he continued, was waning. Circulation of his tabloids was falling and the authority of the internet rising.

By casting himself as the victim, Branson encouraged Murdoch to retaliate. BSkyB demanded more money from Virgin for showing BSkyB's programmes and simultaneously decreased the price BSkyB would pay for the Virgin programmes shown on its channels. The threat was unequivocal. If Virgin refused to pay more, their 3.3 million subscribers would lose BSkyB's most popular shows. 'We have the choice of being hung in the afternoon or shot at dawn,' Branson was told by his executives. 'All we want is a level playing field.' Murdoch, Branson complained, wanted to strangle a weak competitor.

In the rising temperature, on 6 February 2007 Virgin Media was floated on the Nasdaq in New York at $27.90 per share. 'They'll soon be at $30,' predicted Jim Mooney, embarrassed by the low price. Just as Branson arrived in Toronto to promote Virgin Mobile, Virgin Media's shares began tumbling towards $25. His publicity stunt of escaping from an exploding cage suspended above a downtown square secured trifling coverage in the media. Virgin Mobile in Canada would attract fewer than 100,000 active customers among the 18.5 million mobile-phone subscribers, and the service was soon close to collapse. Challenging Goliaths, Branson discovered, was no longer fun.

During February 2007, the fifty-six-year-old in Necker found himself on unfamiliar terrain. He faced an adversary who was richer, faster, younger and more cold-blooded than himself. James Murdoch had no intention of surrendering BSkyB's dominance. Just as Branson vigorously protected Virgin Atlantic's rights at Heathrow, Murdoch planned a publicity campaign to destabilise Branson. First, the controller of one-third of Britain's

newspapers published advertisements encouraging Virgin's customers to switch to BSkyB. 'Virgin Media customers deserve
better,' squealed one BSkyB advertisement. 'If you're a Virgin
Media customer, no one could blame you for feeling disappointed or let down,' preached another in a negative advertising
campaign that was painfully similar to Virgin Atlantic's against
British Airways. Virgin could only minimise the bad news by
offering unprofitable contracts to subscribers and using Branson's
self-promotion to conceal the slide. About 25,000 customers
switched during the first month. While in the past Branson had
aggressively attacked his opponents in the media – reflected by
the regulator's censure of Virgin for issuing misleading advertisements against Orange – he had never been the target of his own
tactics. Virgin retaliated with equally scathing advertisements. In
response, BSkyB offered customers new services, including high-
definition BSkyB Plus and more channels. Virgin Media could
not reply in kind. Gradually, Branson realised that Mooney's
original pitch of 'quick in and out' was 'back-of-the-envelope
bullshit'. In a raw contest for survival, Branson was ill equipped
to land a knockout blow. He decided to surrender.

James Murdoch had set a deadline for cutting off BSkyB's
supply of programmes to Virgin. Branson telephoned him to
offer an additional 19 per cent for access to the company's channels, but twice he was told that Murdoch was in a meeting. 'He
never bothered to return my calls,' complained Branson. On
1 March, Virgin Media's 3.3 million households lost BSkyB's
programmes. 'When Virgin say we did not want to do a deal,'
claimed Murdoch, enjoying Branson's weakness, 'it's just not the
case.' That year, BSkyB would earn profits of £877 million, while
Virgin Media lost £533.9 million. NTL's accumulated global
debts had risen to £12.1 billion. Some Britons sympathised with
Branson's lament about bullies.

'I think it could backfire on the Murdoch empire in quite a

major way,' said Branson. 'I think the son has maybe opened a hornet's nest with this one.' The Office of Fair Trading was already investigating Murdoch's stake in ITV. Branson's lobbying of the government persuaded Ofcom, the broadcasting regulator, also to investigate BSkyB's purchase of the ITV shares. The two inquiries would run in parallel. 'I'm astonished,' commented James Murdoch. The government, he said, was allowing its regulations to be 'manipulated'.

On 26 April, Branson scored a small victory: Ofcom recommended that the Competition Commission should investigate whether BSkyB's purchase of ITV shares was in the public interest. But Branson's revenge barely compensated for the loss of more customers. Despite a rebranding campaign featuring Uma Thurman, his channel was being squeezed. Another 64,300 subscribers had been lost in three months, while BSkyB shares were heading towards a three-year high.

Branson bluffed when he was asked if the battle with Sky was damaging: 'Most of the viewers seem to be staying loyal and I think we won't lose very many.' BSkyB, he demanded, 'should lower its prices' – an unusual sentiment for a capitalist. His solution was for Virgin to make its own programmes 'rather than paying through the nose to BSkyB'.

At Virgin Media's board meeting in Puerto Rico in April 2007, Branson was shown research by UBS, the bank, suggesting that a further 400,000 Virgin Media subscribers might switch to BSkyB. He received the news just as he sought cash for Virgin Galactic – just before the explosion, his team was rushing to meet his first deadline to take passengers into space – and he was investing at least $60 million in renewable energy. In June, he borrowed £113 million over two years from Credit Suisse. His collateral was one-third of his Virgin Media shares, then trading at $24. He gambled that if the shares fell to $19.68, he would compensate the bank, but if the shares rose above $31.98, he would share the profits with it. The risk reflected Branson's weakness. 'It's a bit of financial engineering to get some capital,' he explained. Next, he borrowed a further $80 million – and the news got worse.

After another 70,300 subscribers deserted Virgin Media, Moody's downgraded the company's value from 'stable' to 'negative', and on 26 July the explosion in Mojave killed the three engineers. Then came the first reports of the sub-prime crisis that was threatening America's financial system. Virgin Media abandoned the battle against BSkyB and substantially cut its subscription rates. The losses rose. Branson would later decline to buy back his shares from Credit Suisse.

His only comfort was the Competition Commission's decision that BSkyB's stake in ITV was 'against the public interest'. Sky was ordered to reduce its stake from 17.9 per cent to below 7.5 per cent. Although ITV's shares were cheap at 74 pence, Branson lacked the money to revive his bid. His options as a media mogul in Britain were exhausted. By contrast, Rupert Murdoch could comfortably suffer the loss of over £500 million on his ITV misadventure.

Branson was always looking for opportunities to raise cash. One option was to sell more shares, so during 2007 he approved the sale of Virgin Mobile to the American public. The previous proposed flotation in 2005 valuing the company at $1.6 billion had been abandoned. Two years later, Virgin Mobile had 4.6 million notional 'users' (out of America's 229.6 million mobile-telephone users), but the profits were paltry. Ignoring reality, Branson hyped a 'success' story and pitched the company's value at $2 billion.

During the preparations, he approved a plan which resulted in penalising the key staff who had helped to build the business over the previous seven years. As an incentive at the outset, the thirty had been given share options which they hoped to cash in on after the flotation. Usually, employees do not actually pay for those options but take the profits of a notional 'sale' after the flotation. Branson ignored that convention. Harshly, he insisted that the thirty should actually pay for their options before the flotation and be prevented from selling the shares for a period afterwards. To finance the shares' purchase, the staff would have been obliged to mortgage their homes to gamble that the company's future value did not fall below $650 million. 'They can't take the risk,' Gordon McCallum was told. 'They've made a big contribution, and you're treating them very badly.' McCallum's silence prompted the staff to send messages to Branson. To their surprise, Branson ordered his lawyers to freeze all communications. 'It's out of my control,' said McCallum, finally. 'I can't do anything.' Most of the thirty walked away from Virgin, cursing Branson. His homily in Chapter Eight of *Screw Business as Usual* – 'Screw it, let's do it' – seemed to have been ignored. Under the subheading 'Have Respect', Branson urged his admirers to 'Do the right thing' and 'Be fair in your dealings'.

The flotation on 10 October 2007 raised $412 million (£202 million), valuing Virgin Mobile USA at $800 million, a far cry from the $2 billion Branson had expected. His personal stake was worth about $295 million, much less than he had hoped. Five months later, the share price had fallen by 85 per cent to $7. Branson's 'paper' loss was a further $250 million. Within a year of the flotation, Virgin Mobile's debts were rising and the network was losing 100,000 customers a month. Branson decided to quit, selling his remaining 28 per cent stake to Sprint for $5.50 a share. He claimed to have earned $250 million as pure profit. By the end of the year, Virgin Media's shares had fallen further to $5.76. At the same time, Branson also withdrew from Canada, selling his indebted network to Bell. Even his putative Indian venture was struggling. He had finally found a partner – Tata Teleservices – and would launch the service in March 2008, but three years later Branson abandoned that venture too, giving his 50 per cent stake to his partner.

Regardless of all the setbacks, Branson's magic attracted unrivalled loyalty among the British media. In summer 2007, over a hundred journalists gathered at his Oxfordshire home to report on Virgin Media's glories. All were convinced about the authenticity of his vision. There appeared to be no reason to doubt his self-confidence. In its potted description of the chairman, the *Guardian* reported that Branson 'lives in London', rather than the reality – as a tax exile in Necker. United by a common dislike of Murdoch and empathy for the hippy tycoon, the reporters relished Branson's message that Virgin Media would emerge successfully from its troubles.

'Like Virgin Trains,' he said, 'it'll be like that great success story. Virgin Trains is now one of our top three brands.'

7

Printing Money

In 2002, Branson had conceded that running Britain's trains was not a natural Virgin business. Contrary to his expectations ten years earlier, the railways had not offered a chance for easy profits. His publicised outburst in 1992 that ownership of a railway franchise would be 'a licence to print money' had proved to be mistaken, and in Virgin Trains' early years the brand had been trashed.

Long before he had applied to run two rail networks, Branson had preached to members of the House of Commons Transport Committee about the enviable benefits he would bestow on Britain's dilapidated railways. As the owner of a successful airline, he said, 'Our trains will arrive faster because Virgin drivers will be more motivated.' The image of Virgin Trains overtaking its rivals raised the politicians' eyebrows, as did Branson's advocacy of breaking up British Rail and fragmenting the track authority to encourage competition.

'Your understanding of the railways', said a Labour MP, 'does seem to be on a protozoan level.'

'I have not said anything as daft as you seem to indicate,' replied Branson, who was discomfited whenever his image was scorned.

Branson knew his limitations. His skill was to recruit outstanding advisers. Among those he had selected to help him in his bid for a rail franchise was Jim Steer, a transport consultant who predicted that motorists would ditch their cars and return to modernised railways. Steer also believed that the government was so committed to privatisation that the franchise contracts would guarantee the operators healthy risk-free profits.

Branson's relationship with Steer had begun in 1996 with a blunder over Virgin's participation in launching Eurostar, the new train linking London and Paris through the Channel tunnel. Virgin had won the bid to market the new route. 'I'll be offering a completely different service to travellers, with all the Virgin flair,' Branson told his partners. Their relationship quickly fractured. First, his partners were angered about Branson's poor marketing, and then they were aggravated by his bid to rename the train 'Virgin Eurostar'. In its first year, Eurostar carried half the number of passengers Steer had predicted. Branson was blamed and Virgin was shunted out of the picture. But Steer remained as Branson's adviser. By then, several franchises to run the national rail services had been awarded, and Branson was persuaded to follow the trend. Having missed the best routes, he bid for Cross Country, a ragbag of the remaining network which would not be allocated in other franchises. In 1996, Virgin won the franchise by promising to replace the thirty-year-old trains and attract thousands of new customers.

His next bid was for the West Coast line linking London to Birmingham, Manchester and Glasgow. The north–south artery had been rebuilt in 1965, with a life expectancy of thirty years. In the early 1980s, British Rail's experts had investigated whether the line could be redeveloped for the Advanced Passenger Train, which would connect London with Scotland in four hours and Manchester in two hours. The high speed depended on the train tilting through bends at over 150 mph. The project was abandoned as technically impossible, but was partially revived a few years later. British Rail's engineers had designed the InterCity 250, a non-tilting train which could cruise at 155 mph. The new train required new tracks, and since at that speed the train driver could not see the old signalling lights on the side, the planners discussed inventing a new system whereby the signals would be displayed on a screen inside the driver's cab. The research was stopped when the government decided in 1992 to privatise the railways.

Branson was a natural target for ministers keen for a trophy owner of the West Coast line. 'It's a brave new world where bidders are invited to innovate and take risks,' Branson was told. Scrutiny of the contract's financial terms showed that with minimal risk, Branson could earn a fortune at the taxpayers' expense.

Ever since privatisation was announced, the deterioration of the West Coast's tracks and rolling stock had accelerated, discouraging passengers from using the railway. Branson shared the common prejudice that British Rail was inefficient and unresponsive. He held to the credo that free enterprise would encourage innovation. 'We can make the railways different and better,' said Branson, embracing privatisation.

His team pondered how to build on the requirements stipulated by Railtrack, the franchising agency. 'Let's offer to run tilting trains at 140 mph,' suggested one of Branson's team, 'but only if the government gives us a fifteen-year franchise – and allows no other operator to compete against us on the line.'

'This is all guesswork,' replied Richard Bowker, who had been recruited from London Underground to plan Virgin's bid.

The pitch for a long monopoly contradicted Branson's presentation to the politicians in 1992, but his scenario of trains racing from London to Manchester in 1 hour 50 minutes by 2005 excited John Edmonds, Railtrack's chief executive. Faster trains would generate profits as people abandoned cars and planes. Virgin won the franchise. Tom Winsor, an accomplished lawyer, was assigned by Branson to negotiate a contract which, according to the government's plan, at the outset committed the taxpayer to bear the costs and risk, while Virgin took the profits. Virgin Trains, ultimately owned by Virgin Group Holdings, registered in the Virgin Islands, could expect to earn about 3.5 per cent of the revenue in annual profits.

According to the standard 'cap and collar' contract, Railtrack guaranteed Virgin that there would be tracks and stations to run the trains to an agreed timetable. Virgin would not buy the rolling stock. Instead, the engines and carriages would be leased from Angel, a private company whose income was guaranteed by the government. Virgin risked no money because the lease of the rolling stock would be transferred to whichever operator followed Virgin Trains. Branson's only risk was the amount of money he guaranteed to pay to the government during the franchise. The sliding payments were in two parts, based on Virgin's calculations of its income. In the early years, Virgin stipulated the subsidy required from the government. In the second period, it quantified its payments to the government from the profits. In the jargon, the contract was 'back-end loaded' – Virgin's payments would exceed any continuing subsidy. At the outset in 1997/8, Virgin expected a government subsidy of about £200 million, and by 2012/13 the company would be paying the government a premium of up to £200 million, subject to profits. Those depended on attracting the maximum number of passengers paying for the highest-priced tickets, and Virgin's managers maximising productivity. The unmentioned profit was the cash flow – Virgin could use the cash without paying interest. In the beginning, the company would receive about £900 million from Railtrack and the passengers. Passengers paid in advance, while Virgin paid its suppliers in arrears, so with the exception of season tickets, all the cash could be used by Virgin.

On that basis, in February 1997 Virgin was awarded the contract known as Passenger Upgrade 1 (PUG1). The fifteen-year deal had barely been signed before negotiations began for a revised contract known as PUG2. John Edmonds and Railtrack's directors had embraced Virgin's suggestion that the original specification of new trains running at 125 mph by 2005 should be replaced by trains running at 140 mph. PUG2 would commit Railtrack to building entirely new tracks and installing a new signalling system.

Virgin's directors understood Railtrack's risk. To minimise the cost of failure, Winsor inserted into the contract a series of penalty payments if Railtrack failed to upgrade the network. His irrefutable reasoning was that Virgin's financial model depended on persuading passengers to switch from airlines and cars to trains.

Edmonds did not understand Branson's customary terms of business. Although the new contract was Branson's idea, he expected Railtrack to take the financial risk. Virgin challenged Railtrack's directors and lawyers to resist Branson's familiar ploy. 'We played an A team,' said one of the Virgin negotiators, admiring Branson's talent of employing the best lawyers. 'Railtrack's was a C team.'

By then, most of British Rail's traditional engineers had resigned, but Edmonds did retain Professor Brian Mellitt of Manchester University as Railtrack's director of engineering. Over the years, the professor had promoted his vision of a new signalling system. Called 'moving block', his proposed system combined sensors, wireless technology and computers to monitor a train's speed and flash the relevant signals to the driver's cab. Caught up in Mellitt's enthusiasm, Edmonds did not question why no other railway network in the world operated a similar system or whether wireless could penetrate through tunnels and operate around sharp curves. Remarkably, he did not appear to realise that the introduction of Mellitt's ideas into the London Underground's Jubilee line was proving to be technically unsuccessful. Instead, he relied on a consultants' report which stated that moving-block technology was 'relatively mature', and contracted Alstom in France to develop Mellitt's scheme.

In September 1997, just as the PUG2 contract was presented to Railtrack's board for approval, Edmonds was replaced by Gerald Corbett, the former finance director of Grand Metropolitan, the food and drinks multinational. Corbett knew little about railways or engineering. Like many of the property specialists who were replacing experienced railwaymen, Corbett was certain Railtrack had a glowing future because the company's shares, originally £3, were heading towards £17.

Presented on his arrival with PUG2, Corbett accepted assurances that rebuilding the line and including Mellitt's signalling scheme would cost £800 million. 'We'll just click a switch in 2005 and it'll all be working,' was his understanding. Without further scrutiny, he signed the contract. By then, Branson was energetically imposing Virgin's style upon BR's dilapidated network. 'Call it the Virgin Difference,' he told the marketing staff. Quietly, he had refocused his plans. In 1998, he had bought out his original partners and split the ownership of Virgin Trains with Brian Souter, the founder of Stagecoach, a transport specialist. Souter had proposed a fifty–fifty venture, but Branson insisted on owning 51 per cent.

During 1998, Virgin Trains became notorious for delays and bad service. Plagued by the old infrastructure and disrupted by privatisation, Railtrack was unable to fulfil its commitments. Simultaneously, Virgin lacked the expertise to repair its trains. The public's anger turned against Branson. Daily, the media trashed Virgin for failing to deliver on Branson's promises. To save himself, in January 1999 Branson appointed Chris Green, the former head of InterCity trains, as Virgin Trains' new chief executive. Green was horrified by his inheritance. To save money, Branson had merged the management of Cross Country and the West Coast line and, as Green discovered, appointed 'lots of marketing and customer specialists who were unemployable and knew nothing about railways'. Virgin Trains' management,

Green announced, 'is a nightmare and a mess'. None of his staff knew how to make the old trains work. Service on board was similarly chaotic. Virgin had replaced the traditional service in British Rail's dining cars with airline 'hostesses' serving small portions of food on plastic trays. Passengers frequently complained that Virgin's staff were rude, especially after the trains broke down. Branson did not understand railways, but the criticism, he believed, could be alleviated by good public relations. 'How can I help you?' he regularly asked Green, who had ordered the management of Cross Country and Virgin Trains to be split up once again. Branson wanted to position himself as Corbett's ally.

First, they arranged to meet for a photo shoot at Euston station. Branson's banter with two Virgin stewardesses irritated Corbett. 'He was too smarmy with those girls,' he complained later. 'All those cheap suggestive remarks to the girls, with his hands all over them. I don't like him.' Next, they agreed to meet for dinner. 'I've got to try to get on with him,' Corbett explained. Branson arrived with Holly, his sixteen-year-old daughter. 'That's utterly inappropriate,' thought Corbett. Every attempt he made to engage in a business conversation was forlorn. 'He always feigned ignorance about numbers,' Corbett later reported. 'He kept saying, "I need to ask my team."' Unaware that Branson was genuinely ignorant about detail, Corbett concluded, 'He's wasting my time. He never looks me in the eye. I'm a straightforward bloke, and he just irritates me.' At the end of a frosty meal, Corbett decided to 'quickly bugger off'.

In December 1999, Green was summoned to Railtrack's headquarters. In what was codenamed 'Black Diamond Day', he was told by Corbett that Mellitt's signalling system could not be designed.

'It's all pie in the sky,' said Corbett. 'We've decided to put our hands up now instead of wasting more time and money.'

'You've been chasing a rainbow,' replied Green, with a sense of disbelief.

'We rumbled the mad professor,' continued Corbett, referring to the delays on the London Underground's redevelopment, which had been blamed by some on Mellitt's similar signalling proposals. 'He's got qualifications coming out of his backside, but it hasn't done any good. He's retired.'

Green appeared to be sympathetic.

'We were naive,' said Corbett, defensively. 'We're going back to PUG1 with conventional signalling. We will rebuild the tracks. It will cost £2 billion.' No one queried why the estimated cost had nearly tripled within three years. PUG2 – and the 140 mph trains – was abandoned. Corbett assumed that Virgin would be understanding and, without recrimination, revert to trains travelling at 125 mph. 'If you expect them to be nice guys, you're in for a shock,' he was warned.

'You've been sold something which is not deliverable,' Green reported to Branson in his office in Holland Park.

'Oh shit,' said Branson. 'We must make it work.'

'They haven't even put a spade into the ground to rebuild the track. Nothing's happened,' said Green, incredulously.

Branson was unforgiving. No mercy could be shown even for unforeseen problems. 'We want £1 billion of compensation,' he announced, listing some anticipated losses – the slower service would require extra trains, and the additional passengers he'd hoped for would not now be switching from airlines to faster trains. His attack was based on Tom Winsor's watertight contract – 'One of the best contracts in history,' Green would admit. Virgin demanded that Railtrack immediately pay £250 million in compensation. The relationship between Branson's team – Patrick McCall, Virgin Trains' chairman, and Tony Collins, the contracts director – and Corbett became acrimonious. The arbiter of the dispute was none other than Winsor, who had moved from Virgin to become the rail regulator. As a lawyer, he was unsympathetic to Corbett's plea that the contract should be ignored to save Railtrack from insolvency. Corbett's fate was then further endangered by a terrible accident.

In 2000, soon after a fatal crash in Paddington and the disruption of services by floods, four passengers were killed at Hatfield in an accident caused by a broken rail. In the uproar over Railtrack's failure to maintain safe tracks, speeds were slashed to 20 mph on some sections. On the West Coast line, journey times doubled and the number of passengers halved. Every day, Virgin and Branson were blamed for various disasters. 'The public hate us and it's all going nowhere,' Richard Bowker told his colleagues. 'Everyone is at each other.' In turn, Virgin's publicists encouraged derision to be heaped on to Railtrack. 'Corbett is arrogant and has let us down,' inquirers were told. In private, Corbett was damned by Virgin's executives as 'useless and obsessed by the property business'. There was no sympathy for his plight coping with a poisoned inheritance. The Labour government exploited the political opportunity. Having accurately predicted the disaster of privatisation, senior ministers turned every delayed train into a toxic indictment of Railtrack.

Virgin Trains was trapped. The same contractors blamed for bad maintenance of the tracks were also responsible for the repairs. By exaggerating their problems, they effectively maximised their profits. Corbett discovered that Railtrack could not even fulfil PUG1 – and the cost of replacing the West Coast line had escalated from £2 billion towards £6 billion. Branson's complaints were justified, but he attracted little sympathy.

Corbett considered retaliation. Railtrack could have used the public's anger about the late delivery of Virgin's Pendolino trains as a bargaining chip in the dispute, but he was persuaded to desist. 'We have to show we are partners,' advised John O'Brien, responsible for franchising the network, 'and the government would not like us to use contracts which favour us against the operators.'

Relations between Virgin and Corbett collapsed. With the exception of Chris Green, Corbett disliked the Virgin team. 'I don't like their open-necked shirts, especially Bowker's. He knows nothing,' claimed Corbett. Will Whitehorn, Virgin's spokesman, was deemed unhelpful for 'always talking to the press'. Winsor, the regulator, was criticised as 'clever and confrontational, regulating by megaphone'. Corbett distrusted Branson and was irritated by his Sunday-morning calls. 'My team is pleased . . .' Branson would enthuse about a triviality, confirming Corbett's prejudice: 'He doesn't understand the numbers and relies on those around him.' In their rare meetings, Branson riled the beleaguered executive. 'It's his shifting eyes,' complained Corbett. 'He's all over the place. Always out for himself and being very difficult.'

'Bloody Branson,' Sir David Rowlands, the permanent secretary at the Department for Transport, complained to Corbett. Even John Prescott, the secretary of state for transport, criticised Branson's conduct. The pugnacious politician had already condemned Branson's rebranding of the trains, saying, 'You've done wonders for the paint industry, but what are you going to do for the railways?' Now, he disliked Branson's aggressive demand for hundreds of millions of pounds in compensation from the taxpayer.

In the midst of that argument, Chris Green met Branson in Holland Park. The first Pendolino train had just been delivered. 'They work,' smiled Branson. 'Virgin has been saved.' At that turning point, anticipating that the tracks would be rebuilt, Green asked Branson to lease more Pendolino trains in expectation of extra passengers. To prove his acumen, Branson played a familiar game: he reminded Green about something that had been said six months earlier. Naturally, Green was impressed.

Like others experiencing Branson's apparently 'tremendous' memory for detail, he was convinced that the owner of hundreds of companies was the mastermind of all. Sceptics believed that Branson rehearsed those displays.

'It has been bad,' said Green, 'but all the projections show it can only get better. The West Coast's new tracks will be reliable and carry more trains much faster.' Virgin's risk, he added, was minuscule. Passenger numbers would rise and Virgin only needed 50 per cent occupancy on the extra seats to make a profit. At the end of thirty minutes, Branson agreed. In the old era, Green reflected, British Rail would have taken a year to mull it over. However, Branson's decision did not restore sympathy for him in Whitehall. Tony Collins's remorseless demand for compensation had outwitted Corbett and was pushing Railtrack towards collapse. Technically, Virgin Trains was also facing financial peril.

The first casualty was Corbett, who was replaced by John Armitt, a shrewd engineer. The second was Railtrack itself. In 2002, the company was placed in administration and the public shareholders lost their money. Network Rail emerged as the successor. During that process, Virgin Trains' franchise was suspended and replaced by a risk-free management contract rewarding the company with 1 per cent of the revenue. Armitt also reintegrated track maintenance into Network Rail and started weekly meetings with the operators. 'We can stop lobbing hand grenades at each other now,' said Green, believing that peace had broken out at last. The West Coast track was being improved at a final cost of £8.7 billion – ten times the original estimate – and Network Rail was devising a new timetable to increase traffic, improve punctuality and guarantee more revenue. Once the management contracts were abandoned and the original franchises were restored in 2006, Virgin could anticipate serious profits rolling in. Branson felt the millions of pounds Virgin could expect to earn were justifiable compensation for the damage the botched privatisation had inflicted upon his brand.

The appropriate moment for official acknowledgement of Virgin's sacrifice, in Branson's opinion, occurred in 2004, when the Virgin team were summoned to the Victoria headquarters of the new Strategic Rail Authority (SRA), which was responsible for issuing franchises. The topic was the Cross Country franchise. Virgin's trains were breaking down and achieving only 50 per cent of their punctuality targets, and passenger numbers had collapsed. Virgin's predicted £15 million annual profit had become a £25 million loss. The SRA decided that the size of the subsidy Virgin was receiving for the shoddy service could no longer be justified. Clearly, the company had overbid for the franchise, failed to buy all the new trains and would fail to pay the promised premium to the government.

Nevertheless, Branson led his team confidently into the SRA's offices. The authority's chairman was Richard Bowker, the former director of Virgin Trains, and Branson hoped that his ex-employee might be persuaded to modify the contract's terms in Virgin's favour. Instead, Bowker announced, 'We will not continue the Cross Country franchise and we will not agree to any renegotiation with Virgin. We are going to offer it up for a new tender in 2006.' Green looked at the faces around the table: 'There was surprise, shock and disappointment. Branson was angry.' Virgin, Branson spluttered, was a 'victim' deprived of a just reward.

On reflection, Branson concluded that Virgin needed a tough commercial negotiator. Green had improved the train service but he was unsuited to fight Bowker, so in September 2004 he was replaced by Tony Collins, who had been employed by Virgin Trains since 1999.

As he took over from Green, Collins told an official at Network Rail, 'Richard called from Necker. He's concerned that you're not working fast enough to modify the tracks for the new rolling stock.' The official was irritated. The image of Branson sunbathing on a tax-free beach while dictating how the British railways should be run was shameful. Worse, he recalled Green's joke that 'Richard Branson is not interested in any aspect of the railways except whether the orange juice tastes good.'

Collins's arrival coincided with the climax of a power struggle between Bowker and Alistair Darling, the new secretary of state for transport. To curtail the mayhem, Darling ordered that the SRA be dissolved in 2006. He directed that future franchises and the control of expenditure would become the responsibility of a new director of railways, a new post inside the Department for Transport. That was a good moment for Branson to seek support from his political allies.

Green's departure in September 2004 was to be marked by a lunch at Euston station which would also celebrate naming a new Pendolino train *Chris Green*. Usually, Branson delegated Will Whitehorn or Stephen Murphy to represent him at these functions, but on that occasion he flew from Necker to greet their number-one guest, Tony Blair. Green assumed the prime minister had been invited to boost staff morale, but Branson's agenda during Blair's thirty-minute visit was more political in nature. The Hatfield crash in 2000 had accelerated the government's projected subsidy to rail from £1.3 billion in 1995 to £6.5 billion in 2005. Network Rail was accused of losing control of costs, and many believed Virgin was receiving excessive subsidies. Branson replied that his company deserved even more taxpayers' money. His public assertion that the government had paid Virgin £1 billion in compensation for the delayed rebuilding of the tracks was disputed, but it fuelled public anger. With skill, Virgin's executives were exploiting Whitehall's disarray.

Civil servants were constantly changing rules, appointing and dismissing consultants, scrutinising rolling stock and even dictating the refreshments menu. Untrained officials were approving franchises that would end in disaster. Transport ministers were exerting more control over the railways than their predecessors had over British Rail. This was fertile ground for Virgin's negotiators. Branson expected Blair's team to select someone sympathetic to Virgin as the new director of railways. Instead, Mike Mitchell, a troubleshooting railwayman, was appointed. 'It will take one to get one,' noted one insider, approving the appointment of a tough railwayman to confront Virgin. Mitchell was neither Virgin's natural ally nor was he inclined to continue paying large financial subsidies to the company. Since the collapse of the franchises in 2002, Virgin had received about £338 million for managing the West Coast line and as compensation for the lost revenue caused by the disruption. Once the track was modernised, Mitchell wanted to end the hiatus, revive the PUG1 agreement and reduce the payments to Virgin. With the West Coast franchise restored, he expected Virgin to pay the government about £200 million in 2012/13.

Tony Collins agreed to resume PUG1 but disputed the terms. On Virgin's behalf, he approached Mitchell to negotiate additional subsidies and the submission of a new bid to run the Cross Country franchise. The process was opaque; the cost of so-called 'additional services' was impenetrable. Taxpayers would never know whether Virgin gave value for their money. Helped by that obscurity, Collins played hardball, hammering Virgin's rights as enshrined within the original contract. By 2006, the department's officials were usually in a state of irritation. 'They're getting too much money,' an official complained. 'The haggling doesn't stop.'

On one memorable occasion, the departmental officials wanted to recover £20 million from Virgin Trains. 'It's too advantageous for Virgin,' Collins was told.

'See you in court,' Collins replied. 'If you don't like it, you shouldn't have signed it.'

In running a business, he showed no sentiment. Virgin gave out no favours and, relying on the contracts, did not seek allies. The company only took hostages. Although the government's case was arguable, Collins never concealed his low opinion of the Department for Transport's staff. In the argument over the £20 million, he outfaced his opponents. The civil servants were not prepared to risk a multimillion-pound legal battle. 'You guys are always against Virgin,' Collins complained the following day. Like Branson, he played the underdog.

One victory was not the same as winning the war. For Branson, the prize was restoring the two franchises on favourable terms. He arranged to meet Douglas Alexander, the new secretary of state for transport. His message, the department had been told in advance, was about the advantage of keeping Virgin as a franchisee. Branson arrived wearing an open shirt that revealed the benefits of owning a Caribbean beach. 'We're good and we should be allowed to go on for much longer,' he told Alexander. Virgin's current franchises, he said, should be extended and even last for ever. The minister was non-committal. As usual, Branson asked a technical point – this time about the rolling stock and franchising – suggesting that Virgin should receive more money. An official replied, dismissing Branson's claim. 'That sounds reasonable,' said Branson, surprising everyone who'd assumed he'd been briefed by Collins.

'It's skin-deep understanding,' Alexander agreed after Branson left. 'He has no grasp of detail.'

Shortly after that encounter, in July 2007 the Department for Transport announced that the Cross Country franchise would be awarded to Arriva, a subsidiary of Germany's Deutsche Bahn.

'Why have Arriva got it?' Collins asked angrily.

'They made a better bid,' he was told. 'Virgin overbid.'

'Arriva overbid,' snapped Collins. 'They will never be able to make it pay. It's so unfair.'

Branson took the news badly. Financially, he was told, all the bids were similar. Arriva won by offering a better service compared to Virgin's 'poor' management. Always a bad loser, Branson ensured his anger was translated by his managers into the orchestration of a difficult handover. 'They've turned off the commercial tap,' reported an Arriva executive after taking over Cross Country's offices. Without Virgin's computers, Arriva was deprived of vital information, including essential details about the network's revenue. Virgin, Arriva's executives eventually discovered, had overseen a dramatic fall in passenger numbers. Key employees had also departed. 'And they've alienated the staff who have stayed,' complained one executive. Virgin had demanded the instant return of company cars, uniforms and mobile telephones. The transition was further stymied by a Virgin executive threatening to charge Arriva for exploiting the Virgin brand if the Virgin logo was not removed from all the rolling stock within three months. 'That's down to you,' he was told. 'If you don't paint them out within three months, we'll charge Virgin for advertising.' The anger spread into pettiness, with Virgin refusing to allow Arriva's first-class passengers to share any of Virgin's own station waiting rooms. 'They're not making it easy for us,' complained the Arriva executive. 'They've left everyone demoralised.' On reflection, he agreed that 'Virgin was screwing us.'

8

Ghosts

'Hi, it's Richard here.'

'Richard who?' asked Rowan Gormley, a South African employed in a London private-equity firm.

'Richard Branson. I'm calling because I'd like you to work here at Virgin.'

The two arranged to meet at Branson's house in Holland Park. Neither appeared to know what to say. The year was 1995.

'You called me,' said Gormley, discomfited by the awkward silence.

'Yeah,' mumbled Branson. 'I wanted you to come up with some new ideas. Come and work for us.'

Attracted by Virgin, Gormley soon after delivered his list at a meeting attended by three of Branson's most trusted lieutenants – Stephen Murphy, Will Whitehorn and Trevor Abbott, one of the original architects of Virgin's music business. Gormley listed Virgin hotels, Virgin holidays and, finally, 'What about Virgin financial services?'

'Virgin is about fun,' snorted Abbott derisively.

Murphy and Whitehorn shared his disinterest. Gormley turned to Branson. 'Virgin is trusted, and financial services can make lots of money.'

'Do it,' said Branson.

'Do we have any money?' asked Gormley.

'No,' replied Branson, admitting the reality about his empire. 'Find the money and do it.'

'What about Abbott?' asked Gormley.

'Ignore him,' replied Branson.

Shortly after, Abbott left Virgin on bad terms and subsequently committed suicide, blaming Branson in part. 'Richard broke my back,' he recorded on a video shortly before he hanged himself. In Branson's world, failures were forgotten. Gormley could be the future. His invention was Virgin Direct, which would sell personal equity plans – or PEPs – that were priced by tracking an index of shares quoted on the London Stock Exchange. Its launch depended on finding a suitable partner.

The formula for this start-up was familiar. A potential partner would provide the money and expertise in exchange for using the Virgin brand. Dividing the profits was subject to negotiation but, where possible, the losses would be borne by the partner. In this case, as an added ingredient, Virgin's partner in the banking business needed to be an authorised deposit-taker. In *Screw Business as Usual*, Branson wrote: 'I wanted to get into the banking industry because I saw the money markets and finance as a way to build bridges between the social sector, big government and business.' Banking, he added, would fulfil his ultimate objective of 'a fairer distribution of wealth'.

Most of the City institutions approached by Gormley ridiculed his proposal. The only exception was Norwich Union. The insurer had recently been fined by the government regulator for mis-selling pensions. Associating with Virgin, its directors calculated, would alleviate the opprobrium. Among the attractions to the insurers was the brazenness of Branson's proposed TV promotion: 'For years the pension industry has got away with not telling you how much of our money they cream off in charges.' Branson would promise 'no-nonsense value for money' and the lowest charges.

Gormley's target was to raise £70 million from the public within six weeks. Branson rang daily to check on progress. Two days before the deadline to collect the funds – the end of the financial year – Gormley was desperate. Only £5 million had been committed. On the last day, the security guard rang Gormley to announce that a Royal Mail truck was backing up to their building. Inside the sacks of mail were commitments worth £40 million from the public, who had been attracted by the promise of a safe investment. More followed later.

Gormley's project took off, and within months Virgin Direct was earning good profits. Despite Branson's denunciation of those who 'cream off in charges', Virgin's PEPs, organised by Norwich Union, were among the most expensive for investors. Virgin's annual management fees were 1 per cent of the fund, while M&G and other rivals levied 0.3 per cent. Investors also earned less. Virgin's tracker of unit trusts rose 109 per cent in two years, while the FTSE All Share Index (including dividends) climbed 144 per cent. Few complained. Trust in the Virgin brand suppressed most concerns.

'Let's ramp it up,' suggested Gormley in 1997, eager for expansion. Norwich Union declined, but just then George Trumbull of AMP, an Australian bank, began calling him.

Flush with money, AMP was aggressively buying financial institutions across Europe. Gormley's ambition to offer mortgages, pensions and life-insurance policies matched AMP's resources. The deal they negotiated entirely favoured Branson. AMP carried 100 per cent of the risk in return for using the Virgin brand. The profits would be equally shared, while AMP, who provided the entire infrastructure, would bear any losses. The AMP executive who negotiated the partnership, Paul Batchelor, would be described by his successor as 'a personality who wanted to fall in love with Virgin. He was full of dreams, and Virgin played straight into the space.' Norwich Union sold its share to AMP, and Virgin Direct was relaunched as Virgin Money, with the new attraction of internet banking. The TV advertisements again featured Branson: 'I have identified a sector that is arrogant, complacent and fleecing the customer.' The financial-services industry, he continued, 'specialises in bullshit. Its record includes pensions mis-selling, endowments that don't come up to scratch and massive investment underperformance.' Virgin Money, he promised, offered honest value.

At that moment, Branson's reputation was being challenged elsewhere. Amid considerable noise, he had launched Virgin Brides, Virgin Cosmetics, Virgin Net and Virgin Cola. The drink's sales, he proclaimed loudly, had captured 10 per cent of Britain's market. Independent research showed Virgin Cola's sales were barely 1 per cent of the country's cola consumption, which cast his forecast of earning £1 million in profits every week as fictional. Branson's salesmanship reflected his wishes rather than the reality. His philosophy had become famous – 'It's all about bending the rules or breaking the rules' – yet the same man was a guardian of money. 'I set up Virgin Money to offer people straightforward financial products that are easy to understand,' he claimed.

In 1999, Virgin Money was managing about £1 billion of deposits pledged by the public. Earning good profits, Gormley persuaded Branson to embark on the next stage. His creation was Virgin One, an internet bank offering customers a better rate of interest if they opened a single account for their cheques, savings and mortgages. Half of Virgin One would be owned the Royal Bank of Scotland, with the other half owned equally by Virgin and AMP. Branson would not be earning easy profits in this deal: Virgin was committed to contributing to the costs and to any losses. Virgin One's advertisements showed Branson, dressed in a pin-striped suit and bowler hat, promising to 'turn personal banking on its head'.

The bank gave him the chance to transform his conglomerate into a global giant. The scenario outlined by Gormley utilised the communications revolution: Virgin, he said, should use the internet to forge a closer relationship with its customers. Virgin Atlantic already sold tickets and transferred money via the internet. That was just the start, said Gormley. By fully exploiting the internet's potential, Virgin could use its database to offer all its products to loyal customers, without media advertisements, so reducing the cost of sales. Anyone buying an airline ticket would be automatically offered a special deal to try Virgin One banking, and vice versa. Gormley's suggestion placed Branson at a Rubicon. Virgin Money was his moment to merge all the disparate Virgin companies into one seamless global corporation.

'Let's show them,' was Branson's favoured exhortation during discussions. The words encapsulated the fun he derived from challenging an established giant. On that occasion, the phrase was targeted at the bankers. Virgin One was his opportunity to pocket millions of pounds by transforming Virgin from a branding venture into an integrated empire, with internet marketing to sustain its expansion. That depended on Branson educating himself about the new technology, but instead he deferred to Stephen Murphy's advice. To his misfortune, the Virgin Group's chief executive did not sufficiently grasp the internet's potential in the same way as, for example, Martha Lane Fox had when she co-founded lastminute.com in 1998. Just as Steve Ridgway, another middle-aged conservative, had dismissed Ryanair's exploitation of the internet for its ticket sales since the mid-1990s, Murphy excluded taking advantage of it to promote and cross-sell Virgin's products. Similarly, Jayne-Anne Gadhia, appointed by Branson to manage Virgin One, was flummoxed.

Gadhia was selling Norwich Union's unit trusts when she read an article about Branson in *Hello!* magazine, and through a friend she arranged an introduction. Clever, articulate and sassy, Gadhia shared Branson's qualities as a salesperson. She could sell other people's ideas or improve someone else's design, but unlike Branson she lacked originality. A conventional marketer of savings and loans products, the history graduate from London's Royal Holloway College nonetheless became Branson's principal adviser on financial services. Cautious and uncreative, she did not share Gormley's enthusiasm for a block-buster campaign to persuade the public to abandon traditional banking. Branson himself, mystified by the financial business, was defensive towards those challenging Gadhia. 'We'll think about it,' he answered in reply to any criticism. Branson failed to grasp the paradox. His original fortune had been created by thinking out of the box, but since the sale of Virgin Music he had relied on conventional administrators. His hippy era, when suits were banned and his directors had been summoned to board meetings while he lay in his bath, was gone. His new advisers were ill equipped to compensate for his unfamiliarity with new finance and the internet, and they were sensitive to his dislike of those challenging his supremacy.

In order for Gormley's strategy of unifying the Virgin Group through internet marketing to work, all the Virgin companies needed to co-operate. But collaboration contradicted Branson's philosophy. Since he began in the 1970s, he had encouraged rivalry among his staff, feeding when appropriate their instinc-tive suspicions about each other. He was sanguine about the lack of mutual support between Virgin's companies. For example, Gormley would later discover that Virgin Atlantic refused to buy wine from Virgin Wines. Bewildered outsiders guessed that Branson wanted to avoid either internal conflict or the accusa-tion that one Virgin company was subsidising the other. The truth was more prosaic. Ever since Virgin Music had been cre-ated, Branson had disenfranchised his employees and associates to protect his financial secrets. Compartmentalism entrenched his control but frustrated change.

To promote Virgin Money in 2000, Gadhia relied, as usual, on Branson's appearances in advertisements. A year later, however, a financial crisis began. In 2001, AMP's finances crashed. A raft of senior executives in Sydney were fired. Others were dispatched from Australia to rescue the bank's assets in Britain. 'Branson has taken us for a ride,' a visiting banker told his British staff. AMP, he discovered, had lost at least A$200 million from its relationship with Virgin, while Virgin had earned about A$100 million. 'It's a lousy deal,' he declared. 'It's noise in the system that we don't need. Sell it.'

Branson was furious about AMP's decision to abandon the relationship. In a 'ferocious' call from Necker, he cursed the Australian. 'You can't do that to the staff.'

'You don't understand,' he was told. 'AMP has lost hundreds of millions of dollars in Britain.'

'I'd like to buy AMP,' Branson told Andrew Mohl, the new chief executive.

'At the right price, yes,' replied Mohl, 'but you're dreaming if you think you can buy at this point. You haven't got the money.' In *Screw Business as Usual*, Branson described Virgin Money as 'a community rather than a profit-making vehicle . . .What we want to do is make everyone better off.'

Virgin Money was sold to Henderson, a British company, and Virgin One was offered to RBS. Initially, Fred Goodwin, the bank's chief executive, rejected the offer. 'He's relentlessly negative,' reported an AMP banker. Eight months later, Goodwin changed his mind. He paid £125 million for the bank, a higher price than previously suggested, and a good profit for Branson. Jayne-Anne Gadhia moved to RBS.

By 2002, Virgin's financial business was practically eliminated. Gormley had departed to launch Virgin Wines and would eventually sell that company at a loss. Like so many ideas based on exploiting the Virgin brand, the public were not attracted by a Virgin label on a standard product. Gormley apologised to Branson. 'Don't worry,' Branson replied. 'You made me a pile of money on financial services. You're still in my credit book.'

Sidelined in Britain but hungry for more profits from the money business, Branson sought opportunities in other countries. But rather than developing internet banking, he was transfixed by its traditional side. His best idea was to launch a Virgin credit card in Australia, in collaboration with MasterCard and Westpac.

In 2003, Branson arrived in Sydney accompanied by blondes, a big grin and his familiar promise to take on banks and end 'the rip-offs'. The 'cosy bank oligopoly', his publicists said, was fertile territory for Virgin, with its challenge of lower interest rates and better service. Within a year, the business had evaporated. Privately, Branson blamed Westpac for either poaching Virgin customers or rejecting two million applications in order to protect its own credit-card business, but he must have realised the truth: few customers were attracted to the British company. Unlike AMP, Westpac refused to cover the losses. This disappointment coincided with the sale of Branson's stake in Virgin Mobile Australia, in which he took a A$20 million loss on the shares. Branson had taken a punt that the Virgin label would attract customers and lost.

Repeatedly, Branson was failing to reproduce his British successes in other countries. During one visit to Noosa in Australia in March 2004, he tried to do the opposite – invest in Pulp Juice, a soft-drinks company owned and managed by Ian Duffell, an old friend. 'Pulp is a fantastic concept,' Branson told the media. 'I think it will go down really well in Britain and South Africa.' His assurance that Virgin would build fifty bars sparked a 56 per cent increase in the company's share price and enhanced the credibility of Duffell and another investor as they sought to raise extra funds from shareholders. Four months later, before he had actually invested any money, Branson pulled out. Duffell rued what he called 'a sorry story of big promises, failed ventures and the loss of over $15 million of shareholders' funds'. The business officially collapsed in 2006.

Instead of re-evaluating the strategy, in 2006 Branson arrived in South Africa to launch another credit card, this time in collaboration with the Barclays-owned Absa Bank. Once again, he promised the 'biggest shake-up ever' to end 'rip-offs'. The joint venture to provide insurance, savings, mortgages and pensions would cost, he estimated, $32 million over two and half years. His expectations went unfulfilled.

In early 2007, believing that he had learnt from his mistakes, he welcomed Jayne-Anne Gadhia's return to Virgin. First, she tried to buy back Virgin One from RBS. The preliminary discussions convinced the RBS bankers that 'Branson had not got the money', and their discussions ended. Next, Gadhia wanted to establish Virgin Money in America, to offer Virgin credit cards. Anthony Marino, the head of Virgin's development in America, searched for an opportunity. The hot topic, he reported, was peer-to-peer lenders.

Unregulated by law, peer-to-peer lenders negotiated the terms of personal loans between families and friends for student loans and mortgages. The attraction for the lenders was high profits and special tax benefits. Among the best was CircleLending, created in 2001 by Asheesh Advani in Waltham, near Boston. Marino approached Advani out of the blue. Describing Virgin as a venture-capital company searching for opportunities in the mortgage business, Marino outlined Branson's ambitions to break into banking's internet age. Excited by Virgin's plan, Advani negotiated with Gadhia to sell CircleLending for about $52 million and remain as the chief executive. Weeks later, Advani and Branson stood together in Waltham to launch Virgin's latest investment. Dressed in a black T-shirt bearing the logo 'Go Fund Yourself', Branson gave his audience a familiar message: 'We like shaking up industries, and I think we can give mortgage companies, banks and credit-card companies a run for their money.' Over the next five years, he added, CircleLending would expand from thirty to a thousand employees. 'Richard has told me', said Advani, 'that he'll be investing tens of millions of dollars in the business.' The launch coincided with Branson finding his best chance to break into global finance.

An entrepreneur's success depends on hard work, skill, inspiration, ruthlessness – and also on luck. All those ingredients are necessary when a suitable opportunity arises. In some instances, entrepreneurs create their own chances; at other times, an event materialises that is ripe for exploitation. In Branson's career, he had both created and exploited the breaks. The collapse on 13 September 2007 of Northern Rock, a bank based in Newcastle, was a chance for the latter – and an opportunity for Branson to become a serious banker after ten years on the fringes.

The television pictures of depositors queuing to withdraw their savings – the first run on a British bank in nearly 150 years – terrified Gordon Brown, the prime minister. The government's loan to the bank was rising towards £90 billion as Brown and Alistair Darling, the chancellor of the exchequer, searched forlornly for a saviour among the established banks. After dithering for two months, Brown acknowledged that the government's only alternative to nationalisation was to find a buyer among the minor players, including Branson.

'Go for it,' Branson told Gadhia. By capturing Northern Rock, Gadhia had explained, Virgin would inherit one million customers and a network of branches. She was supported by Stephen Murphy and Peter Norris, the former Barings director blamed by many for contributing to that merchant bank's collapse in 1995. Despite his notoriety, Norris was trusted by Branson. To compensate for Gadhia's lack of experience in retail banking, she secured the financial support of RBS; and, to bolster Virgin Money's credibility, she recruited Sir George

Mathewson, the sixty-seven-year-old retired chairman of RBS and Toscafund, to Virgin Money's executive. Investors in RBS and Toscafund would eventually lose substantial sums of money, and some blamed Mathewson for their losses. To add more gravitas, Branson also recruited Sir Brian Pitman, a seventy-five-year-old former chairman of Lloyds TSB and a director of Virgin Atlantic. Two retired bankers were the stars of the Virgin cast hoping to save the stricken bank.

Kept in the background was Wilbur Ross, the source of Branson's cash. Ross, a sixty-eight-year-old American, had earned his fortune by turning around insolvent steel mills. Since the financial crash, his targets in America and across Europe were failed lenders. Once bought, his plan was to return them to profit within two years and resell them. Northern Rock fitted the profile. The only obstacle in owning a bank notionally worth £94 billion was Virgin Money's credibility.

In 2006, Virgin Money had issued 2.5 million credit cards, but its profits were just £10.6 million. The company had no experience in managing credit cards, and certainly not in banking. Even Gadhia, keen to promote Branson's takeover, unintentionally admitted the weakness. 'We believe the Virgin brand', she explained, 'is exactly what is needed to reassure the public.' Branson's launch of Virgin Cola, she continued, had aroused her enthusiasm for the man and his empire. 'It was great,' she gushed about an outright failure. Branson's bid depended on Gordon Brown's judgement.

Ever since Branson had flown to London in 2003 to travel with Brown on a Virgin train from Euston, he had improved his relations with the politician. Because much of Virgin's business depended on government franchises and regulations – especially its airlines, trains and cable – Branson, who had endorsed Labour in the two previous general elections, had agreed to participate in Brown's 'enterprise' seminars and serve in the 'star chamber' of his Business Council for Britain. He also had good reason to complain about the party: his two bids for the national lottery had failed, he had lost two bids for rail franchises (Cross Country and the East Coast line) and he was angry that his bid in 2006 to buy ITV had been stymied by Labour's support for Murdoch. But bearing grudges, Branson knew, was futile. Instead, he told the prime minister how Virgin's interest in Northern Rock coincided with the government's.

Branson offered to inject £1.3 billion in return for a 55 per cent stake of the bank's £94 billion of assets. Virgin Money, said Branson, would invest up to £250 million, although there were doubts whether this was cash or his valuation of the Virgin Money brand. £400 million in real cash was offered by Wilbur Ross. The remaining £650 million, Branson proposed, should be put up by the existing shareholders, although he did not explain how they could be persuaded to commit more money to a bad investment. To repay the government's loans to the bank, he proposed to raise £11 billion from other banks instantly and to borrow a further £13 billion over the following three years. The security for the huge loan, said Branson, would be a government guarantee. 'We feel we have a winnable [*sic*] package,' he said. 'I believe it's the best option because we would rebrand it the Virgin Bank, which is a very strong brand.' Alistair Darling supported Branson's bid. Critics highlighted Branson's trivial conditions: his proposal to charge £10 million a year for using the Virgin brand and his stipulation that the shareholders should pay £5 million towards his costs for the takeover. The more serious criticism was that he had seemed to have forgotten that Northern Rock had collapsed precisely because established banks had refused to lend money to the insolvent institution. Unable to borrow money themselves, they were unlikely to lend £24 billion to Virgin.

To resolve the doubts about Virgin's plan, Gordon Brown

spoke to Branson over a weekend. Days later, the prime minister announced that Virgin was the government's choice 'to steer the course of stability and protect the taxpayer'. Northern Rock's shares surged by 20 per cent. 'We have made it clear', said a Treasury spokesman on 29 November, 'that we support the Virgin Group as a preferred bidder but we have always said we are keeping all other options open.' There was one other realistic bidder.

Brimming with confidence, Branson issued full-page advertisements in national newspapers addressed to Northern Rock's depositors. 'I have the greatest respect for customers,' he wrote, 'and I hope you will continue to be a valued customer of our new and exciting bank.' Under Virgin, he continued, they would receive better service, their savings would be protected and Northern Rock's debts to the Bank of England would be repaid. The value of Virgin's investment, he predicted, would double within three years. With limited risk, Branson expected to earn £1.5 billion, while the taxpayer would receive at most £500 million in return for risking over £24 billion.

The depiction of Branson paying a fortieth of the bank's original value and channelling the profits into his tax-free Caribbean bank accounts resurrected well-rehearsed questions about his reliability. Ever since his unethical buy-back of Virgin Music shares, the hippy outsider had few friends in the City; not so much because of Virgin's sleight of hand but more on account of the consistent losses suffered by its publicly owned companies. Among his most hostile and prejudiced critics, he called to mind the pavement artist performing the three-card trick instead of a serious financier who could be trusted to care for £65 billion of mortgages and £24 billion of loans. Virgin Money did not have a banking licence to accept deposits of money, but it asserted its directors were 'fit and proper'.

Entrusting Branson with public money roused Vince Cable,

the Liberal Democrats' financial spokesman. Branson's past, said Cable, made him unreliable as the government's partner, even if he would not be a director of the enlarged Virgin Money. 'Branson', he said, 'is the front man for a consortium of hedge funds and private-equity operators whose aim is to make a killing from a highly leveraged acquisition.' Virgin Money, he continued, was a branding and marketing organisation lacking the credibility to manage a bank. Barred by his tax status from spending more than ninety days in any year in Britain, Branson could only fume offshore that 'Virgin's plan and the Virgin brand will attract customers, get growth and earn rewards.' Off the cuff, he promised taxpayers a £5 billion profit. Although the City shared Cable's opinion that Branson's promises were a gamble, Gordon Brown disagreed. To protect his reputation, the prime minister wanted to avoid nationalisation, not least because he would be accused of nationalising the losses. The alternative he favoured was to privatise the profits, although both options were unpalatable to politicians.

Over Christmas, Brown despaired. Treasury officials judged Branson's solution to be credible, but Cable's criticisms had gained sympathy. While the prime minister fretted, Branson jetted around the world on his Falcon, being anointed 'Citizen of the Year' by the UN, meeting Nelson Mandela and addressing pupils at the Branson School of Entrepreneurship in Johannesburg. In the new year, Brown resolved to trust Branson, and the businessman was invited to join the prime minister on a business tour of the Far East on 18 January 2008. Just before leaving from London on a chartered BA flight to Beijing, Branson mentioned that he was 'fairly confident' that a deal could be struck with the government. Soon after take-off, he moved to the front of the plane and sat with Brown, boasting to the accompanying journalists on arrival that during the journey he had presented what he called a 'winnable package' to rescue Northern Rock.

Questioned about giving Branson preferential treatment, Brown denied having any discussions about Northern Rock during the trip. 'I haven't spoken in any detail to Richard Branson,' said the prime minister at Beijing airport. 'There was no cosy arrangement. The commercial decisions are not a matter for me.' Then Branson also went into reverse, denying even speaking 'one to one with Brown' about Northern Rock. 'We avoided discussing the matter,' he insisted. 'If I did want to have a word with the prime minister, I would not board a British Airways plane with 100 journalists aboard.' Two nights later in Shanghai, Brown appeared with his wife at a party hosted by Branson. Cable exploited the contradictions: 'If Gordon Brown's mate Richard Branson is going to become the private buyer, he'll be laughing all the way to the Bank of England.'

Political pressure compelled the government during late January to stiffen the terms of the sale in its favour, forcing any buyer to guarantee repayment of the government's loans. Virgin's only competitor withdrew, and Branson became convinced that he held all the cards. The government had no alternative to accepting his terms – other than nationalising the bank. Then Virgin changed the terms of its offer, reducing its payment. 'There's not much room for sharpening pencils,' said Branson. Brown's negotiators were surprised by the rough tactics. On the same day, the shares of Virgin Mobile USA fell to $6.12 from their $15 flotation price. Virgin Blue's shares in Australia also slipped, to A$1.30, half their flotation price. In the financial crisis, Virgin companies were suffering more than others. Treasury officials perceived a gap between Branson's promises and performance and, after Virgin changed the terms of its offer, started to question the company's sincerity.

Cable returned to the attack. He described Branson's bid as a 'con' and doubted whether he was 'fit and proper' to run Northern Rock. In Cable's opinion, Branson's arrest in 1971 for masterminding over twelve months a tax fraud worth £500,000 in today's values made him unsuitable 'to run a public company, let alone a bank, and let alone as someone responsible for £30 billion of taxpayers' money'. After all, said Cable, Branson's personal tax status in Britain was questionable. 'There are serious public-interest grounds for worrying about the Branson bid,' he wrote. Replying from Necker, Branson accused Cable of 'ignorance' and complained that his request for a meeting had been ignored. 'Perhaps you could explain why this is a sweetheart deal?' he asked from the Caribbean, but the political argument had been lost.

Alistair Darling now switched sides. 'The numbers', he agreed with his advisers, including Goldman Sachs, 'do not stack up.' Virgin's bid, advised the government's bankers, carried 'a degree of risk for taxpayers' because Virgin would be given a 'very significant subsidy' to make a profit, while the taxpayer had no realistic chance of earning any return. In headline terms, the risk of entrusting custody of £94 billion to someone of questionable credibility wrecked Branson's hopes.

During the morning of 17 February 2008, while Virgin's representatives were still negotiating with Treasury officials, Darling composed an announcement nationalising the bank. Branson cursed that Brown had 'bottled out'. His hopes of owning a major bank and earning £1.5 billion had been stymied.

One month later, the financial crash in New York began. First Bear Stearns imploded, and in September Lehman Brothers was declared insolvent. The world's financial system was tipping into the abyss. Despite the havoc, at the end of October Branson stuck to his plan to relaunch Virgin Money in America. As usual, his campaign was contrived to get free publicity – on that occasion by breaking the transatlantic sailing record. Branson would be aboard *Virgin Money*, a yacht with twenty-four crew moored in Manhattan. His timing was odd: not only was Wall Street in crisis but meteorologists were forecasting an imminent storm in the Atlantic. Nonetheless, unwilling to abandon the voyage, Branson ordered *Virgin Money* to sail. Two days later, a huge wave damaged the yacht and the crippled craft crept back to harbour.

Branson began reconsidering his investment in CircleLending. The banking crisis had wrecked the housing and mortgage businesses and many peer-to-peer lenders were insolvent. CircleLending had survived, but Branson and Jayne-Anne Gadhia had lost confidence in Asheesh Advani. The company's founder had bought Lendia, the biggest wholesale mortgage lender in north-east America, but the software of the combined organisation was malfunctioning. The losses were mounting. Branson's hopes of using CircleLending as a foundation of a Virgin bank had foundered, and New York's bankers were ignoring a man they labelled as a music producer. Abruptly, Gadhia changed strategy. Banking was draining Virgin's financial resources. Virgin Money, she recommended, should abandon mortgages and transform itself into a pure bank complying with the regulations which CircleLending had avoided. Branson's promise to Advani to expand the business was forgotten, and in 2008 he merged CircleLending with Graystone Solutions Inc., sold out and made a swift exit from banking in America.

The costly disappointment was once again compensated for by a stroke of luck.

9

Turbulence

On 27 March 2008, British Airways' operations at Heathrow collapsed in chaos. Hours after Terminal 5, the airline's £4.3 billion showcase opened, twenty years of planning were wrecked. Computers malfunctioned and untrained staff shunned desperate passengers. Dozens of flights were cancelled and thousands of suitcases lost. In the terminal, BA's passengers were close to rioting. Incompetent managers offered apologies and shredded BA's reputation. Branson did not conceal his delight. The airline's highly paid cabin staff, he knew, were also planning to strike.

BA was 'doomed', Branson announced in the midst of a party he was hosting to celebrate Virgin Atlantic's launch twenty-five years earlier. As he reminisced about the arrival of Virgin's first flight at JFK, when the doors of the second-hand Boeing 707 were opened to reveal the debris of a wild champagne-soaked party, his abuse escalated. BA's share price, he chortled, had tanked. 'I thought of buying it,' Branson sniffed to admiring journalists, 'but it's not worth much any more.' BA, he scoffed, would soon collapse, 'but it's not worth the government bailing it out'. He added, unsmilingly, 'We're ready to take over British Airways' routes and slots.'

Carping about the vulnerable was Branson's speciality. During the same brief visit to New York, he also mentioned that a major American airline was sinking: 'I don't think I'll get into naming names, but I will be surprised if one, in particular, of the US carriers is around in eighteen months' time.' The demise of rivals evoked no sympathy. 'Let inefficient airlines die peacefully,' he said. Alitalia, he added, should also be allowed to go bankrupt and possibly be taken over by Virgin. Branson's bravado reflected his relief at overcoming a succession of problems.

The most costly burden was Virgin America, his newest airline. Ever since a launch party was disrupted by torrential rain at Kennedy airport in July 2007, Branson's confidence about his challenge to Southwest and JetBlue, the grubby budget airlines, had been shaken. Virgin America's unusual comfort – including leather seats, wireless internet, touch-screen entertainment and attentive service – attracted praise, but Branson's confident forecasts of profits within two years had not materialised. Buffeted by high fuel prices and the financial crash, his entrenched rivals had counter-attacked, cutting their fares by up to 50 per cent. As a last gasp, Alaska Airlines complained that Virgin America was 'operating illegally' after the two original investors sold out. Virgin, the airline complained, was no longer genuinely American. The complaint was rejected, but the dream had been dented. Just ten months after the inaugural flight, Virgin America reduced its capacity by 10 per cent and sought permission to conceal its $227 million losses. Continued survival depended on Branson guaranteeing funding for the airline. Virgin America had been sustained by A$158 million of profits earned by the launch of Virgin Blue in Australia, but in 2008 the battle for survival in America was being mirrored Down Under.

In Branson's topsy-turvy world, he had initially been lukewarm about a cut-price Australian airline. The idea was Brett Godfrey's, whose involvement at Virgin Express, an indebted cut-price European airline, had ended without glory. Ignoring Branson's indifference, Godfrey had established an office in Sydney, and with four others targeted Ansett, Australia's second airline, which operated 40 per cent of the internal flights in Australia. Bad management and trade-union restrictions were wrecking Ansett's finances. 'I don't think it's going to work,' Branson told Godfrey on the telephone. 'I'm not coming to Australia.' Eventually, he invested about A$15 million in exchange for 95 per cent of the company. Godfrey could expect to receive a comparative pittance for his work.

Branson's lure undoubtedly brought opportunities, and occasionally he was blessed. On that occasion, his timing was astonishing. The 9/11 terrorist attacks toppled Ansett. Virgin Blue's planes had just started flying, and the airline was the only bidder for Ansett's check-in desks, equipment and slots at Australia's airports. Branson's low offer, replied the Macquarie bank administering the insolvency, was unacceptable. 'The bank's demands', Branson retorted, 'are extortionate. The public will suffer because fares will be pushed up.' He cut a deal, and one year later his bluster was rewarded when, in March 2002, he sold a 45.5 per cent stake in Virgin Blue for A$500 million (£221 million) to Chris Corrigan, the quietly spoken chief executive of Patrick Corporation, an Australian investment company. In December 2003, a further 25 per cent was sold for US$158.3 million (A$240 million) in a flotation. As usual, to avoid paying tax, he directed that his profits should be transferred to Virgin Holdings and Cricket, a personal trust, both based in Switzerland. He was stopped by the Australian government's insistence that he should first pay capital-gains taxes. His litigation against the government would fail.

In 2005, Virgin Blue carried about a third of the passengers on Australia's internal flights but was losing money battling against Qantas and Jetstar. The value of its shares collapsed. Open warfare broke out between Branson and Corrigan. 'Branson doesn't listen,' said Corrigan, complaining about Branson's obstruction. 'He's an ageing Bee Gee with a beard. You never want to assume he's your friend.' Corrigan became the majority shareholder and referred their argument to arbitration. Testifying under oath, Branson was uncertain about key facts and lost. Later, the two men met for a drink on Bondi Beach and agreed to stop their war. To Corrigan's surprise, Branson withdrew from their truce the moment he heard that Corrigan's company had been targeted for a hostile takeover bid by Paul Little of the Toll Corporation. Branson negotiated with Little that he would buy Corrigan's 62.4 per cent stake in Virgin Blue if Toll was victorious. Little did defeat Corrigan but went back on the agreement. Two years later, Virgin Blue was booming, earning profits of $98 million. Branson's stake was again valuable.

By summer 2008, the fate of all Branson's airlines appeared to be positive: his original A$15 million investment in Virgin Blue had created an airline that at one stage was worth A$2.5 billion (US$1.9 billion); Virgin America was haemorrhaging money but could become profitable; and, thanks to BA's chaos, Virgin Atlantic's profits would double that year to £68.4 million. By contrast, BA's losses were £401 million. Then, suddenly, his good fortune soured.

Virgin Atlantic's fate had always been precarious but it survived by attracting passengers thrilled by the promise of non-stop parties that started in the airport lounge. Branson's cheeky disregard for the truth still won admirers. 'I always travel with a bar of Cadbury's Whole Nut,' he told an interviewer, who then asked, 'Do you fly upper class?' 'No,' replied Branson, 'I always book economy.' By then, Branson regularly flew in his Falcon and had virtually abandoned his popular habit of greeting Virgin Atlantic's passengers with a notebook to record their comments as they crossed the Atlantic. His growing detachment from the day-to-day business was reflected in a complaint posted on the internet by a passenger about the food served on a Virgin flight from Mumbai to Heathrow.

'I love the Virgin brand,' the passenger emailed Branson, 'I really do which is why I continue to use it despite a series of unfortunate incidents over the last few years. This latest incident takes the biscuit. Ironically, by the end of the flight I would have gladly paid over a thousand rupees for a single biscuit following the culinary journey of hell I was subjected to at the hands of your corporation.' The passenger attached photographs of a sponge dessert served with tomato and peas, and a heap of yellow liquid which he assumed was custard but was in fact mustard – 'More mustard than any man could consume in a month.' Starving and distraught, the passenger reached for the cookie on his tray, which came, he wrote, in a 'baffling presentation'. The photograph, he told Branson, suggested that the cookie was an 'evidence bag from the scene of a crime. A crime against bloody cooking. Either that or some sort of back-street underground cookie, purchased off a gun-toting maniac high on his own supply of yeast . . . Imagine biting into a piece of brass, Richard. That would be softer on the teeth than the specimen above.' Exhausted, the man tried to enjoy 'your world-famous onboard entertainment'. He attached a photograph of the image: 'It's just incredibly hard to capture Boris Johnson's face through the flickering white lines running up and down the screen . . . I was the hungriest I'd been in my adult life and I had a splitting headache from squinting at a crackling screen.' He ended his letter: 'My only question is: How can you live like this? I can't imagine what dinner round your house is like. It must be like something out of a nature documentary.' The apology from Virgin's customer-relations department was perfunctory: an employee expressed surprise that the passenger had disliked Virgin's 'award-winning food which is very popular on our Indian routes'.

The complaint was an omen, and in autumn 2008 Branson's *Schadenfreude* over BA's crisis at Heathrow was replaced by a calamity of his own. In common with those of many other carriers, the finances of Virgin's airlines had been wrecked by that summer's financial crash. Virgin Atlantic's profits, earned at BA's expense, would turn into losses of £158 million in 2009. The company's flights to Mumbai were among those cut, stopped after just three years. Branson's expansion into Africa had also imploded, and in Nigeria he was struck by what he called 'Mafioso-style tactics'.

The potential for lucrative profits had lured Branson into launching a new airline in a notoriously corrupt country. Oil-rich Nigerians were paying fortunes to BA for transporting washing machines and other heavy packages as excess luggage from Heathrow to Lagos. Although Branson would say that Kofi Annan had urged him in 2004 to introduce safe planes into a country cursed by fatal crashes, he was also attracted by the potential profits. He planned to start Virgin Nigeria, an airline flying across Africa that would feed passengers on to Virgin Atlantic's flights from Lagos's MMIA airport to London and onwards to New York.

Branson had personally struck the deal to create Virgin Nigeria with President Olusegun Obasanjo in 2005. The president offered Branson concessions in oil and other commodities as an incentive to invest £24 million in return for a 49 per cent stake in the airline. Branson agreed that Nigerian businessmen would own the majority stake. Virgin Atlantic leased six Boeing 737s and transferred them to the new Nigerian airline. However, soon after, Branson and his partners argued: the Nigerians wanted Virgin Nigeria to fly to London and New York, while Branson rejected establishing a competitor to his own airline. After some pressure, he agreed that Virgin Nigeria could fly between Lagos and Gatwick in an old Airbus 340. 'You want our airline to fail,' Branson was told by a partner.

Four years later, President Obasanjo left office. His successor, President YarAdua, assumed that Branson and the ex-president had a close working relationship. Seeing that Branson's bond with his Nigerian partners had crumbled, a member of the president's entourage ended Virgin's investment violently. 'The

Nigerian government ignored our contract and sent in heavies to smash up our lounge in Lagos airport with sledgehammers,' Branson complained. His appeal to President YarAdua for protection against the violent 'dream killers' was rejected. Branson accepted the thugs' message, abandoning the airline and losing his money. 'I think Branson needed to understand the local environment,' observed Jimoh Ibrahim, a Nigerian businessman, after buying the debris.

Misfortune also disrupted Virgin Blue. At the end of 2008, the airline's A$98 million profit had turned into a loss of A$160 million. The shares fell from $2.80 in February 2007 to 29 cents, making the airline worth just A$170 million. Amid fears of an influenza pandemic and ferocious competition, staff were fired and aircraft sold. Paul Little handed control of the airline back to Branson. 'The economy is fucked,' said Branson in 2009. He predicted 'spectacular casualties'.

In a financial crisis, Branson's characteristics were revealed. Virgin, he had often declared, took care not to fire any staff by arranging job shares, part-time work and voluntary unpaid leave. His employees, he repeated, were embraced as members of the Virgin family. 'At least if you've got a job, you've got your dignity and you've got some money coming in,' Branson had told a crowd in Los Angeles while unveiling a new Virgin Boeing 777. 'But for those people who are out of work it can be very, very devastating.' The benevolent self-portrait created by Branson was not quite accurate. To protect his own airlines from insolvency in 2009, he forgot his sermons about Virgin's focus on the consumer's interest and on caring for his workers, described by him as 'the Virgin family': that year, Virgin Atlantic fired 15 per cent of its staff. Those who remained were meant to be reassured by Branson's family mantra, but that comfort had been rattled by his disdain for employees seeking trade-union protection. 'Say "no" to the old way of flying,' he had advised

Virgin America's new staff when considering membership of the Transport Workers Union. 'And say "no" to the TWU.' The price of seeking trade-union protection, he said, was the loss of the Virgin family's 'uniqueness and independent spirit'. Momentarily, there was a stand-off.

Branson was similarly unamused when 4,800 Virgin Atlantic cabin staff threatened a four-day strike, protesting that their pay compared unfavourably to that of BA staff. 'For some of you,' Branson wrote in an open letter, 'more pay than Virgin Atlantic can afford may be critical to your lifestyle; and if that is the case you should consider working elsewhere'. The paternalistic image was damaged. 'What Branson did', a union leader told Steve Ridgway, 'isn't sobering but shocking. He's saying it's his train set and he'll do what he likes with it. But what about his employees? Where does that leave them?'

Virgin's cabin staff eventually backed down. Branson had made no concessions, but a new strike was threatened by the company's pilots. The income gap between those at Virgin Atlantic and those at BA had increased. Virgin's pilots were convinced that Branson was concealing the airline's profits in a myriad of offshore accounts. To offer reassurance, Ridgway had allowed accountants retained by BALPA, the pilots' trade union, to scrutinise the airline's financial records. To the accountants' surprise, the airline appeared to be spending more than it was earning and lacked cash reserves. Baffled but not impotent, the union eventually negotiated a 13 per cent pay rise over three years and a share of future profits. The latter would not be forthcoming. Virgin Atlantic was struggling – not just for profits but also for survival. As his options narrowed, Branson's invective became more strident, especially against BA, itself weakened by strikes and the financial crisis.

Ever since he had launched Virgin Atlantic, Branson had behaved as if his airline's survival and profits depended upon humiliating BA. Among his notable successes was the filibustering campaign in 1996 to prevent BA from forging an alliance with American Airlines, or code sharing, in order to allow seamless interconnections for their passengers between the two airlines anywhere in the world. BA's major rivals in Europe were all grouped into either the Star or SkyTeam global alliances, and Branson lobbied hard in London and Washington to prevent a similar pact based at Heathrow. Consumers, he argued, would be harmed. 'No way BA/AA,' was the winning slogan daubed on the fuselages of Virgin Atlantic planes.

While Branson celebrated victory, transatlantic travellers from Britain were paying higher fares than those flying from Amsterdam and elsewhere in Europe. Although Julie Southern, Virgin Atlantic's commercial manager, insisted, 'We have always provided competition for British Airways. That is Richard's *raison d'être*,' in reality he opposed genuine competition on flights between America and Britain. His self-interest was to protect Virgin's privileged access to Heathrow and compel BA to operate at a disadvantage against the other major European airlines.

In 2008, Branson's bulwark disappeared. The Open Skies Agreement between the EU and the American government allowed any airline to fly between Europe and America. Overnight, the agreements that had previously restricted flights between Heathrow and America to two American and two British airlines (including Virgin) was ended. BA's fate depended on an alliance with American Airlines. 'It'll be the end of Branson within minutes of his rivals announcing their intention to reapply for permission to forge an alliance,' predicted a BA executive in September 2008.

BA and AA did reapply for permission to merge their booking systems. Their putative code share on nearly 5,000 flights would cover about 20 per cent of all transatlantic flights, compared with the Star Alliance's control of 41 per cent and SkyTeam's 29 per cent. The statistics were irrelevant to Branson. 'I'll fight this to the end,' he said. Under the banner of free competition and the consumers' interest, Branson attacked 'a monster monopoly. It's like allowing Coca-Cola and Pepsi to merge.' He pledged to spend 'millions' to prevent a tie-up that would 'crucify' the public. He did not, however, possess 'millions' in a war chest. In private, he admitted that 'the landscape is much tougher'.

Denying any self-interest, he appealed as 'the people's champion' to President Obama to stop 'a monopoly, or near monopoly, on some of the busiest and most profitable routes from the US to Europe causing an unprecedented loss to consumers'. In his letter to a man whom he had recently described as 'the best president America has ever had', Branson urged that the proposed alliance be blocked as it was harmful to consumers. The two airlines combined, Branson told the president, would control 63 per cent of all transatlantic flights between Britain and America. Other statistics showed it would be 44 per cent.

Willie Walsh's first reaction was polite. BA's chief executive restrained himself. But as Branson's campaign developed, Walsh accused his critic of sounding like a 'cracked record' and let it be known that he would 'put the boot into Branson for ducking questions'. Branson, said Walsh, 'should wake up to the economic realities of the business'.

One reality was Virgin's size. Branson's airline leased thirty-eight aircraft flying on thirty routes, while BA dispatched 248 aircraft on 150 routes; BA had 41 per cent of the slots at Heathrow compared to Virgin's 5 per cent; and Virgin Atlantic ranked as the tenth-largest carrier across the Atlantic.

Walsh also questioned Branson's sincerity. In October 2009, Branson criticised US airlines for levying a new $10 fee for baggage. 'Airlines', he said, 'risked alienating travellers by adding so many charges on top of ticket prices. The extra fees are not a good idea.' Branson's condemnation was odd since seven months earlier Virgin America had imposed a $15 fee for checked-in bags. The double standards coincided with the approaching trial of the four BA executives who had allegedly conspired to fix the Passenger Fuel Surcharge with Branson's team. The bitterness among the BA management over Branson's denouncement to the Department of Justice had not disappeared and raised questions about his understanding of the airline business.

Branson acknowledged a major error. For years he had single-mindedly focused on expanding Virgin Atlantic, ridiculing the low-cost airlines. 'EasyJet's a terrible idea,' Steve Ridgway, the chief executive of Virgin Atlantic, had scoffed during the 1990s, adding, 'Ryanair is rubbish.' Branson echoed that opinion. Since then, Ryanair had become more valuable than BA, and easyJet had expanded to become a profitable challenger to BA and all the other European airlines.

The miscalculation exposed a central flaw within Branson's empire. He prided himself on delegation but avoided reading complicated documents, was untrained in finance and copied old ideas which had failed elsewhere. Virgin Mobile had been one of the exceptions: renting network capacity was a genuinely novel concept. By contrast, his airline businesses all relied on an outdated and inflexible financial model. Both Ridgway and Branson had underestimated the potential of the internet. Neither had understood Michael Ryan's genius in creating new routes, new airports and the model for Ryanair's low fares: he priced the aircraft's seats on the assumption that they would all be sold. Accordingly, Ryanair's prices were low. Virgin Atlantic could not break its habit of slavishly shadowing BA.

Belatedly, Branson had tried to replicate the enormous profits reaped by cut-price flights across Europe by expanding Virgin Express, a troubled airline based in Brussels. 'I am absolutely delighted', he exclaimed in 2002, 'that the Virgin Express product will be at the front of the wave of change that will shortly sweep over German aviation.' Twenty Virgin aircraft were to be based in Cologne. Then he abandoned the plan and, once again cursed by falling ticket sales and unreliable aircraft, he dashed for the exit in 2004 by selling Virgin Express to a Belgian rival. The failed venture had cost Branson about $100 million and weakened Virgin Atlantic. Instead of dismissing Ridgway for failing to devise a profitable budget airline, Branson showered praise on the hapless executive. He had one remaining lifeline to save Virgin Atlantic's independence.

Michael Bishop, the owner of BMI, a British airline serving Europe, wanted gradually to sell his business after 2002 and retire. BMI owned 11 per cent of the slots at Heathrow and supplied about a quarter of Virgin Atlantic's transatlantic traffic through code sharing. If Branson bought BMI, Virgin Atlantic would become a credible challenger to BA, easyJet and Ryanair. For several years, Branson had discussed a formal alliance with Bishop, first as a merger and then an outright purchase by Virgin. In Bishop's opinion, their negotiations collapsed after Branson reneged on their oral agreements and tried to cut the purchase price. Bishop criticised Branson's style and suspected at the end of 2008 that his finances were stretched. Even Branson admitted that if HBOS had crashed during the banking crisis, Virgin's credit lifeline would have disappeared and the airline would have been imperilled.

With Branson out of the reckoning, Bishop sold a 30 per cent stake of BMI to Lufthansa, 20 per cent to SAS and kept 50 per cent plus one share. He also negotiated an option with Lufthansa that guaranteed a good price for his remaining shares. In July 2009, after Bishop activated that option, Lufthansa had to buy full control of the loss-making airline for £223 million ($368 million). In the midst of the recession, BMI was a poisoned chalice, and Lufthansa's directors sought a buyer. BMI's slots at Heathrow were worth about £200 million. Virgin Atlantic's independence depended on buying the airline, but Branson did not come up with the money.

As Britain's star entrepreneur, Branson dived for a smoke-screen. 'We would relish the chance to buy Gatwick,' he told his media friends. 'Branson's comments are fantasy,' said a BA spokesman.

The fate of his airlines, Branson knew, was at risk.

10

Green Squib

Virgin Atlantic's losses were matched by Branson's investments in renewable energy. At the end of 2008, he had lost at least $60 million but, as the *New York Times* reported, Virgin had benefited through his championship of the environment.

Interviewing a woman in Manhattan protesting about capitalism and the banks, a journalist from the newspaper inquired how she had travelled from San Francisco. 'Virgin America,' she replied. But, she was asked, wasn't Virgin the sort of corporation she should be opposing? 'Branson', she replied, 'is working on creating solar planes.' Other tycoons would have been damned by a high-carbon lifestyle, but Branson's 'green' activities brought him approval as an environmental crusader. His public relations were masterful.

'Oil is too precious to burn in cars. I drive cars using ethanol,' said the billionaire, adding that Necker was powered entirely by wind and solar energy. Although global aviation was allegedly responsible for 4.9 per cent of man-made climate change, Branson deflected blame by explaining that Virgin Atlantic had ordered fuel-efficient aircraft. Even Virgin Galactic was presented as kind to the environment. 'It produces the same carbon dioxide emissions as a Boeing 747 on a ten-hour flight,' Will Whitehorn had said. Critics trying to monitor the results of Branson's $3 billion pledge to produce non-carbon fuels were flummoxed. The evidence was elusive, but Branson was still the hero.

On 19 February 2008, Virgin Atlantic dispatched invitations to another spectacular environmental event. On the same day,

Branson flew in his Falcon from India to New York. Over the following three days, he continued to jet between San Francisco, San Diego, Los Angeles, Montreal, New York and finally Toronto, where, to 'capture the public's imagination', he committed Virgin's support to Earth Hour, an international gesture of dimming lights from Toronto to Sydney. The eco-entrepreneur arrived at Heathrow airport on 24 February to reassert Virgin's green credentials.

No other businessman could have attracted nearly one hundred journalists to witness what Branson called 'a historic occasion'. Just after 11.30 a.m., he stood in front of a Virgin Atlantic Boeing 747 holding a small bottle. 'Today marks a biofuel breakthrough for the whole airline industry,' said Branson. The bottle contained a mixture of coconut oil and babassu palm oil. He intended to prove that the jet could complete the forty-minute flight to Amsterdam's Schiphol airport using three tanks filled with normal aviation kerosene and a fourth containing kerosene mixed with the biofuel.

The biofuel had been manufactured by Imperium Renewables in Seattle, on America's Pacific coast. The company had imported 150,000 coconuts from plantations in the Philippines and palm oil tapped in the Brazilian wilderness. The product was then flown 4,800 miles to Heathrow.

Branson had chosen coconut fuel after discovering that ethanol froze at 15,000 feet. The switch did not damage his credibility. With a forced smile he drank the fuel. 'My God, it was horrible,' he later admitted. After the plane landed safely in Amsterdam, some environmentalists hailed Branson as 'a game changer in aviation'. His experiment, they said, had started a debate. Other venture capitalists, those environmentalists anticipated, would produce alternative fuels using algae and natural crops. Their enthusiasm was reinforced by Virgin's publicists telling journalists that 20 per cent of the fuel for the fourth engine was the biofuel. Friends of the Earth challenged this assertion, claiming it was only 5 per cent. Among the crowd on the tarmac were representatives of Boeing and General Electric, the engine manufacturer. 'Boeing has done five flights using biofuels,' Virgin's spokesman would later say as proof of the manufacturer's commitment to using alternative fuels. Boeing subsequently explained the company 'supported' Branson's idea but denied any 'commitment'.

In the aftermath of the flight, Branson was asked whether burning biofuels in a jet engine was cleaner than kerosene. 'Yes,' he replied. Environmental campaigners, including Friends of the Earth, contradicted him. Burning biofuels is not cleaner than aviation fuel. Moreover, highlighting the production of crops for biofuels, his critics argued, had buried inconvenient truths about the carbon emissions needed to gather the coconuts and palm oil. Farmland and forests were being destroyed to grow the crops, and excessive carbon was emitted by manufacturing the fuel and shipping it around the globe. Branson's performance, said his opponents, was a cheap alternative to greenwash advertising. As ever, Branson was not embarrassed. Although he admitted that there was insufficient palm oil and coconuts to manufacture the fuel regularly, even for a single Boeing engine, their objections were peripheral to one reality: on the same day as that flight to Amsterdam, the price of oil was $100 a barrel, the highest since 1980, and was certain to rise further. Virgin Atlantic's financial hedging to protect itself from increased prices had been inept. His airline's finances were deteriorating, and his investment in green technology was similarly hit.

Virgin's Green Fund, based in London, was seeking, said Branson, a 30 per cent return from investments. 'Up to now,' he said, perplexingly, in 2009, 'we've spent $300 million on this, so we're ahead of the game because we haven't actually made that amount of profit.' A few weeks later, he spoke about the imminent 'completion' of raising another $400 million for the Virgin Green Fund. The manager of the fund, Shai Weiss, he said, would be investing between $5 million and $100 million in projects to develop renewable energy. Weiss's record was inconsistent. In 2008, Virgin had invested $14.5 million in Green Road Technologies, a research group seeking to reduce cars' fuel consumption. Within two years, the company was in financial difficulties. Alongside that loss was Virgin's faltering investment in Cilion.

Soon after Vinod Khosla had opened the first ethanol plant in Keyes, California, he announced its closure 'for technical and market reasons'. His plan to build eight others was abandoned in January 2009. Despite government subsidies, the project was unprofitable and, worse, ethanol had become unpopular among environmentalists. The conversion of natural land into cropland was destroying ecosystems, including the sponges and rainforests that absorb greenhouse gases. Khosla's $200 million investment in Cilion was sold for $20 million in cash and shares to Aetatis. An evangelical advocate of green innovation, Khosla was burning money rather than producing biofuel. But his reputation did not suffer.

Khosla sermonised about 'the green-technology revolution' and dismissed critics as 'Luddite jokers'. His interest in biofuels as 'the single most important tool we have so far for alleviating climate change' and his justification of profiting from environmental investments were opinions Branson easily agreed with. 'The only way to predict the future is to invent it,' was Khosla's golden phrase. He ridiculed the notion that the world could reduce its energy consumption. The trick, said the billionaire, was to find alternatives to oil, coal, cement and steel. Like any disciple, Branson repeated the gospel to his friends, including Tony Blair, who in 2010 agreed to join Khosla as a paid adviser on 'global relationships'.

Blair's endorsement coincided with increased stridency in the US Congress about reversing climate change. The politicians spoke about a $500 billion green economy creating two million new jobs in pollution control and conservation. Their conviction that entrepreneurs would make a difference to the world reassured Branson about the profitability of green industries.

Among his new investments was Solyndra, a manufacturer of solar panels based in California. $600 million had already been pledged to that 'clean tech' industry, whose advantage, said Khosla and others, was that its panels were made from a substitute for high-priced silicon. Virgin Green, said Branson, had scrutinised 117 different panel producers before investing $31.9 million in Solyndra. Joining other high-profile investors from Silicon Valley seemed a one-way bet after Khosla reaped a 100 per cent profit by selling Ausra, a solar thermal company, for $250 million. Soon after Branson's investment, the *Wall Street Journal* praised Solyndra as America's top 'clean tech' company. The seal of approval came in the form of President Obama's personal support. The federal government advanced a $535 million loan to Solyndra, which triggered investors to pour in another $600 million. Holding on to Khosla's coat-tails represented a break in Branson's routine pattern of business. Usually he copied and challenged Goliaths. But Khosla's mastery of government subsidies and regulations – mirroring Branson's methods – was tantalisingly persuasive.

At that moment, Khosla was negotiating with the administration of Atlanta, Georgia, for a $162 million grant. He planned to build a factory to produce forty million gallons of cellulosic ethanol every year from local pine trees. Enthusiastic officials hailed Range Fuels, Khosla's enterprise, as 'liquid gold'. Warnings from sceptics about 'a high-risk venture' and 'still unproven technologies' were silenced by his admirers.

Branson did not invest in Range Fuels but, encouraged by

Khosla's overall success, in 2008 he entrusted more millions to Gevo, Khosla's next venture, which planned to manufacture butanol rather than ethanol as a renewable fuel. Manufactured by fermenting sugar and yeast, butanol produces more energy and is easier to blend with petrol than ethanol. After raising $199 million from investors, including a 10 per cent stake for Branson's Green Fund, Khosla began planning production in Luverne, Minnesota. Once again, Branson confidently predicted success: 'Butanol will replace jet fuel within five years. We've set ourselves a target of using butanol instead of jet fuel on Virgin Atlantic within five years.' He also pledged to use it on Virgin Trains. However, within weeks of announcing the venture, Khosla ran into legal problems. Butamax, a company jointly created by BP and Dupont in 2003 to make butanol, had patented their perfected process in 2005. After three years' research in a plant in Hull, north-east England, Butamax announced their intention to exploit their patent in an American factory. One year later, in 2009, Gevo applied for US government funding to develop butanol and was granted $1.8 million. The application revealed the company's intention to use the identical process that Butamax had pioneered in Hull, prompting Butamax to sue Gevo for infringing its patents. Branson's Green Fund now owned a stake in a company accused of unethical behaviour. Gevo denied the allegation and claimed to be more advanced in butanol production than Butamax. The dispute coincided with Khosla's receipt of $76 million of taxpayers' funds in Georgia to produce cellulosic ethanol. Despite receiving this money, Khosla had to delay starting production and reduced his forecasted output from forty million to twelve million gallons a year.

The setbacks did not damage Branson's reputation. The few cynics were silenced by the favourable publicity still surrounding the $25 million Earth Challenge. Few seemed to be aware that no winner had been named and that the prize remained unpaid.

Among the hundreds of disappointed applicants was James Lovelock, a Branson favourite. Lovelock proposed laying pipes across the surface of the oceans to suck carbon dioxide into the sea. 'Richard has been in touch with Jim Lovelock about this idea', said a Virgin spokesman, 'and is very interested. We are looking into it to see if we can fund a trial.' Nothing happened but, at no cost, Branson's image was enhanced by his continuing association with three other outstanding environmentalists: Tim Flannery, Crispin Tickell and James Hansen.

That coterie of stars, combined with his own activities, elevated Branson's standing among the environmental clan as preparations for the meeting of the UN Climate Change Conference in Copenhagen in December 2009 were concluded. The organisers were appointing 'world business leaders' to inspire the expected 15,000 delegates, 5,000 journalists and ninety-eight political leaders, including President Obama. With Al Gore's help, Branson was given a starring role in the conference as a 'councillor' among the business leaders.

Branson adopted a Churchillian pose. Britain's prime minister had directed the nation's defence against Nazi Germany from a subterranean war room. To conjure a similar image, Branson created the Carbon War Room in Washington. Several passionate climate campaigners joined Branson to, in the jargon he adopted, 'enhance low-carbon economic development, remake the carbon-industrial complex into a post-carbon economy and accelerate green solutions'. 'Black Gold', a War Room slogan, was dedicated to removing carbon dioxide from the atmosphere.

Naturally, Branson sought others to help finance his 'think tank'. Two of the 'founding partners' were unusual: Novamedia, which manages the Dutch Postcode Lottery, and Strive Masiyiwa, the Zimbabwean owner of Econet Telecom, a mobile network in Africa. Branson and the other founders, who chose to remain anonymous, committed $3 million each over three years. Branson's contribution was sourced from the fees paid for his public speeches.

A head-hunting agency recruited the executive directors through unsolicited telephone calls. Jigar Shah, who had created and then sold for $200 million SunEdison, a provider of solar-energy systems, agreed to be chief executive for $253,001 a year. 'I want to give something back,' he said, adding to Branson's delight that 'climate change is the largest wealth-creation opportunity of our lifetime'. The director of operations was to be Peter Boyd, Virgin Cola's former head of marketing, who later worked for Virgin Mobile in America and South Africa. Travis Bradford, an investment-fund manager, was Shah's deputy on $209,091 per annum. Mark Grundy, previously employed to promote Coca-Cola and PepsiCo and an advocate of greenwashing, was responsible for publicity. 'Companies', he said, on Branson's behalf, 'will be most successful if they tie their green efforts to a specific cause or issue – whether that is personal health, sustainable business practices or climate change.' In the aftermath of the 2008 crash, he linked the environment to money-making: 'Green is now always going to be part of marketing in a way that it wasn't before 2007.'

To improve Virgin's image through the War Room, Branson transferred Jean Oelwang, a Virgin marketing executive in Australia, to London to manage his charity, Virgin Unite. The symmetry between helping the poor and saving the planet was, in Branson's opinion, natural. Oelwang explained that her purpose at the War Room was to 'really drive business as a force for good in the world'. A similar role was assigned to Sean Cleary, a former South African diplomat who represented the white apartheid government between 1970 and 1980. Subsequently, Cleary represented the South African government in the regime's wars against the liberation armies in Namibia and Angola.

Branson was good at recruiting idealists. Claire Tomkins,

an engineer specialising in clean-energy technology, accepted his offer 'at a moment in time when we all believed we would get an agreement in Copenhagen', she said. 'It was a super-charged atmosphere.' But Tomkins was under no illusion about Branson's motives: 'Richard was looking for interesting deals out of the War Room. He was looking for money.' Shah and Bradford were partners in his quest. 'Many environmentalists', Bradford believed, 'are myopic. They act out of a false paradigm that earning money from innovation is a conflict of interest with the environment. They put their faith in bad solutions. They suffer from a perception gap about getting a good return on environmental energy-saving measures. You can make millions and simultaneously help the climate.'

Branson tasked the new team to provide a tub-thumping speech for him to deliver in Copenhagen. He wanted a theme that deflected attention from the aviation industry's culpability. Jigar Shah suggested shipping. The industry admitted producing 250,000 tons of carbon every year, or about 3 per cent of annual emissions. 'The shipping industry has no incentive to improve,' Shah told Branson.

The International Maritime Organization, Shah discovered, had meticulously collected data showing the carbon footprint of 60,000 individual ships. In Shah's plan, to be explained by Branson in his speech, the IMO's data would be published on the War Room's website. 'We'll put ships of the same weight side by side,' continued Shah, 'and show which ship is emitting more carbon than another ship of the same weight.' By comparing every ship's carbon emissions, charterers would be encouraged to reject the contaminators. 'We'll send a shock wave through the industry.' This new territory, Branson agreed, would grab the delegates' attention. It was so simple. 'This is exciting and sexy,' added Shah. 'We'll be catalysts, creating an irreversible momentum. We will prove that capitalism can solve climate change.' Artlessly, he added, 'This is the easiest one to pull off.'

In full flight, Branson stepped on to the podium at the Copenhagen headquarters of Maersk, one of the world's biggest shipping groups. 'The shipping industry', he said, enjoying the possibility of denouncing his hosts, 'is just as big a polluter as the airline industry, if not more. But they've managed to keep under the radar and have done almost nothing about their carbon footprint.' Shipping, he said, should be subject to a global tax on emissions. Thanks to the War Room's database, charterers could force the industry to change. With a smile acknowledging the applause, he stepped down to accept congratulations from the delegates.

One man in the audience was outraged. Peter Hinchliffe, the IMO's secretary general, condemned Branson's speech as 'dismissive and aggressive'. Hinchliffe had previously accused Peter Boyd of misinterpreting the IMO's data, but he had been ignored. As Branson mingled with the audience in the auditorium, he was introduced to Hinchliffe.

'You're completely wrong in everything you said,' Hinchliffe told him. 'You're not giving the true picture. You can't compare ships as if they were all Boeing aircraft. Even if two ships are the same weight, you can't compare a tanker and a container ship. Every ship is a different trade and type, and has different safety requirements. So the energy consumption varies.' Branson fell silent. 'And we're already doing a lot,' added Hinchliffe, listing the industry's initiatives.

'I didn't know anything about that,' stuttered Branson, who Hinchliffe believed 'seemed quite shocked'.

'And why are you attacking us?' continued Hinchliffe. 'Shipping emits 3 per cent of the world's carbon and carries 90 per cent of the world's trade. Planes emit 4 per cent and carry only 10 per cent. You're not telling the true story.'

Branson shuffled away, promising to 'look at everything'.

Travis Bradford was not surprised by the exchange he had witnessed. 'Branson's very good at raising awareness,' he said, 'even when he doesn't understand what we are saying.'

The exchange delighted Jigar Shah. 'We're completely disrupting the shipping industry,' he chortled. 'They're completely pissed off.'

To Hinchliffe's disappointment, Branson did not live up to his assurance. 'It's become impossible to work with the Carbon War Room,' he reported to his members. 'Branson pulled a stunt, got good publicity, but they've got no influence.' On reflection, he asked rhetorically, 'And why is Branson lecturing shipping, considering all the energy his planes use?' He was baffled when Branson subsequently wrote, 'We have gathered a tremendous amount of support for our vision of a low-carbon shipping industry.'

The contradiction was highlighted by questions to Branson during the conference. One year earlier, Branson had supported a global tax on aircraft to reduce carbon and had criticised those who resisted his campaign. But in Copenhagen he somersaulted. Like all airlines, that year Virgin Atlantic was fighting for survival. A global tax on emissions, he told the delegates, was 'unrealistic'. Airlines, he said, should be exempt, otherwise they would be 'taxed out of existence'. He even joined those demanding that carbon trading be removed from the agenda.

The inconsistencies reflected Branson's fixation with the price of oil. About one-third of an airline's costs is jet fuel, and after the oil price spiked at $147 a barrel in July 2008, Branson feared that the world's economy was doomed. His airlines and his lifestyle were threatened. Searching for culprits, he placed the blame on a cartel of oil traders who were secretly rigging the prices. He had no evidence of a conspiracy, but at the time Branson was preoccupied by price-fixing. Virgin had just confessed to manipulating the Passenger Fuel Surcharge, so his conflation of oil prices, renewable fuels and cartels was understandable. In his reliance on Will Whitehorn, Virgin's media supremo, for facts, he was unaware of the unique circumstances causing the oil-price spike: namely, thanks to America's new environmental laws there was a shortage of special oil products, which coincided with China's high demand for those same goods in anticipation of the 2008 Olympics. By relying on the peak-oil illusionists, Whitehorn also apparently omitted to tell him that every official inquiry in Washington had failed to discover hard evidence that the oil market was artificially fixed.

After the Olympics, oil prices fell below $100 a barrel, and in September 2008 Branson did an about-turn. Visiting Lisbon, he explained that the economic crash had changed his philosophy. 'I think a real collapse of oil prices is possible at this time,' he said with relief. 'Maybe back down to $56 a barrel.' One month later, he somersaulted again. Cheap oil was anathema to environmentalists convinced that governments should be compelled to embrace renewable energy. Virgin's task force on fuel prices, chaired by Whitehorn, predicted that a 'peak in cheap, easily available oil production is likely to be hit by 2013'. Branson fell into line. He joined the chorus predicting oil prices of $200 a barrel by 2010, and even announced the creation of Virgin Oil – his plan to build a £1 billion refinery to supply aviation fuel. This was pure fantasy. Faced with a surplus of refining capacity in Europe, the major oil producers were selling or closing their plants. Investing in a new refinery was far beyond Branson's finances.

On the same day in September 2009 that Branson urged business leaders from over fifty countries meeting in London that recovery from recession 'must be environmentally sustainable, moving away from the excesses of the Industrial Revolution to a new future based on protecting and valuing our natural resources', he flew on his Falcon to New York to attend that year's Clinton Global Initiative. (At least three scheduled flights departed every hour from Heathrow to New York.) He was met by staff from the War Room.

Their idealism was evaporating. The financial crisis had destroyed the evangelism espoused by Claire Tomkins and other campaigners. 'Everyone is in shock,' Tomkins declared. 'What can we do next? Whatever, it will be a long slog.' Looking at Branson's team, she decided, 'It's the end of euphoria. There are too many defeats and negative rhetoric against climate change. We can't run any campaigns. It's too hard to raise money. At the beginning we'd been told that they would be raising tens of millions of dollars, but that hasn't happened. It was the inflection point.' The War Room was to be shrunk. Its income from the trustees had fallen from $5.5 million to $1.1 million and its losses stood at $2.5 million. She and others decided it was time to leave. By then, Travis Bradford had also left. 'Nothing new was launched,' he said about an organisation struggling to survive. 'They were looking for the next big thing to grab attention and build momentum.' Four years later, the War Room had still failed to find a new 'big thing'.

In 2010, oil prices did not hit $200. Branson postponed the 'apocalypse'. In another report, he now predicted that the oil crunch would occur in 2015. His warning of a world without oil was endorsed by Sir David King, the British government's former chief scientist. King pronounced in 2010 that the world's oil reserves had been exaggerated by 33 per cent and that by 2014 demand would exceed supply, causing shortages and price spikes. To support the doomsayers who claimed peak oil was just four years away, Branson published the *Virgin Review of the Environment*. The 'proof' was provided to him by experts including Jeremy Leggett, a manufacturer of solar panels who predicted an oil crunch within five years. Helped by Virgin publicists to appear on BBC TV's *Newsnight*, Leggett argued on

Branson's behalf that the only alternative to oil's gradual disappearance was renewable energies and, particularly, solar panels – produced by himself.

To promote the accelerated use of renewables, in December 2010 Branson jetted to the World Climate Summit in Cancún. Unusually emotional, he told his audience that oil prices would soon hit $200 and never fall. The world's reliance on oil, he continued, would cause the American unemployment rate to rise to 15 per cent. 'The next five years will see us face another crunch – the oil crunch. Our supplies of oil and natural gas are being rapidly depleted.' Governments and business, he urged, needed to switch rapidly from oil to renewable energy. 'Just do it,' he pleaded. 'For God's sake. Get off your arses and get on with it.' If governments failed to do more, he predicted, the world would suffer an 'unbelievably painful' economic slump. 'We're going to have the mother of all recessions if we don't sort out our energy policy fast.' To his audience, he was a crusader. Encouraged by their response, Branson added an attack on the world's shipping companies as 'culprits' for emitting 'one billion tons of carbon dioxide every year'. He won applause by demanding that shipping be instantly taxed to encourage them to cut their emissions by 25 per cent over the following twenty years. Pertinently, he forgot Hinchliffe's reprimands and side-stepped the IMO's statistics stating that emissions were a quarter of his assertion, while taxes on air travel were not even mentioned.

Beyond the media and supportive audiences, Branson was struggling. He and Whitehorn had set themselves up as leaders of the environmental campaign in Britain but their forecasts were unconvincing. 'Because we've been believers that the possibility of peak oil is real,' Whitehorn said, 'we've been investing in diversifying our businesses. That's why we've become one of the UK's largest long-distance train operators.' In reality, Virgin Trains started in 1992, long before Branson's interest in the environment. 'We've also been investing', continued Whitehorn, 'in new aircraft types, which are more efficient, and we're looking at issues such as carbon composites.' The choice of materials used to manufacture planes was beyond Virgin Atlantic's influence. The small British airline had no option other than to lease aircraft offered by the two principal manufacturers. Whitehorn's opinions, he discovered, were disregarded in Whitehall. The Department of Energy, he complained, 'ignores not just our conclusions but our very existence'. Both Branson and Whitehorn wrongly assumed that Virgin's admission of participation in the cartel to fix the fuel surcharge had been forgotten.

Rebuffed by civil servants, Branson once more appealed directly to the prime minister. He urged David Cameron to prevent oil traders from speculating and, through price-fixing, being 'allowed to make large sums at the expense of us all'. Prices, he said, were artificially increased by 30 per cent. 'I think there should be strict rules set as to how much trading can be done in the oil market,' he wrote. 'Billions of dollars is being traded on oil futures which is falsely pushing up the price of oil.' He provided no evidence to support his allegations. On the contrary, the proof gathered in America showed that the oil market was too diverse to manipulate, except for brief moments in unusual circumstances.

The disconnect between Branson's convictions and reality could be explained by his lifestyle. Cocooned on Necker, travelling on his private jet among like-minded billionaires, he was isolated from the wider debate. His predictions of an apocalypse were contradicted by the facts: the West's demand for oil was falling; new supplies had been found in Brazil, Kazakhstan and Iraq; and with new technology additional oil was being extracted from existing wells. 'Peak demand' for oil was more likely than a peak in supplies. Rising oil prices were caused not by shortages or speculation by traders but by OPEC, the cartel of the world's major oil producers, who daily limited the amount of oil produced to protect the high prices. Oil's politics and technology were a foreign language to Branson. Simplicity was his credo: the inevitable end of oil would be followed by the era of renewable fuels.

The popularity of alternative jet fuels had been boosted by Branson. As his publicists highlighted, his advocacy had been followed by BA's agreement in February 2010 to buy jet fuel manufactured from organic waste by the Solena Group in the US once the factory was completed in 2014. Branson himself had invested in Solazyme, a Californian biotech company that was spending $60 million to produce fuel from algae. An alternative supplier puffed by Virgin was AltAir Fuels. Based in Seattle, the embryonic company committed itself to supply 750 million gallons of jet fuel manufactured from farmed saltwater-plant and camelina feedstock to fourteen airlines.

The parade of Virgin's investments was applauded by environmentalists. Despite the lack of progress and dubious science, the Virgin brand benefited from the portrayal of Branson as a concerned citizen spending millions of dollars to save the world. The jigsaw was completed by Virgin Unite, the charity set up by Branson.

Many billionaires in their sixties present themselves as benefactors by giving away in excess of $50 million every year from their bank accounts or a trust to the underprivileged. Branson took a different path. Business, he believed, should help the disadvantaged to help themselves. Under the banner of Virgin Unite, he cast business as 'a force for good, helping people to thrive in balance with our planet'. He offered Virgin and himself as a beacon of selflessness. 'We unite people', he wrote, 'to tackle tough social and environmental problems in an entrepreneurial way for the public benefit.' Branson was not offering charitable funds like Bill Gates to eradicate Aids and malaria or the Rockefellers to foster education; he said his fortune would 'focus on great ideas and areas where we feel there is a gap'. In a declamation placing Virgin among the global leaders, he explained: 'Our aim is to help revolutionise the way that governments, businesses and the social sector work together, in order to address the scale and urgency of the challenges facing the world today.' His proof of Virgin's contribution to the cause was to have 'incubated and launched the Carbon War Room and the Elders' – a group of retired politicians financed by Branson to dispense advice to the world. The next stage was 'a new Global Leadership Initiative driving a new model of business leadership which would see businesses achieving charitable objectives as a fundamental part of doing business'.

Virgin Unite's lofty ambitions in 2011 amounted to encouraging volunteering, campaigning in the media against homelessness, and making Virgin employees aware that they should encourage entrepreneurship. The charity's principal bequests were £209,000 towards the establishment of an HIV clinic in South Africa and a small contribution towards maternity clinics in northern Nigeria. The accounts did not clarify all the bequests made from the £5.7 million budget – except that the source was £3 million in cash, with the remainder in-kind resources donated by Virgin companies. The first accounts reported that staff costs were £2.2 million, while £1 million was lost in an investment managed by a hedge fund. The charity claimed to have generated '£20 million of free media coverage'. Spending less than £1 million on two health projects represented, in Branson's words, funding 'to tackle tough social and environmental problems in an entrepreneurial way for the public benefit'. Some had noticed a disparity between Branson's promises and delivery.

Tim Flannery and Crispin Tickell had been pleased to be associated with Branson's Earth Challenge. Since the triumphant meeting in Kensington, Branson had praised 'a bold call to action which stimulated a lot of thinking around the world'. In the four years since the $25 million prize had been offered, Virgin had received 2,600 proposals. Among them was a submission by Alex Michaelis, the designer of David Cameron's eco-home in London. Michaelis was among the many waiting to hear a response. After examining the submissions, Alan Knight, the Earth Challenge director, had announced that there was no winner. 'There's no silver bullet,' he explained in November 2011. Flannery and Tickell were surprised. Both understood that Branson would immediately give $5 million to the winner. 'It might have come across as a beauty contest with an instant prize,' Knight replied, 'but we said it would take ten years before a winner was announced. It was never going to be a quick cheque.' That was not Tickell's recollection about the original invitation. Branson's staff seemed to be prevaricating.

'You have to announce a winner,' he told Knight's staff.

Instead, Knight produced a shortlist of eleven 'pioneers' with whom, he said, 'we will work'. He added, 'Richard is very excited we have eleven pioneers. It's first past the post, not the best at the date. We will decide.' The prize seemed impossible to win.

'It's not thought 100 per cent through,' said another person involved with the contest, suspicious whether Branson would ever pay the money.

'Branson launches something on Monday', concluded Tickell, 'and has forgotten it on Tuesday.'

The competition began to attract criticism from environmentalists as 'barmy geo-engineering which is speculative and useless', motivated by a man responsible for 'a carbon-manufacturing business who promises to make it better'. Branson's arrival in Calgary, the capital of Canada's polluting tar-oil industry, to promote the competition's shortlist brought him criticism for being the 'friend' of Big Oil, for being 'ill informed' and for causing the public to be 'duped by projects based on incomplete and in some cases downright false information'. His carbon-capture schemes were described as 'nonsensical'. No one even mentioned any more his $3 billion contribution to Clinton's campaign against global warming.

11

Virgin Speed

Defeat, Branson enjoyed saying, caused him little fear. 'My mother taught me never to look back in regret but to move on to the next thing. I have fun running all the Virgin businesses so a setback is never a bad experience, just a learning curve.'

Virgin's name had been slapped on to many ventures that had failed but, until 2008, pictures of Branson surrounded by blonde Virgin Atlantic hostesses or kite-surfing across the Caribbean with a nude 'girlfriend' clinging to his back had entrenched Virgin as the brand for the hip to fly, for the cool to buy their music and for the healthy to work out with at Virgin Active. Virgin at its peak epitomised the crazy spirit of teenagers disrupting the Establishment. Aspiring rebels worshipped Branson as the champion of the counter-culture. He was the modish billionaire inviting the public to party and profit, and Virgin's customers defied convention by subscribing to a heroic maverick. Across the globe, his image as an intrepid buccaneer mitigated his declining fortunes.

An attempt to launch Virgin Radio in Dubai had been unsuccessful. Virgin Vie, his clothing company, was heading for closure, joining Virgin Cars. Virgin Cosmetics, which Branson had said in 1997 would have a hundred stores within five years, was running into insolvency. To save embarrassment, the founders were paid £8.8 million and the company's name was changed to Effective Cosmetics. In America, the Virgin Megastores, which had opened in Los Angeles in 1992 and peaked in 2002 with twenty-three shops, were dying. Branson blamed supermarkets for selling CDs too cheaply, an odd stance for the self-proclaimed consumers' champion, who regularly accused rivals of 'ripping off' the public. In Britain, after transferring twenty-two Megastores rebranded as Zavvi to its managers, he watched the chain crash with losses of £122.5 million, exposing Virgin to liabilities of £57 million. In New York, an attempt to launch Virgin Comics in collaboration with Gotham Entertainment of India ended less than two years after it began. Virgin Vine, a new wine label, was launched and disappeared, and at the same time Branson finally quit the music business. V2, the successor to Virgin Music, had been established in 1996 with finance from the McCarthy brothers. Two years later, the business was bust and the brothers could barely afford to buy a pint of milk. After squeezing the McCarthys out of the business, Branson transferred V2 to Morgan Stanley, the bank who had loaned money to the failed venture, and Virgin abandoned the music business. Virgin Health Bank was another transitory business, unveiled in 2007 and encouraged by Gordon Brown, the then chancellor of the exchequer. Flagged as a non-profit blood bank to store stem cells taken from umbilical cords, Virgin Health Bank was established in partnership with Professor Christopher Evans, a biotechnology entrepreneur. Sufficient space was available, said Branson, to store 300,000 frozen samples for twenty years in order to regenerate tissue and treat blood cancers. Within the first months, the £1,500 ($2,940) charge was considered too high and the service was rejected by parents and the NHS. The facility disappeared from Britain.

Junking failed businesses never deterred Branson from announcing new ventures. In Miami, he told local journalists that Virgin was going into cruise holidays, but he failed to interest the owners of existing cruise lines in a partnership, so his idea was forgotten. During a visit in 2008 to Macau, in the Far East, he announced that, in co-operation with Tabcorp, an

Australian gambling company, he was going to compete against Las Vegas's moguls and open a Virgin casino there. Although he had no experience of gambling – unlike other tycoons he rarely played roulette or blackjack in Las Vegas – Branson announced at the end of his first day in the city that he was 'in advanced talks' with Edmund Ho, Macau's chief executive, to build a $3 billion resort. He was 'close to buying', he said, a fifty-acre plot for three hotels and a casino. 'We hope to get all the boxes ticked in the next couple of months and start developing the site soon afterwards.' Once Ho realised that Branson offered no money and expected Macau to pay for hosting the Virgin brand, the discussions ended. Virgin's substitute was a virtual casino on the internet.

Casting around for other opportunities, Branson envied the fortunes earned in Russia's mineral-rich economy. He flew to Moscow in search of business and associates. Virgin Atlantic, he announced, would soon be flying to the city from London, followed by the launch of a Virgin airline flying within Russia. 'We're in discussions with two or three different partners in Russia,' said Branson, predicting an agreement within three months. He also announced the launch in Russia of Virgin Mobile and Virgin Connect, his new internet company. Virgin Connect, he said, under the management of Rostislav Gromov of Trivon, a Swiss company, would capture 10 per cent of Russia's market within five years. 'We will demystify the complex tariff jungle and bureaucracy seen in the market.' His script was identical in every country, but, surprisingly perhaps, he attacked the oligarchs, his putative partners. 'Having a large boat', he said, 'isn't going to give you a lot of satisfaction and it gives capitalism a bad name.' Branson believed that owning private islands and a fleet of planes distinguished him from the oligarchs' gin palaces. Virgin made no progress in Moscow.

In his search for new ventures, he revisited past failures,

especially Britain's national lottery. The combination of a vast cash flow and perpetual publicity by unveiling that week's winner as a 'Virgin Millionaire' would undoubtedly have guaranteed Branson's fortune. To deflect those suspicious of his personal enrichment, Branson had called his supposedly non-profit company the 'People's Lottery'. Not everyone was persuaded by his apparent altruism. The first rejection of his bid in 1994 in favour of Camelot had provoked Branson's tearful anger. His second bid was rejected on similar grounds, amid questions about his suitability. In-between was the libel trial destroying the reputation of Guy Snowden, the American founder of Camelot. Ignoring his promise not to make a third attempt, in spring 2008 Branson sought partners to win an auction for Camelot, which was valued at about £450 million. After his attempt to raise sufficient money from Dubai International, a $12 billion wealth fund, failed, he withdrew.

Successive disappointments risked damaging Virgin's image. Although his admirers at *Forbes* magazine had in 2002 rated Virgin as the fourth-best marketed brand in the world and probably the best in Europe, diversification was jeopardising the brand. Pertinently, after the death of Steve Jobs, Branson praised him as 'the entrepreneur I most admired'. Both Jobs and Branson understood that brands created premium value, but the Apple boss focused on the innovation of a few unique products. He avoided Branson's scattergun hunt for a windfall. While Apple's reputation continued to grow, the Virgin brand was losing its youthful allure. Virgin had become mature and mainstream. The fizz had gone. Away from the interaction of a buzzing office and street culture, Branson was relying on managers regarded as conventional rather than adventurous. Belatedly, he realised they had squeezed the pips of Virgin's original rebellious spirit. With them, he struggled to rekindle the zest and reinvent Virgin's image.

His catalyst for regenerating the excitement was Virgin Galactic. In America, advertisements promoting Virgin Atlantic and Virgin America regularly featured the space pioneer offering relaxing intercontinental travel. The mocked-up images of the tycoon flying on a Virgin Galactic spacecraft encouraged American commentators to exaggerate Virgin's empire as consisting of anything between 200 and 400 companies with an annual turnover, according to *Forbes*, of $17 billion. Branson's publicists never contradicted the hyperbole. Contrary to the public's perception, Branson owned only half of Virgin Atlantic and half of Virgin Trains, and only a small percentage of the other Virgin companies. Adding together the turnover of all the businesses bearing the Virgin name – and less than forty were active – Branson controlled outright at most four major companies with an annual turnover of about £6 billion.

The empire's seed corn was the Virgin brand, owned by Virgin Group Holdings. Most companies carrying the Virgin label paid 0.5 per cent of their annual revenues for using the brand. In 2009, the licence fees earned about £35 million. Branson's hope, said Peter Norris, Virgin Group Holdings' chairman, was to double that income within five years. Future success depended on reglamorising Virgin and attaching the reinvigorated brand to profitable new businesses. Finding an opportunity was down to chance, but the financial crash in 2008 did throw up one unexpected punt – Formula One motor racing.

Hit by losses, Honda abandoned its sponsorship of motor racing. The most prominent casualty was the company's Formula One team, which was managed by Ross Brawn, an outstanding designer. In the midst of the financial crisis, Brawn's chance of finding a new sponsor with sufficient money was slim, not least because of the technical uncertainties which would inevitably follow his decision to replace Honda's engine with one bought from Mercedes. Installing the German engine on to a chassis designed for Honda's jeopardised Brawn's chances of winning the championship. Among the potential saviours of his team and 700 employees was none other than Richard Branson.

Trying to coax Virgin into Formula One was nothing new. At their occasional meetings, Bernie Ecclestone, the sport's ringmaster, had tried to tempt Branson. 'We would welcome you with open arms,' said Ecclestone, mentioning Virgin's guaranteed global exposure. 'You're exactly the type of person we want.' Branson's reluctance always puzzled Ecclestone. Unknown to the former car trader, who had personally pocketed over $4 billion in cash from the sport, he had overestimated Branson's wealth. While Branson presented himself as a billionaire, he was unwilling to risk $80 million a year, the minimum required to run a Formula One team. Although Ecclestone paid at least $30 million of the TV rights to the weakest teams, their remaining income depended on attracting sponsors willing to buy media exposure. Champions like McLaren recovered their $300 million annual costs with the help of Vodafone and Santander each paying about $60 million for their logos to feature on the car's body and the drivers' outfits. Red Bull, the multibillion-pound global energy-drink company, flourished thanks to the success of its Formula One team. The sport would be ideal for promoting Virgin, but Branson had never been sufficiently rich to play.

The financial terms changed after Honda abandoned Brawn. The news prompted one of Branson's executives to call Brawn. Decent but not supremely gifted, Alex Tai, a Virgin pilot, was also employed to hunt down new businesses. Brawn's reaction to Tai's call was predictable. After the mention of 'Richard', Brawn leapt at Tai's hint that Virgin might be interested in investing millions of pounds. He hurried with Nick Fry, his chief executive, to the School House, Virgin's headquarters in Hammersmith. Branson, appearing via video conference from Necker, shared Tai's enthusiasm but dithered about commitment. 'I don't see the commercial sense of Formula One,' Gordon McCallum repeated.

'Sponsors are as rare now as hens' teeth,' Fry grunted after they departed. To safeguard the survival of the Brawn outfit, half the Honda team's staff had to be dismissed.

Over the following days, Branson was urged by Tai to take the risk. Without any competitors for the sponsorship, Tai said, Virgin's fees could be minuscule. Branson agreed. 'We'd like to sponsor the team,' Tai now told Fry.

Promising sponsorship was, in Branson's lexicon, an offer to use the Virgin brand without Branson paying any money. Fry grimaced. Hard cash was required, and the deadline was 28 March 2009, the eve of the first race of the season, in Melbourne.

Branson invited Brawn and Fry for dinner at his home, Kidlington Mill, in Oxfordshire. The atmosphere was jovial, but Branson could not mistake the resolution of his guests. Thanks to Ecclestone's normal contribution to all the teams, they had nearly enough money to start the season but needed cash to get to halfway. Then, they would hope for the best. Branson again refused to commit himself. He would decide, he said, after Tai watched the teams' trials in Barcelona on 9 March. By then, Branson's interest had become known. 'Formula One must tidy itself up,' Branson commented in response to a newspaper's inquiry about his possible involvement.

The Brawn team arrived late in Barcelona. The rival teams' strengths and weaknesses had been registered during their test runs. No one expected Jenson Button, driving the Brawn, to pose a threat. Within minutes of him speeding around the track, the shock was palpable. Button completed the circuit a full second ahead of every other car, thanks to Brawn's unexpected introduction of a double diffuser. By the end of the day, the car was recategorised as the favourite. Visibly excited, Tai telephoned Branson. Virgin, he said, could sponsor the winner. He urged a deal. Branson called Brawn, again stipulating sponsorship without any payment. 'No,' replied Brawn, and flew to Melbourne. Just days before the deadline, Branson offered about £6 million in a mixture of cash and Virgin airline tickets. With the deal sealed, he rushed to Melbourne and headed for the racetrack laid out through the city's park to watch the Virgin-sponsored team perform in the practice sessions.

Formula One fetes its heroes in a perpetual spotlight. This suited Branson perfectly. Inside the VIP paddock, he basked among the famous personalities. Pleased to have attracted an exceptional media scrum around himself, he was overwhelmed when Button, driving Virgin's car, won pole position for the following day's race. The spotlight intensified on the favourite to win. 'You're going to be my other Burt Rutan,' Branson told Fry. 'You can pull rabbits out of a hat.'

That evening, the whole team arranged to eat at Nobu. Fry arrived two hours late, to discover that Branson and his family had waited for him, drinking champagne but not eating. Minutes later, Branson headed for the lavatory. On his way back, he stopped by Jenson Button's table. Suddenly, Button began remonstrating with Branson over his proposition to Jessica Michibata, his girlfriend. Branson returned to his table without Fry noticing the commotion. The following morning, they met in the hotel lobby. 'I'm going to stop drinking,' Branson told Brawn and Fry after describing his misbehaviour. 'And I'll apologise.' The race was due to start, and neither man was interested.

Branson's misfortune was that Button's anger leaked amid a spate of unflattering publicity about the Virgin boss. The hostility fell on fertile ground. Some Australians were already critical of Branson's use of scantily clad women to advertise his airline. Others disliked the projection of his face – 100 feet high – on to Sydney Harbour Bridge. To limit the damage, Virgin's publicists replied to questions about Button's complaint with: 'Richard has no memory of anything happening. They had a great night with lots of celebrating.' But after Button described the incident to Piers Morgan in a newspaper interview, Branson's spokesman admitted the truth: Branson had been drunk and was 'embarrassed'. He subsequently gave up drinking for three months.

The season's opening race ended spectacularly, with Jenson Button and Rubens Barrichello coming first and second in Brawn's cars. The image of Branson standing between the winning drivers astride the Virgin logo on the car's white metal body was seen by 100 million people across the globe. Nothing could have prevented him from stealing the limelight and saying things that created headlines. He had pulled off a brilliant deal. The publicity in Melbourne would have been worth about £20 million. Branson paid £200,000 per race and Virgin was the only sponsor of a team that looked certain to win more Grand Prix races. The hot question was whether Branson had become wedded to the sport.

'I have been friends with Bernie and known him for many years,' Branson told inquirers. 'He has tried to tempt us in, and we have been a reluctant bride up until now. It appears we have chosen a good time to enter into this relationship; and I am glad I have resisted Bernie in the past, as timing is everything in life.' Branson could not curb his habits and offered to improve Ecclestone's business. 'We plan to thoroughly enjoy our involvement in Formula One and bring some extra life to it and do things the Virgin way. We plan to be innovative and I want to pursue Bernie and Max [Mosley], not only to pioneer great engineering but also pioneer clean fuels. We have been developing a clean fuel for F1 which works, and hope to introduce it to Formula One.' He offered to help Ecclestone reduce costs and 'encourage more brands to join Formula One to keep it exciting'.

Ecclestone barely considered Branson's comments. He doubted if Branson understood Formula One's unique engineering or its aerodynamics, and the idea of clean fuels was of no interest. Branson would be automatically excluded from any influence on the business, but Ecclestone did expect Virgin's car to excite Formula One's circus.

Instead, Branson posed as a global financier. His investment in Formula One, Branson spelled out, was a contribution towards rescuing the world's economy. 'Everyone is just frozen in the headlights of this recession,' he told the *New York Times*, 'and if everybody stays frozen in the headlights, it'll just get worse and worse. If you get out there and try and invest, we can start pulling the world out of this recession.' Branson spoke as if £6 million would influence the slump.

Virgin's victory in Melbourne had been carefully scrutinised by Graeme Lowdon, a British IT specialist. Before flying to Australia, he had established Manor GP Racing as a putative Formula One team for the following season. Watching Branson hugging Brawn, Lowdon identified a man caught by the Formula One bug.

Six days later, he again observed Branson enjoying the spotlight at the Malaysian Grand Prix. Brawn had won again, and the team was being tipped to become the overall champion. Branson's hopes of continuing the sponsorship the following season for £6 million had disappeared. Brawn would be looking for at least $80 million. The billionaire, Lowdon decided, had to be persuaded to sponsor his own nascent team.

Although neither Lowdon nor his partner, John Booth, were wealthy, their motor-racing expertise had been established in Formula Three. Their chance to enter Formula One had been stoked by Max Mosley, the president of FIA, the Formula One regulator. Mosley planned to introduce new rules to limit every team's annual expenditure to $42 million, an edict aimed at Ferrari, Red Bull and the other leading teams. Their huge budget, in Mosley's opinion, deterred new entrants, who were needed after the departure of both Honda and Toyota. He feared that other engine manufacturers – Mercedes and Renault – might follow.

With a $42 million cap and an experienced car designer, Lowdon believed he had a good chance of success. Fortuitously, Nick Wirth, also made redundant by Honda, agreed to develop a car for Lowdon within the limit. To save money, he would design and test the car using a computer model rather a wind tunnel, saving at least $35 million. That still left Lowdon searching for $42 million.

Lowdon introduced himself to Darryl Eales, the managing director of Lloyds Development Capital (LDC), a private-equity group attached to the bank. Over a cup of coffee in Kensington, Lowdon persuaded Eales that Mosley's proposed new rules gave Manor a chance of success. Financing the team, said Lowdon, should be seen as support for British engineering – a scenario Eales accepted. Over the next eight weeks, said Eales, he would scrutinise the investment and prepare the contracts.

Lowdon's next stop was Virgin. His contact there was Tony Collins, the chief executive of Virgin Trains, to whom Lowdon had sold his latest invention – wireless internet for passengers. Collins, a motor-racing fan, introduced Alex Tai, and in mid-April Lowdon and Wirth were pitching in Hammersmith, feeding Tai's ambition to stay in the spotlight and enjoy more glory. As Tai pondered the proposition, Wirth threw down his chips: 'Branson will never get the same deal with Brawn again. Brawn will want $20 million next season just for a sticker on the car. And $80 million minimum for the team to be called Virgin.' Tai remained silent about the reality: ever since Brawn's third victory, there had been no conversations between Branson and Brawn. Branson had been discarded by the winners as a man without the money in favour of serious suitors, including Mercedes, a Malaysian oil company and several European banks.

'You personally can move up in the racing world,' Wirth told

Tai. 'Brawn can't offer you that.' Lowdon massaged Tai's ego: 'You could be Virgin Racing's team manager.' With the same studious manner that persuaded Darryl Eales about Manor's destiny, Lowdon spelled out how Max Mosley's new rules should attract Virgin because 'you can take advantage of the dislocated market'. Virgin's exposure with Brawn, he said, proved the value of sponsorship. The branding experts had valued Branson's £6 million investment as already worth £60 million – and rising – in TV exposure. 'Do you think you can persuade Richard to sponsor Manor?' asked Lowdon.

To remain in Formula One, Tai knew, Branson's decision would need to be swift. Mosley's deadline for applications to enter Formula One's 2010/11 season was 28 May. To qualify, Lowdon would need to name a major sponsor. His case was strengthened by Eales's agreement to invest £12 million. 'The prospects of healthy profits and a return on the investment are excellent,' Eales would tell the *Financial Times*.

The bulk of the money depended on Tai's support. In the course of their conversations, the Virgin executive told Lowdon that if his company became committed, he personally could recruit at least ten other sponsors, especially from the Virgin empire.

'Richard likes it,' Tai told Lowdon in mid-May. Brawn had won four out of five races, and Branson was loving the global publicity. Mixing with the rich and famous hit a high point in Monaco at the end of May. By the Mediterranean, the VIP paddock was heaving with celebrities, many greeting Branson as a hero. On the day before the race, Branson stood in the pit chatting with billionaires and occasionally boarding their shimmering yachts. That night, he hosted his own party in nearby Villefranche. Brawn had won pole position and, barring a crash, the team was almost certain to win the following day. Virgin's executives appeared to think of little else other than the image of two cars adorned with the Virgin logo being seen by 100 million viewers.

Nonetheless, Branson's excitement and Brawn's success were not the gossip in the paddock. Formula One's insiders were discussing a spectacular argument the previous night in Monaco's Automobile Club between Mosley and the team leaders about his plan to limit costs. Mosley's survival was in doubt.

Mosley's financial cap had always been opposed by Formula One's established teams. Led by Luca Montezemolo, the chief executive of Ferrari, the managers rejected any restrictions on spending. Their opposition was the pretext for either ousting Mosley or breaking away from FIA and Ecclestone to establish their own competition. In his fight for survival, Mosley had encouraged Lowdon to embrace the financial cap he wanted to impose on Formula One to wreck Ferrari's dominance. Inevitably, Ferrari led the coup against Mosley. Influenced by Ross Brawn, who supported the anti-Mosley breakaway, to form their own Formula One business, Branson told Donald Mackenzie, the financier who had bought into Ecclestone's Formula One, 'I'm going to back the breakaway.' 'Good luck,' replied Mackenzie, and walked out of Branson's office. Bizarrely, Branson failed to understand that his own interests lay with Mosley's scheme, not with the spendthrifts. Ecclestone scoffed at Branson's confusion.

The following morning, just before the Grand Prix, Lowdon took Tai to *Lionheart*, a large yacht moored in Monaco's bay owned by Philip Green, the billionaire clothing retailer. He wanted a quiet conversation to secure an agreement. Tai, Lowdon realised, was 'hotter than ever'. Enraptured by playing among the rich in Monaco's sunlight, Branson's envoy wanted more of the same. Lowdon played on the euphoria. To keep Branson involved, he maintained the fiction that Mosley's $42 million cap would be implemented in the new season. 'Richard won't win next year,' said Lowdon, 'but we'll be the challenger.

That's Virgin – the challenger brand.' If Branson signed the deal, Tai was promised again, he would be Virgin's team manager and receive shares in the company. Tai smiled and returned to shore.

At nightfall, after Brawn had won his fifth victory, Branson landed in Marrakech. In his last conversation with Ecclestone, he had been encouraged to fund a Virgin team and start on the grid at Melbourne in 2010. The negative voice was that of Gordon McCallum, the chief executive in charge of Virgin's commercial investments. 'This isn't going to work,' he repeated. But, gripped by Formula One's marketing power and the parties, Branson ignored the advice and succumbed to Lowdon's assurances that success was possible without spending $80 million. Neither Branson nor Tai seemed to have questioned whether Ferrari intended to design their cars by computer rather than in a wind tunnel.

Lowdon spent the evening drinking in Monaco, waiting for Tai to telephone. Eventually Tai called. 'Richard really likes it,' he said. 'We're on.'

'Alex has been brilliant to persuade Richard to do it,' Wirth sighed.

The sting was Branson's refusal to pay any money. He offered only the brand. The attraction, Tai explained, was that the Virgin wrapper would encourage other corporations to pledge real money as co-sponsors, and Tai would deliver sponsors from Virgin's 300 companies. With his dream of competing at next year's Monaco Grand Prix in jeopardy, Lowdon accepted the terms. His vision depended on securing Virgin's name. Wirth, he knew, could not solve the technical problems with a computer rather than a wind tunnel, but that was irrelevant compared to the glory of a guaranteed place on the grid. Tai's personal commitment was the purchase of shares worth about £4,000. Branson himself believed there was nothing to lose.

'They've certainly got me addicted,' he said after the next race in Turkey – Button's sixth victory. 'We got in when it was very cheap and it's been great for us with global coverage, but I suspect next year the price will be astronomical and we may have to look somewhere else with a smaller team. We at Virgin have most likely got the mileage we needed from it. We'll have had a fantastic year with them, so it'd be a good time to sit down and have a word about upping my interest.'

Three days later, Lowdon's application was submitted to Mosley. Virgin Racing was competing against other aspiring newcomers for three places on the grid. At the hearing, the FIA committee was sceptical that Virgin would want to be associated with losers, but Tai offered an Oscar-winning performance in response. 'We don't want to piggy-back on Brawn,' said the team's director. 'Virgin likes taking risks and being the underdog.'

'You were brilliant,' Wirth told Tai, enthralled by the pilot's eloquence. 'You've got us on to the grid.'

'With Branson's involvement,' he later said, 'we stood half a chance to be successful.'

'Super,' said Ecclestone, delighted that another billionaire had joined the club. He assumed that Branson and the Virgin Group would invest about $80 million and raise another $100 million from sponsors.

Alex Tai was appointed director of Virgin Racing. 'We're the new car on the block,' he told Reuters. 'Hopefully we'll be here for sixty years to come and making money during that time and not pouring money into it. It's possible to have a Formula One team that actually makes money.'

In late June, Mosley was forced to resign, and the financial cap was buried. Lowdon and Wirth were now faced with what they described as a 'nightmare'. Instead of telling Tai that their financial plan was wrecked, when Lowdon arrived at the British Grand Prix at Silverstone in July he mentioned his hope of getting the rules adjusted without Mosley. Tai wanted to believe that fiction, as did Darryl Eales and his deputy, Carl Wormald. Both had arrived in Silverstone to finalise LDC's investment. The party atmosphere pulped the bankers' commercial scepticism, and both accepted the assurances from Tai and Branson that Virgin companies would be sponsoring the team. Branson, Eales noted, spoke warmly about Tai's close relationships with Virgin's directors. There was sufficient money, everyone believed, for Virgin Racing. The payroll was increased from five to seventy employees.

By September, the truth was unavoidable. Designing and testing the car by computer rather than in a wind tunnel was technically impossible. 'This is a crisis meeting,' Wirth told Tai. 'We're exposed to failure. We're going to be bloody slow.' If Tai was confused, Wirth was forthright. 'It's not too late to change anything, but it'll only get better if you get some money.' The bankers were not told the bad news by Tai. Eales and Wormald only recall being told that everything was going to plan. To bridge the gap, Lowdon relied on Branson's assurance that Virgin companies would sponsor the team. Tai repeated his pledge: 'I've got a pipeline of opportunities I'm working on.'

'The Virgin Group have the skills to get the jigsaw together in the right order,' Lowdon reassured Wirth.

Many potential sponsors did listen to Tai's pitch, but none committed themselves to what they considered was an inevitable loser.

'There's been a huge search for money,' Wirth reported, 'but we've got none.' He was paying suppliers out of his own pocket, hoping that Virgin would at least lend $3 million. Tai refused: 'I've got a pipeline of opportunities but it's just taking longer than I hoped to convert.'

'We'll be at the back from the outset,' Wirth told Tai. 'You're fucked. You'll be there for ever.'

'We'll be racing with one hand tied behind our back and hopping on one leg,' Lowdon warned Tai. With 'Virgin' emblazoned

Branson was thrilled that Governor Bill Richardson of New Mexico spent $210 million to build Spaceport America as the base for Virgin Galactic, although the rocket – seven years after its first deadline – is yet to reach space.

Branson's goal in 2002 was to firmly establish Virgin in America. In his search for allies, he embraced environmentalism and aligned himself with Bill Clinton and Al Gore, pledging $3 billion in 2006 to fight climate change. Just how much has been handed over is uncertain. But the pledge, and Virgin Galactic, attracted Arnold Schwarzenegger, then governor of California, as a key Branson ally.

Branson's hopes for American stardom, thanks to a Fox TV series called 'The Rebel Billionaire: Branson's Quest for the Best', ended in a ratings flop.

Similarly, his bitter battle to protect Virgin's privileges – by preventing collaboration between British Airways and American Airlines – was lost after Virgin pleaded guilty to participating in an illegal cartel.

Virgin's financial crisis in 2000 was overcome after the company embraced Tom Alexander's idea to launch low-cost mobile phones. Despite Branson's familiar publicity stunts around the world, Virgin Mobile succeeded only in Britain.

Much of Branson's success depended on his close relationships with politicians, not least Tony Blair, who supported the nomination of Branson for a knighthood in 1999.

In his search for new businesses, Branson repeatedly tried to break into banking. Unsuccessful in Australia and America, he relied on Jayne-Anne Gadhia, Virgin Money's chief executive, to finally make the breakthrough in Britain after buying Northern Rock.

Just as the launch of Virgin Blue in Australia started strongly, Branson has so far found that stunts are no match for entrenched competitors in the British banking and Australian airlines sectors.

Unusually, Branson invested substantial sums of his own money in manufacturing renewable fuels. His reliance on Vinod Khosla, an American billionaire, gained him favourable publicity, not least with Gordon Brown when he launched a train powered by biodiesel in 2007. The project was soon abandoned, and Branson's investments in renewable fuels have so far lost money.

Branson, however, gained huge and comparatively free global publicity by sponsoring Brawn's winning Formula One team in 2009. Virgin's foray into Formula One ended in tears – but not for Branson.

Branson appears to thrive on conflict, not least with British Airways. Posing as a pirate in July 1991, he enjoyed antagonising Lord King, then chairman of BA, by changing the livery on BA's iconic Concorde to Virgin. Their battle climaxed in 2006 when Virgin executives admitted involvement in an illegal cartel with BA. Iain Burns and three other BA executives stood trial for price fixing. On the eve of Virgin executives testifying for the prosecution in 2010, the trial collapsed and the four were acquitted. The legacy was BA's enduring hatred of Branson.

The two faces of Branson: the lovable hero promoting Virgin Media with Olympic sprint champion, Usain Bolt, in a successful campaign which the regulator criticised for misleading the public. His attempts to earn a similar fortune from privatised NHS services, however, have so far attracted only protests.

on the car, he imagined that Branson would spend some money to protect his brand.

On the eve of the season's final race in Abu Dhabi, Branson jetted in to celebrate Brawn's triumph in the 2009 championship, host a party and enjoy the last benefits of the publicity. Formula One sponsorship normally cost about £125 million. Branson had paid just £6 million. Among the visitors to his hotel suite was Darryl Eales. LDC was about to invest another £6 million in Virgin Racing, and Eales wanted to test Branson's commitment. To his relief, Branson was reassuring.

'I'm in,' said Branson.

'We need more money, and I wondered if you would mind if we found another investor?' asked Eales.

'I'm flexible,' replied Branson. 'Get someone else if you can.'

'And can you get Virgin companies to sponsor the team?' asked Eales.

Branson became coy. Stutteringly, he explained that while he personally would want Virgin companies to sponsor the team, he was having difficulty persuading members of his board. In particular, Stephen Murphy, said Branson, was proving to be an obstacle. In spite of Branson's mumbles, discomfiting body language and failure to look him in the eye, Eales accepted Branson's explanation without considering that, as the sole proprietor, Branson could do what he liked. With hindsight, Eales regretted falling for a Hollywood performance.

The formal unveiling of Virgin Racing was promoted by the FIA as a feature of the 2010 season, and Virgin's publicists became unusually motivated. An all-night rock 'n' roll party in Notting Hill Gate, hosted by Branson, was arranged for 15 December. The theme was 'Virgin the Challenger', and everyone wore leather bomber jackets adorned with the Virgin logo. As the champagne sprayed over the guests, Lowdon momentarily dreamt that Virgin's billions would come to the rescue. Wirth was more realistic. Spotting that the alcohol, food and even the jackets were all provided free by sponsors, the engineer looked at Branson. 'He's not tight,' he realised. 'Just poor.'

In public, the story was different. 'Richard Branson', John Booth, the joint manager of the racing team, told journalists on the eve of presenting Virgin's car, 'will bring credibility to Formula One. To have somebody like Sir Richard and Virgin on board is a dream come true for us. He's a global media figure and one of the most recognised faces on the planet. Sponsors want to be with him, and he brings a real buzz to the whole operation.' Converted to Branson's credo, Booth exaggerated Virgin Racing's prospects, predicting that as the most advanced of the new teams, it was certain to have success in the opening race of the new season in Bahrain. 'It's great to have someone whose name is on the team, who is interested and passionate about it,' agreed Wirth.

Privately, Branson understood the problem. Underdogs did not win motor races. He grappled for excuses. Formula One, he complained, should 'reduce its embarrassing costs. You don't need to spend hundreds of millions to have fun.' Virgin, he promised, would 'make Formula One sexier'. Without spending the same as Ferrari, he pledged to make the sport 'even more of a sexy beast. The Virgin team will prove that you can have a really good racing team, running very fast, within a very tight budget.' Then he slipped up: 'There is no need to do massively expensive wind-tunnel testing or all the other things that they do to get an extra second or two.' He had revealed his ignorance of the sport.

Formula One races are decided by fractions of a second. Each season, every leading team employs around fifty PhD graduates and spends upwards of $300 million to shave a fraction of a second off their best times. Virgin Racing was ignoring the sport's fundamentals, but Branson demanded to be heard as an equal.

He wanted Virgin Racing to get the same publicity as Ferrari, for no money. As the master of so many arts, he persuaded himself that teams who had been racing for forty years would welcome, as he put it, 'Virgin as a valuable marketing tool for our partners.'

Darryl Eales spotted the looming calamity. Ever since Mosley's removal, his disillusion had grown. 'It's become a tough deal,' he said, admitting his mistake. Lloyds had agreed to increase its loan to Virgin Racing from £12 million to £30 million. Eales's attempt to persuade Branson that Virgin should contribute some money had left him with doubts. In one-to-one conversations, he noted, Branson was 'enigmatic and not so sure-footed'. Eales's faith in Alex Tai's assurance of the Virgin Group's support had also been mistaken. Other than a solitary advertisement in Australia, no Virgin company would agree to sponsor any race. Outsiders could not imagine the stubborn rivalry among Virgin's executives. Eales was unaware of a recent admission uttered by David Baxby, a senior Virgin executive based in Geneva: 'We don't have a grand vision joined up where everything has to work at the group level.' Every Virgin company, Baxby explained, was expected to swim or sink on its own by making itself 'relevant'.

'Tai is a good self-salesman,' Eales decided, 'but over-optimistic. He's not a hard-nosed racing man. We need a professional CEO. He's inappropriate.' Before delivering the news, he consulted Gordon McCallum over a cup of tea. 'You must do what's right for the business,' said Branson's chief executive.

In a brief, emotional meeting, Tai was removed and replaced by John Booth. 'We now need to find an investor with deep pockets,' said Eales.

In the test runs during the weeks before the first race of the championship, Ferrari's managers watched their rivals. 'Virgin cars will limp to the starting line,' they agreed.

'Ferrari is sad,' countered Branson, stung by the criticism. 'Ultimately, I think the new teams will give Ferrari a run for their

money. I didn't want to write a very large cheque for an established team,' he added. 'Virgin is Formula One's last 100-per-
cent-owned British team.' McCallum was more realistic. 'We
shouldn't risk the brand unless we know the team can complete
a season,' he told Tai, asking a member of the team, 'Can you
guarantee that no Virgin car will stop in the middle of a race?'
The question dangled, unanswered.

The Virgin team arrived in Bahrain in early March 2010 for the
season's first race to discover that Ecclestone had turned against
Branson. Slow cars, in Ecclestone's opinion, cluttered the track.
Branson was dismissed as a whinging loser. Branson understood
Ecclestone's message when he was led to Virgin's motor home in
the paddock. Every team was assigned a minimum fifteen-metre
plot for their mobile headquarters and hospitality suite. Red
Bull's and Ferrari's were thirty-five metres long. On Ecclestone's
orders, Virgin's frontage was reduced to five metres and located
at the very end of the parade. Branson had been exiled.

The reality of Virgin's disarray dawned on Carl Wormald and
Darryl Eales as they looked down on to Bahrain's track awaiting
the first practice session. Suddenly, two Virgin cars roared out of
their pit. 'Fuck me,' exclaimed Wormald. 'I didn't realise we had
two cars.'

To celebrate the beginning of the season, the team owners
were invited to dinner by Bahrain's crown prince. Branson was
placed at the far end of a long table. After an abrupt end to a
desultory meal, the prince's favoured confidants were invited
to a glamorous party at a palace on the beach. Branson looked
forlorn. The following day, after bantering in the pit with the
mechanics, he took a pair of headphones and gazed over the
wall for the start of the two-hour race. As usual, Ecclestone
watched the contest on television in his hospitality tent. After
forty minutes, he saw Virgin's cars pull out. 'A nickel-and-dime
operation,' Ecclestone jeered.

'It's the rigid budget,' said Wirth.

'Shit or get off the pot,' Ecclestone told Branson as they passed in the paddock. The ringmaster disliked men who lacked conviction. Branson lurked around his cramped headquarters, pondering his future in the sport. Formula One was everything he loved: speed, risk, glamour, beautiful women, parties – an extraordinary business enriching many people. He wanted to share the cake. How he hated raw competition. There was no place for the underdog punching above his weight. 'One day hopefully Virgin will overtake Red Bull,' he told an aficionado. Formula One, he added, could only prosper if the teams' budgets were forcibly reduced to $40 million.

Two weeks later in Melbourne, Branson's embarrassment grew. During the practice sessions, Virgin revealed that Wirth's computer design had produced a car with fuel tanks which were too small to complete the distance at full speed. 'Fuck me,' exclaimed Branson, visualising the effect on Virgin's image as a spluttering car was pushed off the track. Pulling out of Formula One was not an option. Delivering a positive message while drowning was, however, Branson's accomplished art. 'We're still hoping to be the best of the new teams,' he told sceptical journalists at the track. 'We know we have a fast car.'

The next humiliation was in Monaco, the scene of the previous year's Brawn triumph. The wheels of one of the Virgin cars came off – literally fell on to the tarmac. A mechanic had failed to properly tighten the wheel nuts. 'We can't even finish the fucking race,' a Virgin executive told Wirth. Ecclestone dismissed Branson as a nonentity.

In their dreams, the Singapore race in September should have been a climax for Virgin. As usual, Asia's richest power brokers had arrived on the island for a weekend of business and partying. For ten years, Branson had tried to build an airline and telephone business among those inscrutable billionaires, with mixed results. If Virgin's car could be successful, his status would rise. Instead, he was mired in embarrassment. 'It's been a fun season,' he said, watching the practice sessions. 'We knew we were the underdogs again and we went into it with our eyes open, and it is fun building a team from scratch.' At that moment, a computer glitch was disrupting Virgin Blue's flights in Australia, and thousands of passengers were stranded. Branson always delighted in his rivals' misery, but he could not understand it when others shared that sentiment about him. Before leaving, he was asked whether he was fully committed to Virgin Racing for next season. 'Yep, for sure,' he replied.

Branson cut an isolated figure as he walked through the paddock before the last race of the season in Abu Dhabi. Ignored by journalists and TV cameras, he had no excuses for the Virgin cars being ranked at the bottom of the table. The team's debts had risen to over £60 million, with LDC owed £44 million. Eales decided to sell Lloyds' shares to Andrei Cheglakov, a Russian electronics millionaire whose ambition for Marussia, his motor company, was for it to compete at Sochi in 2014, in the first Formula One race ever to be held in Russia. Branson agreed that the new team would be called Marussia Virgin; naturally, Virgin would not pay anything. Through Cheglakov, he hoped Virgin might finally develop a presence in Russia. 'This cements our place on the Formula One grid,' said Branson, before heading to a party with King Juan Carlos of Spain and Niki Lauda, whom he had persuaded to buy a ticket for Virgin Galactic.

Nick Wirth did not party. A bitter row was brewing between himself and Lowdon over Wirth's claim that he was owed over £15 million. 'Graeme Lowdon', claimed Wirth angrily, 'is one of the nastiest men I have ever met. It took every molecule of my life to avoid the train wreck they tried to bestow on me.' Although Wirth received some money, Lowdon strenuously denied any wrongdoing.

At the end of 2011, contrary to Branson's statements, Virgin abandoned Formula One. Branson extricated himself, leaving a legacy of resentment. 'I got in at the right time and then got out,' he told his executives. 'We didn't risk or lose any money.' Like all Virgin's casualties, Lowdon did not want to be identified as the loser. 'We didn't get more from Virgin than we expected or was promised,' he said.

Soon after this latest setback, Branson posted a message on his blog: 'After reflecting across forty years and thinking about what characterises so many successful Virgin ventures, I have come up with five secrets to business success: enjoy what you're doing; create something that stands out; create something that everybody who works for you is really proud of; be a good leader; and be visible.' Joining Formula One had breached several of his own rules, but there was always an antidote. Days after leaving Abu Dhabi, Media Control, a German data corporation, awarded him a prize previously won by Bill Clinton, Nelson Mandela and the Dalai Lama. 'The jury', read the citation, 'is honouring a globally active businessman whose creativity and innovation has become a force for good in international co-operation, human development and preservation of the environment.'

Prizes naturally made Branson feel special.

12

Virgin's Crime: The Trial

Branson's genius is to blur and bury jarring inconsistencies. To the public, he appeared as the billionaire sponsor of a Formula One team, the owner of exotic islands and the master of a global empire. His status was enhanced by Virgin publicists generating a stream of stories and photographs illustrating his relationship with celebrities. 'Kate Middleton turns to Sir Richard Branson for advice,' was a newspaper caption in August 2009 highlighting his intimacy with the future queen not long before the announcement of the royal engagement. A photo taken for former South African president Nelson Mandela's ninetieth birthday showed Branson alongside Robert De Niro, Oprah Winfrey, Will and Jada Pinkett Smith, Naomi Campbell and Neil Diamond. 'It's a fantastic halo' effect, he admitted.

That coup was followed by photos of Branson alongside Queen Noor of Jordan. Together, they had launched Global Zero, an organisation dedicated to eradicating the world's nuclear weapons within the next twenty-five years. Shortly after, there were photos of Branson visiting Darfur in the Sudan with Jimmy Carter, the former American president and a leading Elder, a member of the global advisory group sponsored by Branson. The journey of an elderly politician, an ageing hippy and Mia Farrow was planned, said Branson, 'in solidarity with people in Darfur' to highlight the famine and civil war. The journey ended in disarray. The local government was irritated by the outsiders' interference, and the ex-president was manhandled. In the years since the al-Qaeda attacks on New York and Washington, the invasion of Iraq and the bombings on the London Underground, the antagonism between Muslims and Christians like Carter had grown. Angered that his group of self-appointed 'civilisers' were treated without respect, Branson committed himself to a three-day fast in sympathy with the suffering Sudanese. 'The Elders', he said, 'are in a position of moral authority and respect and play a key role in world peace.'

Proud of his creation, Branson was blind to Carter's eccentricity. The former president was proposing to end strife in 'the Holy Land'. Israel, urged Carter, should negotiate with Hezbollah and Hamas, whom he called 'peace-loving organisations'. Since the two groups regularly organise terrorist attacks against Jews and deny the Jewish state's right to exist, Carter's prejudice was unlikely to win sympathy among Israelis. The resentment towards him baffled Branson, who praised 'the beauty of the Arab Spring as inspirational'.

Ignorant of the complexities of the Middle East's torturous conflicts and the centuries-old religious wars between the Muslim sects, Branson had become dismayed by politicians. In his opinion, they were a transitory breed incapable of improving the world. He genuinely believed that sticking Virgin's label on a discredited former president could influence international statesmen. Eric Bost, the American ambassador in Pretoria, reported to the State Department in 2007 that Branson was participating in discussions led by Nelson Mandela to offer Robert Mugabe, the president of Zimbabwe, £6.5 million if he retired immediately. Branson denied Bost's report, but it was not inconsistent with his conviction that government should be entrusted to entrepreneurs blessed with decades of experience. He prided himself on his abilities but preferred to ignore the public's expectation that politicians behave with transparency. He thrived on ambiguity.

Secrecy had always been Branson's preference. Ever since

1969, when he had concealed Virgin Records' true profits from some of his associates, he had guarded his finances in offshore companies. Over the years, he had also ensured that his cabal of executives, especially Gordon McCallum and Stephen Murphy, rarely emerged from the shadows, yet the contrast between his clandestine financial management and his political gestures passed unnoticed among the admiring public. Branson was accepted on his own terms. Even when his ventures faltered, his halo remained fixed. He was universally hailed as an outstanding businessman, even when cracks exposed his empire's financial vulnerability. At this stage, Virgin Atlantic had soaring losses.

The recession was damaging all the major airlines. The number of lucrative business-class passengers had fallen. Virgin Atlantic was vulnerable in July 2010. Without the benefit of BA's disasters at Terminal 5, the £36 million profits in 2008 turned in 2009 to a record loss of £132 million. To survive, Branson had to forget his homily about caring for Virgin's employees. He cut flights, reduced his staff by 10 per cent, delayed the delivery of new aircraft and did not announce any further renewable-fuel experiments. His airline had shrunk by 20 per cent. Many blamed Steve Ridgway for missing too many opportunities. The revelation of the airline's problems coincided with the start of the trial against the four BA executives for conspiring with Virgin Atlantic's senior staff to fix the Passenger Fuel Surcharge. The trial was certain to dominate the media, and Ridgway was at the heart of the prosecution case, giving Branson good reason to be nervous.

Throughout his career, Branson had concealed his methods of operating. He had lied about his purchase-tax fraud – in his version the fraud was perpetuated 'only three times', whereas it had continued for nearly a year. He had said, when victorious in the Camelot libel trial, 'My mother always taught me to tell the truth,' yet in his own books he advised aspiring disciples, 'I have always enjoyed breaking the rules.' Ruthlessness camouflaged by smiles had been a good weapon against competitors. In *Screw Business as Usual* he had written, 'Do good, don't do harm. Give back if you can' – a homily that was no protection when Virgin's executives confessed to a criminal conspiracy to fix the fuel surcharge. Their confession was matched by BA's admission of guilt in America and agreement to pay a combined $300 million fine for the cargo and fuel-surcharge cartels.

With Virgin's and BA's admissions of criminality, the case for the prosecution in London appeared to be watertight. Steve Ridgway had signed a statement that read, 'I apologise unreservedly for my involvement in this case.' Although he denied having 'direct contact' with BA, he did admit encouraging Paul Moore, Virgin Atlantic's public-relations officer, to arrange the announcement of the surcharge with BA's executives. 'I did not stop the discussions,' Ridgway said. Despite his confession, Branson never suggested that his job was in jeopardy. Some assumed Branson's benevolence was influenced by a degree of prudence. The prosecutors in Washington and London believed that the emails between Ridgway and Branson confirmed that the airline's owner was aware of Virgin's secret discussions with BA. Richard Latham QC, the British prosecutor, intended to name Branson as a participant in the conspiracy during the trial, as did lawyers for the defence. Virgin's immunity agreement compelled the executives to give unequivocal support to the prosecution, but although Branson had been put firmly in the frame, his inability to recall receiving Ridgway's emails and his professions of ignorance about the discussions with BA posed a problem for Ali Nikpay, the Office of Fair Trading's legal director. Potentially, Branson's testimony could confuse the jury, and hostile cross-examination could threaten his reputation, so in the end Nikpay decided that he should not be called as a witness. Branson had good reason to be grateful. At that moment he was still hoping to buy Northern Rock, and Virgin had sub-mitted an application for a banking licence. The preliminaries of the criminal trial due to start in April 2010 would jeopardise that breakthrough. However, beyond public view, the prosecu-tion's case was struggling.

The defence noticed that Nikpay had failed to commission a report on the pricing of airline tickets. Nor, the defence lawyers realised, had the prosecution commissioned an expert to explain to the jury the financial consequences of the alleged cartel. Without evidence of financial loss, submitted the defence, how could the prosecution establish a crime? 'A staggering omission by the OFT,' a defence lawyer told the judge, Mr Justice Owen.

By contrast, the defence had obtained expert evidence sug-gesting that the prosecution was misrepresenting how the sur-charge had affected ticket prices. The surcharge, according to this evidence, was never simply added on to fares. Rather, it was another component churned by the computers as they endlessly recalculated a myriad of prices. The consequence of this evidence was critical: the prosecution would be pressed by the defence to prove that the surcharge had actually cost an individual passen-ger an identifiable amount of additional money.

There was another complication that the OFT ignored. BA had applied surcharges to many of its 219 routes, but the airline competed exclusively with Virgin Atlantic on only three routes to the Caribbean. The extent of the alleged cartel would have been minuscule. The OFT had apparently also failed to take into account the fact that all of BA's bigger competitors were excluded from the alleged cartel, so how could price-fixing operate?

Most importantly, a crime would have been committed only if BA and Virgin had made a binding agreement to restrict their freedom to price tickets. Yet throughout that period, the two airlines were competing furiously against each other on prices. Every lawyer in the courtroom noted the judge's displeasure at the OFT's misunderstanding of airline finances and competition laws. And then it got worse for the prosecution.

From the outset, the four accused had insisted that all of BA's surcharges had been agreed internally before any of the conversations with Virgin's executives had occurred. BA's executives could not understand how innocuous conversations about the timing of public announcements could be construed by Branson and Virgin as an admission of a criminal cartel to fix prices. The explanation, BA hoped, would be found in Virgin's internal emails. The disclosure of Virgin Atlantic's emails and documents during the period of the alleged cartel was critical to the defence. Under British law, the defendants were entitled to read all of the airline's relevant communications, but access to them depended upon the OFT, Virgin and Herbert Smith, the airline's solicitors.

During the two years before the trial, the four accused claimed to have become exasperated by the reluctance of the OFT, Herbert Smith and Virgin to disclose critical emails and documents. According to the defence's claims, Virgin was refusing to divulge what it called 'core legal advice', including the statements made by its executives to their lawyers. Among those statements, BA suspected, were protestations of innocence by Virgin's executives.

In total, each of the three executives had made nine successive statements. In sharpening their memories, they had changed their vague testimony to precise admissions of guilt in a criminal conspiracy. Any inconsistencies in those statements would be dream material for a defence lawyer's cross-examination. The most important was the one provided by Paul Moore, the cornerstone of the prosecution and due to appear as the first witness.

To Moore's initial surprise, he had been told by lawyers representing the US Department of Justice and Virgin that his conduct had been illegal. He eventually accepted his lawyers' advice that his conversations with his counterpart at BA, Iain Burns, had materially influenced the price of airline tickets, which amounted to criminal price-fixing. That belief, he understood, was essential in supporting Virgin's immunity agreement.

BA argued that the legal advice given to Moore was mistaken. Virgin's executives, claimed a defence lawyer, 'thought it was in their interests to make the case against British Airways stronger, and that's why they were persuaded to say what they said'. Virgin's bid to retain its immunity was, according to the defence, compounded by the OFT's 'extraordinary degree of deference to Virgin's interests'. In other words, the OFT relied on Virgin's own investigation to confirm that a crime had been committed.

By the closing stages of the pre-trial hearings, Ali Nikpay had yet to provide the defence with copies of the twenty-seven statements signed by Virgin's three executives for the American Department of Justice apparently admitting their own dishonesty. The absence of those statements alienated the trial judge. He told the OFT and the prosecutor that the BA executives could not get a fair trial without reading the evidence. Access to the statements depended on the Virgin executives waiving their privilege of confidentiality. Herbert Smith's letter to Moore asking for permission to hand his statements to the defence was posed in language which, the judge subsequently noted while approving a defence lawyer's argument, had shown 'cynical miscompliance' with the judge's own rulings about the evidence.

Virgin was faced with a dilemma. Regardless of the trial's outcome, the company's reputation would be damaged. The harm could be minimised by ending the trial in one of two ways: first, by Virgin executives denying in their testimony that they had acted illegally; and second, by releasing their inconsistent statements. Taken together, the prosecution's case would be weakened.

Just before the trial started, Virgin agreed to show the defence the twenty-seven statements. Herbert Smith, however, declined to disclose the documents they had used in their interviews with

Branson in March and April 2006. Branson's own statement had been largely redacted. The defence's quest for Virgin's documents assumed even greater importance on the day the trial formally started – 27 April 2010.

On the first day, Branson was put firmly in the frame by the prosecutor, but once again the media's generous treatment of Virgin Atlantic smothered the prosecutor's allegations and the references to Branson were not highlighted in the following day's newspapers. Until the end of the week, Latham's address to the jury followed a predictable course, but then, after the prosecutor and the defence lawyers had completed their speeches to the jury, a series of revelations began to destabilise the trial. The judge was compelled to delay proceedings, exclude the jury from the courtroom and listen to the defence lawyers' bitter accusations about reputations, motives and suspicious conduct.

During the two-year campaign by the defence lawyers for access to more of Virgin's internal records, the airline and the OFT replied that software glitches had prevented the computer experts from retrieving 'some corrupted' messages. The OFT's lawyers, after mentioning the huge harvest of data already disclosed, dismissed the few missing files as irrelevant. Surprisingly, no one precisely identified those absent files.

The first hint of an unusual course of events was the disclosure by Herbert Smith during the first week of the trial of eleven significant, previously unseen documents. Each document had been requested two years earlier. 'This is deeply disquieting,' said the judge, after hearing that the paper documents had been 'on the top of the pile', not 'in the back of the filing cabinet'. Just before the lawyers ended that day's arguments, the prosecution announced that a new batch of emails had been disclosed to the defence that afternoon. Everyone assumed the following day would be difficult because this correspondence referred to the foundation of the prosecution's case.

Richard Latham had focused on the conversation between Moore and Burns on 21 March 2005 about another surcharge increase. According to Moore's statement and Virgin's version of events, Virgin had been discussing an increase of its own surcharge by £3 or £5. Ridgway had told Moore to telephone Burns. Moore obeyed and opened with the words, 'This is one of those conversations we're not going have.' Moore described how he revealed to Burns that Virgin intended to raise the surcharge by £5. According to Moore's evidence, Burns instantly replied, 'You might well want to think about going up by £6.' His swift answer reflected BA's own intentions.

'That sounds good to me,' said Moore. 'I'll expect we'll do that then.'

Critically, the prosecution emphasised to the jury that the public had paid £6 rather than the £5 originally proposed by Virgin because Burns had influenced Moore. In other words, the conspiracy between the airlines had cost the public real money. An email disclosed at a late stage appeared to confirm the prosecution's case.

Timed at 1.46 p.m. on 21 March – after Ridgway had spoken to Moore, but before Moore spoke to Burns – Moore had emailed his team that Ridgway had decided to impose an additional surcharge. The message included his proposed press statement: 'Virgin Atlantic has reluctantly decided to increase its fuel surcharge by £5 . . . from Tuesday 22 March.' As the prosecution emphasised, just twenty-nine minutes later, at 2.15 p.m., Moore telephoned Burns to seek agreement for a joint announcement.

But a newly disclosed email emanating from Moore's department contradicted the prosecutor's version. The new correspondence showed that Virgin Atlantic had decided to increase the surcharge by £6 *before* Moore telephoned Burns. At exactly 1.56 p.m., ten minutes after Moore sent his internal email, Anna Knowles, a member of his team, sent an email disclosing that

Virgin had decided to fix the surcharge at £6 – in other words, the same amount as BA, and that email was sent before the conversation, which the prosecution argued amounted to collusion. Nineteen minutes later, Moore spoke to Burns. To the judge's evident surprise, the defence alleged that the prosecution and Virgin had discovered the new email in 2008 but had not revealed it to the defence for two years – after the trial started. In its defence, Virgin claimed that Knowles' message was discovered only by accident and her original email was missing. According to Virgin, Knowles' message was a copy which had been forwarded to others in the airline's headquarters by Polly Hardiman, another member of Moore's staff. Therefore, it could not be verified as genuine. That explanation was dismissed by the defence. Nevertheless, the disclosure of the new email dispatched a torpedo towards the OFT's case. Other conduct by Virgin and its lawyers now took on a more colourful meaning so far as the defence was concerned.

The defence had been denied access to documents used by the US Department of Justice during their interviews with Moore on the grounds that they 'were not material'. Virgin was now accused by the defence of a 'close-fisted approach to disclosure' by withholding 'potentially highly relevant material going to the heart of the case'. Herbert Smith found themselves criticised for choosing which documents to release to suit Virgin. 'My feelings are of grave disquiet,' said the judge. His mood was further aggravated after being told that on the eve of the trial, Moore had been professionally coached on how to give evidence. Training witnesses in a criminal trial is controversial and was compounded by the defence's allegation that a key email 'may have been modified' by some unknown person prior to the trial. 'That is an extraordinary state of affairs,' said a lawyer.

Other inconsistencies now assumed greater importance. The prosecution's case was based on Burns making the first call to

Moore in August 2004. Moore emphatically insisted that Burns's call had 'come of the blue'. The BA man's initiative, the prosecution alleged, took Moore by surprise. In that conversation, said the prosecutor, Burns had started by saying to Moore, 'This is a conversation we're not having.' Burns had always denied that suggestion, insisting that Moore had called *him* first. After they had examined the new emails, the defence confidently asserted that Burns's version seemed to have been endorsed.

The defence lawyers found a message sent by Moore to his staff, 'Anna and Polly', before his first conversation with Burns in August 2004. In it he described to his two assistants how Virgin intended to raise the surcharge by £5. Importantly, he explained how he had heard from a *Financial Times* journalist that BA intended to increase its surcharge by £6 to £8 and suggested that Virgin wait for BA's announcement. Moore added, 'I might ring Iain Burns at British Airways in the meantime and agree a joint date.' Pertinently, Moore did not write 'a joint price'.

The defence investigators produced Virgin's telephone records and a log book compiled by Burns's personal assistant. The records suggested that Moore had called Burns first and, finding that he was out, left a message. Moore then called again and heard that BA had already decided to increase its own surcharge by £6. Virgin then decided to match BA.

The defence lawyers seized on the new evidence to allege that Moore's statements were unreliable. If there was a conspiracy, suggested the defence, it might have been initiated by Virgin. The contradictions would be tested during Moore's cross-examination. But then the trial was shaken by another surprise.

The prosecutor revealed to the judge that the computer program that had scanned the Virgin documents for the trial had not copied some material dated after 10 February 2005. Accordingly, some emails around the critical date of 21 March were probably missing, as were those referring to Branson's cricket match and much more. Apparently, no one at the OFT, Herbert Smith or Virgin had noticed that omission. That revelation was followed by another surprise. For over a year, Herbert Smith and Virgin had insisted that some computer files had been corrupted and were beyond retrieval. Now, the prosecutor revealed, those 'few' files had been almost miraculously rescued by technicians over the previous days. Suddenly, 70,000 new emails were available, and 12,000 of them were Moore's.

'Somewhere there's a smoking gun,' griped a defence insider, uncertain as to whether the prosecution had been sabotaged or whether the OFT was simply incompetent. The defence demanded that the trial be delayed while all 70,000 emails were scrutinised. The judge refused. Instead, at the end of a weekend's frenzied work, the prosecutor announced that the OFT had withdrawn the case. The four BA executives walked out of the court as innocent men. The collapse of the trial was a relief for Virgin, as their executives would avoid being exposed as self-confessed criminals offering contested evidence. BA would successfully negotiate a reduction of its fines in London and Washington.

After his client's acquittal, Ben Emmerson QC, one of the defence lawyers, criticised the OFT's lawyers for being 'ludicrous', 'disgraceful', 'shabby', 'cynical', 'not fit for purpose' and 'guilty of incompetence on a monumental scale'. 'Ali Nikpay', he said, 'must shoulder the personal responsibility for this fiasco.' The newly released emails, Emmerson asserted to the judge, showed that the Virgin witnesses 'seemed to have changed their accounts, from the accounts entirely consistent with innocence that they first gave to their lawyers to what seems to be more manipulated accounts in the final witness statements'. He blamed the OFT for 'delegating disclosure [of the emails] to lawyers whose job it was to protect and advance the interests of Virgin Atlantic'. That, he claimed, was 'a disgraceful situation'.

In reply, Ali Nikpay focused on 'the role played by Virgin to provide the OFT with continuous and complete co-operation. This may have potential consequences for Virgin's immunity.' The OFT's mismanagement of the case would prompt the new Conservative-led government to close the agency.

The OFT's last gasp was an announcement soon after the trial's collapse. Cathay Pacific, stated the agency, had sought immunity from prosecution for fixing passenger fares between London and Hong Kong with Virgin Atlantic. 'The parties', Nikpay said, 'will now have an opportunity to respond to our proposed findings before we decide whether competition law has in fact been infringed.' Virgin Atlantic set aside £35.4 million as 'administrative expenses' in the event of a conviction for the offence. Two years later, in 2012, the OFT's officials admitted they were confused by the conflicting evidence. Virgin Atlantic, the OFT announced, would not be prosecuted. Branson's good relations with the media limited any negative comments. His airline's fate, however, remained precarious.

'Business is way down,' said Steve Ridgway in 2010. 'I think we are probably at the bottom and there is no sign of the green shoots. Business travellers have not come back.' He dismissed a further 600 employees and cut more routes. Branson predicted that Virgin America would lose another $48 million in 2010. The continued independence of his airline depended on President Obama vetoing BA's proposed alliance with American Airlines. Branson's usual reliance on Virgin's self-professed decency was vulnerable.

'I wouldn't forgive anybody for what they did there,' said Willie Walsh, still outraged by Branson's dash to the American prosecutors. The payback was delivered in a few sentences. Washington's officials were reminded by BA's representatives that Branson was not the disinterested champion of consumers. Contrary to his self-portrayal as 'the cool David taking on the world's corporate Goliaths', Virgin had confessed to a serious crime. The masquerade of the underdog, argued BA's lawyers, should end henceforth.

Officials at the US Department of Transportation approved BA's alliance with AA in February 2010, on condition that four pairs of daily slots at Heathrow be sold. 'The preliminary decision beggars belief,' exclaimed Branson. 'Four slots is a complete joke and those responsible should hang their heads in shame.' Over the following weeks, he fumed that the alliance provided 'no evidence of consumer benefits'. BA and AA would enjoy 'a massive frequency advantage' over Virgin Atlantic, he complained, an obvious consequence of the two airlines operating more planes than Virgin. A few weeks later, BA and Iberia, the Spanish airline, merged. BA–AA–Iberia offered 5,200 daily departures from over 400 cities. Branson's protests were again ignored, not least because his complaints coincided with his own bid for alliances.

On 13 September 2010, Branson protested that Australia's regulator had refused to allow Virgin Blue to code-share with Air New Zealand across the Tasman Sea. 'We're losing money,' Branson retorted, 'and if we don't get the code share we'll pull out of the flights.' At the same time, he applied to code-share Virgin Atlantic's flights to Australia with Etihad, the Gulf airline; and also Virgin's flights from Australia to Los Angeles with Delta.

Virgin justified that hypocrisy as necessary for survival. But in September 2010, Branson's poise was disrupted. Scrabbling for solutions, he spoke about integrating the three Virgin airlines and Virgin Galactic into a 'quality alliance'. His scheme bore a hint of desperation. 'Don't underestimate the halo effect the new alliance will have on the brand,' Branson told the single journalist invited to witness him walking through a Dallas convention centre accompanied by two blonde Virgin America stewardesses. He was handing out free tickets for the airline's new service between Dallas and San Francisco. 'I've long argued with my wife, size isn't everything.'

Amusing quips and his description of himself as 'the rebel mogul' shaking up markets could not compensate for the erosion of his commercial strength. Branson's airline, he finally conceded, needed a lifeline. Asked, 'Is Virgin Atlantic going to be around in fifty years' time?' he replied, 'I think we realise that we need a big brother or we need a partnership.' The obstacle was his past. He was not everyone's favourite business partner.

Cheong Choong Kong, the former chief executive of Singapore Airlines, cursed his purchase of 49 per cent of Virgin Atlantic for £630 million in December 1999. The anticipated profits had not materialised, and Branson had aggravated his partner by expanding Virgin Blue's network across Asia in direct competition with Singapore Airlines. 'God help us,' said Cheong. 'He's unreliable,' declared one of those close to Cheong. 'He's never there. He's not interested in day-to-day results. He's a lightweight.' Cheong often lamented an exchange with one British businessman. 'You should have called me,' said the industrialist. 'I would have told you not to touch it.' Cheong and his successors rejected Branson's plea for money to expand the airline. 'He's got so many inter-company loans', observed a Singaporean executive on Virgin Atlantic's board, 'that one should run for the hills.' Since 2006, the Singaporeans had sought a buyer for their devalued stake. 'Anyone can make an offer and we will evaluate it,' confirmed Goh Choon Phong, the airline's new chief executive. There was no apparent interest.

The Singaporeans' irritation with Branson was shared by the directors of Lufthansa. In late 2009, the Germans decided to cut their losses and sell BMI. Although the airline, which had 11 per cent of Heathrow's slots (fifty-six pairs), was worth around £200 million, Branson offered just £50 million. The Germans were unsure whether he should be taken seriously. He presented himself as a committed environmentalist, yet he supported a third runway at Heathrow and criticised the decision not to open one as 'purely political and incredibly damaging'. The Germans were equally bewildered by a capitalist who frequently advocated the benevolent treatment of employees but condemned Virgin pilots for voting overwhelmingly to strike over their working conditions. Finally, they were baffled as to why Branson offered to pay only a quarter of BMI's true value. Their discussions struggled until the Germans concluded that Virgin Atlantic could not raise the required bank loan. Branson was offering a pittance in the hope that there would be no other offer. At the end of 2010, the negotiations collapsed, but to Branson's distress Willie Walsh appeared with an offer of £172.5 million. Combined with BMI, BA would own 53 per cent of Heathrow's slots. Since Lufthansa controlled 66 per cent of the slots at Frankfurt, and Air France owned 59 per cent of those in Paris, the regulators had no reason to oppose a buyout just because Virgin owned only 3 per cent. 'It is vital', Branson protested immediately, 'that the regulatory authorities in the UK as well as Europe give this merger the fullest possible scrutiny and ensure it is stopped.'

For Walsh, the battle was personal. Recalling the harm inflicted on BA by Branson's successful libel writ in 1993, he anticipated his own triumph with relish. 'I don't get on at all with him,' he said. 'I don't think I'm expected to. I've made no secret of the fact I don't think he likes me either.' Others in London shared that opinion but had no opportunity to voice their sentiments. They had secretly been pleased by Virgin Atlantic's embarrassment when an employee was exposed for selling confidential information about celebrity passengers arriving at Heathrow to the Big Pictures photo agency. They recalled that in 1993, Branson won his libel action against BA by denying Virgin had financial problems. His enemies did not fail to notice the irony when it subsequently appeared that the company was facing difficulties. Those critics applauded Walsh for adding, 'I don't see any value in the Virgin brand. It's not a global brand.'

Branson hated criticism. He also hated losing – especially to people like Walsh. His reaction to any humiliation followed a familiar pattern. First came the bluster. BA's purchase of BMI, he protested, would harm consumers. 'The only reason that British Airways have offered to write out this massive cheque for this massive loss-making company is to stop Virgin Atlantic doing it – so it is purely an anti-competitive move.' Then came the appeal of last resort.

Throughout his career, when faced with commercial defeat, Branson appealed to regulators. In bidding for radio and TV franchises, the national lottery, his various airlines, trains and the use of renewable fuels, Virgin's success had depended upon the regulators' help. Posing as the people's champion, he expected a government to rescue Virgin, the righteous underdog. 'We will challenge every aspect of this process,' Branson now said, 'which if allowed to stand will undoubtedly damage the British airline industry for years to come.' He demanded that government regulators ignore market values, block the deal and favour him, 'in the consumers' interest'. After his appeals was rejected in London, he complained to the EU in Brussels. Without BMI, he said, flights from London to Glasgow, Aberdeen and Edinburgh would become a BA monopoly. He described how the airline had increased the fares between Glasgow and Heathrow by 34 per cent during the six months since BMI had pulled out. That, said Branson, confirmed the danger of monopolies. 'Competition regulation should protect the customer from monopoly situations where companies can set whatever prices they like and stop investing in their product.' The deal, he said, would 'screw the travelling public'. One hundred BMI employees at Belfast airport cheered Branson. Many were convinced he would save their jobs.

In March 2012, BA's purchase of BMI was approved by the regulator. 'The decision is a travesty, just unbelievable,' said

Branson. 'You just wonder whoever's working in the competition authority, whether they realised which department they were walking into the morning they made that decision.'

'Whatever he says', replied Walsh in celebration, 'is largely irrelevant as we have the approval and we're not in any way going to be distracted by anything Branson says.' He added, 'I don't see him as someone who deserves my admiration. Other people have done more in the airline industry. I'm not one of his admirers.'

The regulator's approval was subject to BA selling twelve pairs of slots at Heathrow. Seven would be awarded to an airline flying between Heathrow and Scotland. Branson said that Virgin Atlantic would bid for all twelve slots. He wanted to fly the profitable routes to Cairo, Riyadh, Nice and Moscow. The unprofitable flights to Scotland were less attractive. He had often spoken about Virgin Trains 'wiping the floor' with the operators of the domestic airline routes. Not only were the trains cheaper and faster but, as his spokesmen had often repeated, flights from Manchester to London emitted five times more carbon. Now the environmental argument was junked, as Virgin Atlantic needed transit passengers. Virgin, Branson announced, would replace BMI's flights to Manchester. Walsh seized on another chance to embarrass his foe. 'I would expect Virgin to honour the commitments they have made', he said, 'and fly to Scotland. They now have the ideal opportunity.' To Branson's misfortune, the regulators were weary of the special pleading from a company that had confessed to its involvement in a cartel.

Virgin was, however, given permission to fly on the loss-making routes to Scotland, but easyJet was awarded the profitable route to Moscow. Branson's back was against the wall. Isolated, he was now compelled to search for an alliance – or an outright sale. In May 2011, he admitted that he was in talks with 'two or three' airlines. 'Within the next two or three months we should be clear whether there's an alliance we're happy with or not,' Branson said in Chicago. 'If it means selling shares, I'll consider that. My principal interest is in an alliance.' His potential partners were Air France and Delta. His contemplation of the sale of his own 51 per cent stake signalled an unexpected twist in his fortunes.

13

Virgin Taxes

The day before Branson implied that he had no cash to buy BMI, he announced Virgin Money's intention to buy 632 branches of Lloyds Bank. 'This can happen quickly and smoothly,' he said in May 2011, on behalf of a company back under his control. 'We're a serious bidder and can give the government what it wants through tough competition.' He would need to borrow about £3 billion ($4.87 billion). This was the sort of bargain that Stephen Murphy and Branson had expected the economic crisis to throw up: namely, a good business teetering towards bankruptcy.

The sale of the 632 branches arose in the aftermath of the banking meltdown. In 2008, Lloyds had been encouraged by Gordon Brown to rescue HBOS from insolvency. The result was that Lloyds, a previously sound bank, was decimated by huge debt and its shares lost over 90 per cent in value. Two years later, the regulators ordered both banks to sell branches in order to improve competition on the high street.

Banking's profits attracted Branson, but his ambitions had been frustrated. In early 2010, the Royal Bank of Scotland (RBS) had offered to sell 316 high-street branches for a minimum of £1.3 billion. To avoid one of the hurdles raised during the failed bid for Northern Rock, Virgin Money had obtained a banking licence by purchasing the Church House Trust for £12.28 million. The obscure private bank, founded in 1792, had no branches and fewer than three thousand customers, and its pre-tax profits in 2008 were £450,000. After Virgin Money invested

£37.3 million into the trust, Jayne-Anne Gadhia said that the bank would offer current and fixed-term savings accounts 'by the end of this year'. Gadhia did not have a background as a banker and was always likely to struggle in establishing the complicated machinery. Her forecast did not materialise.

Gadhia now hoped to transform Virgin Money into a proper bank through the purchase of RBS's branches. After the FSA, the government regulator, approved Virgin Money's bid, Branson persuaded Wilbur Ross to pledge $152 million for a 21 per cent stake in the prospective company. On any reckoning, Ross was investing in a dream. Virgin Money did not rank highly among hundreds of competing fund managers, was known only for offering credit cards and mortgages, and had no surplus money. Branson offered less than £400 million for RBS's 316 branches and promised 'to save jobs'. RBS rejected his bid, accepting instead Santander's offer of £1.65 billion.

Buying the Lloyds branches was Branson's next opportunity, but soon after expressing his interest, he was asked to show that he could raise £3 billion. He retreated without bidding. Unwilling to scale back his ambitions, he would need to change his tactics.

The limitations identified by Rowan Gormley had resurfaced. Branson lacked the expertise and money to create a Virgin bank. Unlike Vernon Hill, the American who had introduced Metro Bank in London in 2010, neither Branson nor Gadhia had a clear-cut, futuristic strategy. Successful banking depended upon faultless computer technology and specialist staff. Based on a perfected model, Metro Bank intended to open 200 branches across Britain by 2016, dependent on training sufficient staff to sustain Metro's culture. Gadhia lacked the experience to start a similar bank. Surrounded by loyalists, she disliked critics and had not recruited banking experts. Like Branson, she preferred to shine by reviving familiar ideas.

In July 2010, Branson had returned to Sydney – again with a grin and a blonde – to relaunch low-cost Virgin Money credit cards and low-interest loans. 'We've come to Australia to give the banks a run for their money,' he repeated. 'Virgin loves coming in where people are being ripped off and there's no question that people are being ripped off in the banking sector, and in every single product that we're launching we're much, much better value.' Four years earlier, he had acrimoniously divorced Virgin from Westpac after attracting only 6 per cent of the market. He had blamed the collapse on Westpac poaching Virgin customers, but that explanation appeared to be bluster. The business was later reported to have closed after the auditor raised issues about its financial security.

Since that collapse, Australia's nine banks had consolidated into what Branson called a 'cosy oligopoly'. 'There isn't a lot of competition,' he said, 'and the banks are making a lot of money.' Targeting the 84 per cent of Australians who had never bought life insurance, Virgin needed a partner since the company was not licensed to accept deposits or operate as a bank. Citibank's executives were persuaded to provide the money and administration to sell Virgin's investment products, believing that the Virgin brand would attract young investors. The lure was promises of lower interest rates, discounts and free tickets on Virgin airlines. Three years later, Virgin Money had attracted no more than 90,000 active customers. Potential customers were resistant even to Virgin's advertising campaign. Despite his repeated claims of success, the business lost money every year until Branson quit.

Hype rather than substance characterised his ambitions. His best hope now was to buy the discards of Britain's banking collapse. The remaining prize was Northern Rock. His fate depended upon the British government.

In 2010, Labour faced certain defeat in the general election. Unconcerned by Gordon Brown's distress, Branson switched his support to the Tories and urged his new allies to tackle Labour's £178 billion deficit with immediate spending cuts. 'It would be dangerous', said Branson, 'if we lost the confidence of the markets through delayed action. We're going to have to cut our spending.' The Tories were delighted that wooing Branson had paid off. His support, said the then shadow chancellor, George Osborne, was 'hugely welcome. As Britain's best-known entrepreneur, he knows more about creating jobs and building an economic recovery than the entire Labour Cabinet put together.' In private, Osborne was sceptical about Branson but he would not voice any public doubts about Britain's most popular businessman.

Branson was not surprised by the Tories' gush but he did not anticipate any profound relationship, just a continuation of the stand-off. The sympathy of British politicians was essential to his commercial survival, and he expected their silence over his legitimate tax-avoidance schemes. Nothing would be said, he expected, about the recent relocation from London to Geneva of the Virgin company responsible for licensing the Virgin brand. In 2009/10, Virgin Group Holdings had paid £10.1 million taxes on revenues of £32.4 million, and still owed £26.9 million in corporation tax. By moving to Switzerland, Branson reduced the company's future taxes. To satisfy the Inland Revenue's conditions, Stephen Murphy had personally relocated to Geneva to prove that Virgin's management was taking all its decisions offshore. Simultaneously, to remove any trace of his domicile or residency in Britain, Branson transferred ownership of his home in Kidlington to his two children. For the same reason, his second Holland Park home had been sold, although he justified it by writing, 'I came to the conclusion that I didn't need such a large base in London.' The completion of Branson's tax exile passed without comment in Westminster. Too much was at stake on both sides to disrupt the truce.

Soon after the election and the Conservative-led coalition government was formed, one of Branson's advisers had heard about the secret agreement between the Labour government and the EU Commission that the sale of Northern Rock would have to be completed before December 2013. George Osborne, the new chancellor of the exchequer, decided to advance the sale to 2011. Bids were invited for the bank's savings and mortgage business, which controlled £21 billion and had a million customers and seventy-five branches. The government's price of about £1.5 billion excluded the 'bad' bank with mortgage loans of £54 billion, which the government planned to discharge separately at no loss to the taxpayer.

The political sensitivities were considerable. Osborne needed to avoid the impression that Northern Rock would be sold cheap or that he would allow the purchaser to earn easy profits. The risks would be particularly high if the buyer was Branson.

To avoid the criticism voiced of him two years earlier, Branson entrusted the negotiations to Jayne-Anne Gadhia. During the ensuing period, she had become a familiar visitor at the Treasury and its agencies, calling regularly to judge the mood and win the officials' trust. Everyone, she knew, needed to be persuaded that Branson was not involved in the management of Virgin Money. With him excluded, she assured the officials there would be no repeat of Virgin seeking to renegotiate the price after a 'handshake agreement'. The public, however, would be unaware of Branson's exclusion as all the announcements were made in his name.

To establish Virgin Money's trustworthiness, Virgin's publicists announced that Branson had promised not to fire any of the 2,100 staff and to protect all the branches. For the Treasury, that was a compelling scenario. Gadhia paraded Virgin's additional credentials, focusing on the appointment of Brian Pitman, a retired banker, as chairman. 'Even at seventy-five,' Branson said, 'he is exactly the cool-headed, strategic banker that the situation demands.' However, during the negotiations with the government, Pitman died. His replacement was David Clementi, a former deputy governor of the Bank of England and completely trusted by the Treasury. The heavyweight investor was again Wilbur Ross.

Virgin's opening bid in July 2011 was £1.17 billion, matching the government's secret valuation. Soon after, Virgin discovered that American investment firm J. C. Flowers, the only rival, had bid considerably less and then withdrawn. To maintain the fiction of a competition, the government conceded 'exclusive' negotiating rights to Virgin. In October, the company reduced its bid to £800 million, blaming deteriorating economic conditions and a fall in bank share prices. After negotiations, Virgin's final offer was £863 million, rising to £977 million if certain profit benchmarks were passed. With no other bidder, the government accepted. The taxpayer had lost £480 million, prompting Labour's inevitable complaint that Branson had snatched a bargain. The government replied that Virgin was 'the best available option to minimise future losses'. Branson had done well, although the financing displayed Virgin's limitations. The cash price was £747 million plus other costs. Wilbur Ross gave £269 million, Stanhope Investments of Abu Dhabi invested £50 million, Northern Rock 'lent' Virgin Money £253 million in a convoluted asset purchase, and £150 million was borrowed. Virgin Money contributed just £50 million, and in return owned about 45 per cent of the institution. The sale was announced in November 2011. In Virgin's first press release, Ross's 45 per cent stake was not mentioned. Subsequently, Ross said that he intended to 'sell out a few years down the road for 1.5 times book value'. In other words, he expected his investment to produce a notional 50 per cent profit.

The news coincided with Branson's arrival in New York to

promote *Screw Business as Usual*, the book which outlined his despair about the morality of capitalism. 'My message is a simple one,' he told invited journalists: 'business as usual isn't working. In fact it's "business as usual" that's wrecking our planet. We must change the way we do business.'

His message about Virgin 'transforming itself into a force for good for people and the planet' was directed at corporations. Instead of seeking profits, he told interviewers, corporations should be doing good for 'humanity and the environment'. In Branson's new ethics, there would be no casualties.

At the very moment Branson was preaching social responsibility in New York in 2011, David Baxby, the Australian chief executive of the Virgin Group, was relocating from Virgin's headquarters in Geneva to Singapore – from one tax haven to another. Baxby praised 'a very charismatic founder in Richard. He appeals to a lot of consumers that we're aiming to target.' While mentioning Virgin's airlines, mobile telephones and financial services, Baxby revealed that Branson and the Virgin Group were withdrawing from direct management and wealth creation. In the future, he said, Virgin would offer the brand rather than expertise, money, management and a new product. At best, Branson was consolidating Virgin as a venture capitalist selling its label to innovators and risk-takers and avoiding the hard work.

Curiously, Branson's new book focused praise on minuscule businesses. He identified a grocery, a clothing manufacturer and a producer of frozen organic meals and Cornish pasties. Implicitly, he disliked rival tycoons. After forty-five years, he recognised his weakness. The magic of the early era, when he had employed like-minded mavericks seeking fun and cash, had gradually been diluted, until finally the spell of creativity had evaporated. The pioneers' replacements were traditional managers whose conservative accountancy suffocated risky originality.

The idol feared that his flame was dying, and *Screw Business as Usual* was his latest intuitive attempt at renewal. Virgin needed to be redefined with a new sense of purpose. Implicitly, Branson admitted an inability to beat his rivals. Instead, he mocked them.

During those weeks promoting the book, Branson disparaged Steve Jobs – then still alive – as a ruthless executive. 'That isn't the way it should be done,' he said about Jobs's management of Apple. 'An entrepreneur who treads over people to get to the top is rare. Too many business leaders are too quick to jump down people's throats, or rule by fear, which is foolish. You should lead by praise – you can't launch an idea if no one likes you.'

In New York, he told his audience about Northern Rock, 'We're sitting back trying to work out radical ways of running it differently than banks have been run in the past.' As a new banker, he said, he would be offering small loans to the poor at advantageous rates. He appealed to his brethren in Wall Street to follow his example by no longer 'ripping off their customers' and asked them to 'use their bonuses to repair the damage they have caused'.

'The richest clown on earth,' was a polite riposte from Wall Street. Corporate America was not minded to take lessons from Branson, but some executives were interested to watch whether he practised what he preached. Branson's purchase of Northern Rock would be the test of Virgin's new saintliness as his corporation aimed to fulfil, as he wrote in his book, his ultimate object of 'a fairer distribution of wealth'.

Back in the UK, and dressed in a Newcastle United football shirt, Branson arrived at the bank's headquarters to repeat his promise to neither close branches nor dismiss any staff. Virgin, he told his audience, planned to double the number of customers from four million to eight million (the numbers kept changing) and to triple the number of branches. 'Our customers', he said, 'showed that they trusted the Virgin brand to the extent they would stop withdrawing money on the basis that Virgin would buy it.' In reality, the withdrawals had stopped within hours of the government promising in 2009 to protect all deposits and loans. He also pledged that Virgin Money would offer free banking to those with current accounts, which would be introduced 'by 2013'. With pride, he boasted that the bank was worth £1 billion, a quarter more than he had paid four weeks earlier. Boasting about windfall profits at the taxpayers' expense seemed to contradict his sermon advocating the alternative to 'business as usual'.

The reality was unveiled one month after he had attacked banks in New York for 'ripping off' their customers. Virgin Money announced charges on current accounts which had previously been free, and declared that the interest rates for 25,000 credit-card customers judged to be 'risky' would rise by 50 per cent. How much Branson knew about those changes was uncertain. In *Screw Business*, he had criticised pure profiteering by the banking community for 'wrecking our planet'. He continued, 'We can't charge one group of customers more than another or less than another. We can't find a way to tack on a hidden charge . . . Why? Because none of those things make everyone better off.' To some, Virgin Money appeared to be no different from other building societies, except that, in this case, British taxpayers, on Branson's own account, had lost out to a tax exile.

The blowback of Branson's triumphalism provoked a *Guardian* writer to suggest that 'Virgin is built on the back of taxpayer subsidies.' The company's profits, he wrote, depended upon 'operating heavily protected businesses'. Among the examples managed by Virgin itself were the company's airlines, Virgin Trains, Virgin Care and now Virgin Money. All were dependent on protection by government regulations, government contracts or the provision of taxpayers' money. Together they amounted to over 80 per cent of Virgin's revenues.

'This is of course complete garbage,' replied Branson the following day. 'Ninety-nine per cent of our businesses have nothing to do with government at all and have been built in the face of ferocious competition.' The *Guardian*'s allegation, he continued, is 'an insult to our 50,000 wonderful staff'. He claimed that Virgin Trains was not dependent on the state. 'Far from receiving subsidies, we now pay more than £100 million a year to the taxpayer' – a comment which was somewhat difficult to reconcile with the fact that Virgin Trains was receiving more than £100 million in profits and subsidies from a government franchise.

The more profound weakness went unmentioned in Branson's reply: the absence of a coherent strategy at Virgin Money to guarantee success. In Branson's mind, the merger of Virgin Money with Northern Rock was accomplished by replacing the signs on the high street. Both he and Gadhia heralded Virgin's banking revolution, but neither fully understood the enormity of removing what the industry called 'the legacy products' or 'the platform' from Northern Rock. To modernise Northern Rock's technology, its staff and the branches was complex. Merging it with Virgin Money under a single ethos was challenging. Gadhia had not yet mastered the detail of creating a bank to offer customers current accounts and banking cards. She lacked personal experience of the design of modern banking emporiums. Her expertise lay in paying commission to brokers for selling mortgages and insurance. The result was that one year after the purchase, Virgin Money's branches still resembled historic edifices. The four new Virgin Money Lounges scattered around Britain were small and appeared to be deserted. Other than pledging to offer current accounts by the end of 2013, Gadhia had not produced profitable results from a convincing strategy.

The truth about Virgin Money was portrayed after Santander abandoned the £1.65 billion purchase of 316 RBS branches.

Santander's explanation was the incompatibility of the two banks' IT systems. Even for a banking giant, the cost of solving this would dwarf any potential profits. Within hours of the announcement, Virgin's publicists encouraged newspapers to report that 'Virgin Money pounces on RBS branches'. Reflecting Branson's bravado, Virgin Money was characterised as 'the most credible competitive threat to Britain's big banks'. Previously, Branson had offered less than £400 million for the branches but, given another chance, he slunk away. Virgin Money was still a building society, not a bank.

In the background, Branson knew, Wilbur Ross was waiting for Virgin Money to be floated so he could collect his profits. Branson spoke about a £2 billion sale – an ambitious target with Virgin Money struggling to break out of a financial straitjacket. Branson was searching for other sources of income. As usual, the most attractive was taxpayers' money.

14

'Virgin Dope'

'That's music to our ears,' said a Virgin executive after hearing Tony Blair announce in 2003 that the NHS would buy services from private hospitals. Private contractors would be guaranteed earnings from the NHS's annual £100 billion budget. For Virgin, profiting from the NHS appeared to be similar to the millions of pounds the company received from British taxpayers for running Virgin Trains.

Virgin had already researched the health market. Three years earlier, Branson had been asked by Alan Milburn, the secretary of state for health, to report on how hospitals could improve their food, care and cleanliness. In Milburn's words, the 'award-winning Virgin Group', renowned for its customer services, was best suited to advise the government. The report, 'Customer Service in the NHS', was written by two Virgin Atlantic employees and a consultant. In unpublished appendices, the authors strayed from the simplicities of 'care' to recommending that the government consider privatising parts of the NHS, establishing specialist units, changing NHS contracts and salaries, creating competition by encouraging private health companies to bid for contracts, and encouraging 'entrepreneurial' GPs to create polyclinics to offer services to the local community.

Three years later, the Labour government's reorganisation of the NHS included some of Virgin's recommendations in a scenario outlined by Lord Ara Darzi, a renowned surgeon. GP practices, Darzi believed, were inefficient. Even if seven GPs were grouped together in a community centre, their isolation from other medical services wasted money. His solution was polyclinics established by private companies under contract to the NHS to provide a range of services. GPs, agreed Tony Blair, should turn themselves into private businesses with a guaranteed income by providing services to the local primary-care trusts.

Guaranteed income from the state appealed to Virgin's directors. Private medical providers already sold surgical services to NHS hospitals, but Stephen Murphy eschewed what he called the 'blood and blade business'. Community services were more appealing. Together with Gordon McCallum and Virgin Trains chief Patrick McCall, he searched for an expert to design Virgin's 'market-entry strategy'. One model had been developed in South Africa by Netcare. Mark Adams, Netcare's chief executive in Britain, was called by McCallum to discuss the creation of Virgin clinics. Over eighteen months, Adams discussed the approach Virgin should take with GPs, a conservative branch of a truculent profession. Virgin's success would depend on securing their support, since they would co-operate only on their own terms.

To position Virgin without offending political sensitivities, McCallum commissioned Goodstuff, a market-research consultancy, to plan a strategy. The consultants summarised their overall purpose as 'engendering general warmth to avoid negative press/sentiment'. Their report, which was codenamed 'Project Cocktail', described, with the help of advertisers and specialists in 'healthcare communication', the approach and allies Virgin would need in order to avoid suspicions that the company's involvement in health was 'only for the money'.

That prejudice could be dismissed, Goodstuff suggested, by deploying Branson: 'With Richard as the face of Virgin, consumers believe he aims to put the consumer first.' There was no mention of how Virgin could improve healthcare. Rather, Goodstuff focused on the salesmanship necessary to make Virgin acceptable. 'Putting the consumer at the heart of healthcare', recommended the report, would reflect 'Virgin's holistic offering' of 'always putting the customer first'.

The absence of any medical expertise troubled the agency. Virgin's airlines and trains were not relevant. Slightly more helpful was Virgin Active, the fitness chain labelled by Goodstuff as a 'venture into well-being', taking a cue from Stephen Murphy's belief that 'Virgin is very interested in health and wellness.' Sifting through Virgin Money's website, the consultants discovered the sale of an insurance policy called 'Cancer Cover', but they were uncertain whether profiteering from the illness would attract criticism. The best self-advertisement should have been the stem-cell banking services established with Christopher Evans back in 2007. Branson had hailed the venture as Virgin's response to 'distraught parents' and doctors. But it was doctors and the NHS who rejected his service. He relocated the freezers to Qatar. Within the first two years, the company lost £1.7 million on a turnover of £220,000; and in 2011, turnover fell to £138,000. The annual losses were £404,000. Virgin's investment was depleted.

Ultimately, Goodstuff acknowledged the absence of any pedigree to justify Virgin's entry into the health business. The rationalisation would rely entirely on Branson's image. Doctors and patients, suggested Goodstuff, could be seduced by 'an emotive promise of Virginess' encapsulating 'Virgin's values and service that reflects modern life'. 'Virginess' would be explained by publishing the 'Virgin Pledge for Patients', under the striking headline: 'Virgin will be working with the medical professionals to make healthcare better for both medical practitioners and their patients.'

The pertinent issue was Virgin's intention to maximise its profits. Under the government's rules, each clinic was assigned a quota of patients. The finesse, recommended Goodstuff, was to fill the quota with patients who did not visit GPs. Accordingly,

Virgin should be cautious about admitting 'the 55–65-year-olds who seek advice (perhaps too) regularly from their friendly GP', and be wary of women aged thirty-five to forty-five with children. The most welcome, reported Goodstuff, were young male professionals who 'are the most lucrative to recruit – they help fill a quota without putting a great strain on resources'.

With that brief, McCallum offered Adams a budget of £300 million to develop clinics in eighteen towns. 'Richard wants about twenty Virgin clinics over five years,' he told him. Attracted to Virgin's success in 'shaking up old industries', Adams accepted.

Adams's target was GPs who, after their fortieth birthday, he believed, lost their altruism and tempered their frustration by playing golf. Ideally, he was looking for middle-aged GPs who wanted to become wealthy businessmen by encouraging their patients to buy private treatment from Virgin to cure obesity, diabetes and alcoholism.

McCallum's interest was not only commercial. 'Holly's doing medicine, let's use that,' he told Adams. After studying medicine for five years, Branson's twenty-six-year-old daughter had deferred her second year of training at Chelsea and Westminster Hospital to join her father. She would not return to the hospital. Branson wanted his daughter to become involved in the management of his empire, believing that 'Virgin would definitely benefit if Holly was willing to be more of a face of it.' Virgin Care was ideal for his daughter, he thought. Fearing the erosion of the brand's youthful image, he was equally keen that Sam, his son, should also join the family business.

In January 2007, Adams and his team of NHS experts recruited from leading London hospitals began a three-month national tour. Invitations were sent to over 3,000 doctors in twenty-six towns to attend a three-hour session designed, said McCallum, to 'win their hearts and minds'. Holly was expected to accompany Richard McMahon, Virgin's new health supremo.

The first session introduced by Adams at the London Planetarium began soberly until he showed photographs of Virgin doctors wearing red uniforms. The audience became restless and the session slid towards farce after Adams introduced a message from Branson. The chairman's face appeared on the ceiling. His oration urged the assembled doctors below to save mankind – a calling, he said, which was shared by himself and the Virgin family. 'We can have a fantastic future together,' the God-like recording concluded. Before the finish, Adams realised that his congregation had lost interest. The only excitement was shown by the NHS's civil servants. A few weeks later, they flocked at Virgin's expense to the company's new headquarters in Swindon for a party.

The script was rewritten for the first meeting outside London. About a hundred GPs and protesters organised by Unite, the trade union, disrupted the meeting, but peace was restored once Adams assured the audience that Virgin did not intend to replace doctors' clinical authority but merely help their organisation. Among Virgin's attractions, he explained, was humour. Envelopes containing information about sexual diseases would be marked 'Not for Virgins' and those referring to testicular illnesses would be marked 'Always Mind the Bollocks'. GPs would work for the NHS but would receive 10 per cent of the profits if their patients used Virgin's private services located in the same building, including dentists, therapists and eye surgeons offering laser treatment. As the road tour progressed, Adams became more confident, although Holly – apparently uninterested – had disappeared. By the end, about 200 doctors agreed to join a Virgin polyclinic.

While Adams planned to open the first clinics, McCallum was having second thoughts. Virgin could not afford to guarantee paying the doctors any profits while Virgin Atlantic was losing money. Launching Virgin Care, McCallum decided, was too difficult. The headquarters in Swindon was suddenly closed and Adams and his team were paid off. The plans for Virgin's clinics were abandoned. Adams blamed 'wild optimism' for the failure, while Virgin blamed the NHS trust in Swindon.

Branson had not lost interest, however. Any assured income from the government was attractive. In Virgin's headquarters, Gaurav Batra, another of Branson's fortune-hunters, knew the importance of finding new opportunities and, in the fall-out from the financial crisis, he heard that Assura Medical was for sale. Buying the company, Batra knew, offered a special advantage: involving Holly Branson in the family business – and preferably in healthcare – was a priority for her father.

In 2005, Assura was a property fund managed by Richard Burrell. That year, like Gordon McCallum, Burrell spotted the potential profits offered by Labour's privatisation of GP services. The medicine did not interest Burrell. Instead, he bought the properties used by GPs for their surgeries and rented them back to the doctors. But in 2006, encouraged by the government's promise of contracts for primary-care trusts offering 'integrated' services to hospitals, he plunged deeper into healthcare. The government's formula was for GPs to form commercial groups and offer their services to the NHS. Burrell signed joint partnerships with about thirty GPs' surgeries employing 350 doctors and serving three million patients. Assura Medical was established in 2008, and Burrell planned to attach pharmacies and other private services to each practice. But despite the government's edict, individual NHS administrators opposed to the policy refused to co-operate with Assura's GPs, and Assura's debts rose to £4.4 million. In the midst of the financial crash, the company's directors lost confidence in Burrell's forecasts. 'There's no evidence that it's a growth market,' said one. 'The only growth in the NHS is confusion. Mixing private capital with public policy is tricky. The government doesn't know where it wants to go and doctors are too political. Partnerships with doctors is one step too far.' In January 2009, the board decided to sell the medical business.

'I hear you're for sale,' Batra told Burrell. 'We'd like to look at you. We cocked it up the first time round. We stubbed our toe with Mark Adams by going after the wrong business model, but we want to get into the health business.'

The first visit by Batra, McCallum and Holly Branson was to Reading. Assura, the Virgin team realised, had laid the foundations for a business suitable for Holly to develop. In a buyer's market, Virgin would offer a low price. After Burrell returned to London, the negotiations between Batra and the deputy managers would be helped during their journey across Britain by Batra's suggestion to two Assura directors that their contracts would continue if Virgin bought the business. The only person showing no obvious interest in the discussions, the Assura team noticed, was Holly Branson. 'She didn't ask a single difficult question,' said one director.

McCallum invited Burrell and his two senior directors to discuss the sale at a Virgin board meeting on 16 October 2009 in Geneva. The Virgin team all flew from London to meet the Assura management, who also flew from the capital. The inconvenient logistics, the Assura team assumed, were to satisfy Branson's tax arrangements.

'We're not really sure that we want to buy your company,' said McCallum, 'but let's see what you've got.'

The deflating opening remarks destabilised the visitors. The PowerPoint presentation predicted that Assura was poised to capture £100 million in revenues by 2012, rising eventually to £1.2 billion. The profit margin was a hefty 20 per cent. McCallum could quietly giggle. This was a fire sale of a good business, and Vivienne McVey, Assura's deputy director, was urging Virgin to buy it. McCallum offered £7.5 million for a 75 per cent stake. To finance the purchase, he expected Assura to lend £4 million to Virgin. The loan would be repaid only after Virgin Care became profitable.

'That's derisory,' commented one director. 'Virgin are playing dirty here,' he protested to the fund manager of Invesco Perpetual, an investor. 'We should get a higher price.'

'Even if the offer's too low,' the fund manager replied, 'it's the market price. We accept.'

Virgin appeared to have secured a bargain and, to reduce the price further, it sold off the pharmacies for £3.5 million. The ultimate owner of Virgin Care Ltd was a holding company registered in the Virgin Islands. McVey, appointed as Virgin Care's new managing director, pledged that the company would provide better care at lower cost. Virgin, said Branson, would be 'working alongside our NHS partners'. In *Screw Business as Usual* he wrote that health 'fits perfectly with our focus on doing good to do well'.

Within a year, Virgin realised that Assura's business was unprofitable. Without the promised bonuses, most GPs complained that their relationship with Virgin was 'not going anywhere'. Doctors suggested that their partnerships were being 'taken over by stealth by Virgin', and that once in control, as one doctor discovered, 'Virgin got rid of the GPs because they thought they could do better than us.' At the Virgin clinic in Surrey, doctors were replaced by locums. Virgin's costs fell, while patients complained about the disruption of their treatment. At the Health and Wellness Centre in Liverpool and the Birkenhead Medical Centre in the Wirral, the qualifications of the specialists hired by Virgin were questionable. Biopsies of suspected skin cancers sent to the Sefton dermatology unit in Southport were either mislabelled or incompetently excised, and patients discovered that Virgin was employing an unregistered German locum there. Civil servants at the Department of Health dismissed the grievances as trivial. Their priority was to attract more private companies, and Virgin's managers were uttering soothing reassurances.

Based on Assura's network, Virgin bid to supply care for dermatology, ophthalmology, ultrasound, podiatry, fractures and back and neck injuries in ten areas across the UK. In 2012, the company won a five-year contract to employ 2,500 NHS staff in Surrey to manage eight community hospitals and provide community nurses and health visitors, breast-cancer screenings, sexual-health clinics, specialist dental work and physiotherapy. The budget was £500 million. Virgin also won an £8.5 million contract in Dorset and a £132 million three-year contract in Devon to provide school nurses, health visitors and care for children with disabilities. An objection by the mother of a disabled child to the tendering process was dismissed by a judge.

The protests, combined with Virgin's disruption of established services, antagonised some medical professionals. Across the country, NHS trusts rejected Virgin's bids in favour of in-house providers. Virgin protested. In the East Riding of Yorkshire, Assura's chairman complained that the local NHS had won a contract for bone treatment by tendering less than Virgin. By selecting the lowest offer, the chairman explained, the NHS had deprived patients of choice. The arbitrator, the Co-operation and Competition Panel, ruled against Virgin. The NHS, the panel stated, could not be expected to pay more for a service just to provide a choice. 'Virgin's a bunch of parasites,' commented Lucy Reynolds, an NHS executive. 'They even want their surgeries to be located in Virgin gyms so that their red-uniformed doctors can direct patients to use Virgin facilities.' The original expectation that Branson's reputation would disarm the critics was misplaced.

The GPs joined the disenchanted. Virgin's pressure upon them to direct patients to use private services provided by Virgin – the source of Branson's anticipated profits – had proved to be a conflict of interest. In 2012, the 329 GPs who were Virgin's partners in twenty-five polyclinics agreed that their contractual ownership of the community-service companies should be terminated. GPs would continue to provide NHS services inside buildings owned by Virgin Care, but would have no financial interest in the provision of Virgin's private treatments. Virgin was the sole owner of the business. Virgin Care's losses in 2011 grew to £8.5 million. The following year, the pre-tax losses rose to £9.9 million, and the company's revenue was a mere £23 million. Struggling to succeed, in 2012 Virgin invested £11 million of its own money in the business. For a supposedly global, multibillion-pound corporation, these sums were peanuts – unless Branson was pursuing another strategy, as was suspected by his harshest critics.

Over the previous decade, Branson had championed the decriminalisation of drug use. He had argued stridently that the $1 trillion war against drugs had been lost amid corruption and violence. The only profiteers were the criminal cartels. 'Global drug strategy should be based on evidence not ideology,' he wrote. In arguing for a change in government policy, Branson disputed that drugs were a 'menace' and that the campaign to stop drug use was a choice between 'good and evil'. His first-hand experience with the Sex Pistols' Sid Vicious, a heroin addict who murdered his girlfriend and then committed suicide, and watching Boy George struggling with addiction had persuaded him to write, 'There is absolutely no evidence that the threat of incarceration deters drug use.' Instead of jailing tens of thousands of users as criminals, he wanted the use of drugs to be decriminalised and the scourge treated as a health issue.

Those opposed to decriminalisation criticised Branson's campaign for being self-interested. After all, in the past he had admitted taking drugs and agreed that he would sell cannabis if it was decriminalised. Critics dubbed it 'Virgin Dope', a term that had a special ring for those who associated decriminalisation with an explosion in drug use and the legitimate enrichment of the producers and dealers. The social harm, said Branson's critics, would be incalculable. One beneficiary would be Virgin Care. The health clinics would be ideally suited to bid for NHS contracts to provide treatment. Branson's proposed model had been described by Jamen Shively, a former Microsoft executive who planned to sell his brand of marijuana across America. Since the use of cannabis for medicinal purposes had been approved in eighteen American states, Shively spoke about opening a Starbucks-like chain of medical dispensaries to satisfy his nation's $200 billion annual habit. He launched his idea in Seattle alongside Vicente Fox, the former president of Mexico and an associate of Branson on the Global Commission on Drug Policy.

Branson frequently paraded his relationship with the well-funded international movement to decriminalise drugs. In June 2011, he had joined George Soros, Kofi Annan, George Shultz, Paul Volcker, Carlos Fuentes, Mario Vargas Llosa and the former leaders of Colombia, Greece, Mexico and Switzerland at New York's Waldorf Astoria hotel to launch a campaign in favour of legalisation. Against the backdrop of the ferocious drugs war in Mexico, Branson quoted statistics allegedly published by the United Nations showing that, despite the war against drugs, consumption had increased between 1998 and 2008. 'Stop criminal penalties for people who use drugs but do no harm to others,' he wrote. 'A focus on education and treatment will be much better for society than locking people up for drug use.' He cited Portugal's 2001 decriminalisation as proof that drug use falls after criminal sanctions are removed and users receive health treatment. 'Portugal is the best example,' he wrote. 'The amount of heroin addicts has dropped by half . . . The amount of cannabis use is the lowest in Europe.'

Many of Branson's arguments were contradicted by those opposed to decriminalisation. In Portugal, they replied, decriminalisation had caused an increase in consumption and deaths caused by drug abuse. Similarly, his citation of UN statistics showing a dramatic increase in drug consumption between 1998 and 2008 was described by his critics as inaccurate. The actual United Nations Office on Drugs and Crime World Drug Report showed that the use of hard drugs had declined around the world. On one interpretation, the UN's report suggested that the use of cannabis was only rising because of decriminalisation. The British government's own statistics also showed that hard-drug consumption had declined since 1996. The American figures were comparable. Cocaine use had fallen by 75 per cent over the previous 25 years; cannabis consumption, however, had risen because of legislation to decriminalise its use. Branson did not engage with those figures, instead focusing his arguments on the benefits resulting from Portugal's drug laws. His opponents countered that the Portuguese government's statistics contradicted Branson's assertions: drug use among schoolchildren had increased since decriminalisation, and greater availability had encouraged greater use. They accused him of wishful thinking.

Inconvenient facts did not trouble Branson but, in criticising the drugs war, he refused to address why drug use had fallen wherever the criminal law was applied. In his own words, 'I dislike silly rules,' and in his opinion the criminal laws he disliked ranked as 'silly rules'.

His critics replied that criminalisation is society's warning that drugs are dangerous. Opinion polls showed that the public was consistently against Branson's argument, believing that drugs ruin lives. The fall in consumption in Britain, the critics argued, partly reflected the effect of the law but also an understanding that hospital admissions for mental disorders linked to cannabis use, especially schizophrenia, had increased.

There was no doubt, however, that the laws had failed to put an end to drug use. But all wars against crime have been lost because crime continues, yet no one has suggested that the state abolish all criminal laws. Branson ignored that argument. Drugs, he said, were different. He could not, however, explain away the fact that in Britain, cigarette smoking has declined dramatically ever since the prohibition of smoking in public places, yet alcohol consumption and its associated illnesses have soared as prices have fallen and it has become more readily available. The correlation suggested that relaxing the drugs laws risked increasing consumption. In January 2012, Branson was quoted as saying that if cannabis was decriminalised, he would agree to sell it.

Regardless of those arguments, Branson's opinions were supported by some in Westminster. In particular, he attracted the sympathy of Keith Vaz MP, the chairman of the House of Commons Home Affairs Committee. In 2012, Vaz decided to chair an inquiry into the decriminalisation of drugs. Branson's critics were shocked. In their opinion, Vaz had lost much of his credibility after his suspension from the Commons for one month in 2002 for breaking parliamentary rules. They did not believe his professions of independence and his denial that he was influenced by Branson's Global Commission on Drug Policy. In a letter to Kathy Gyngell, a campaigner against decriminalisation, Vaz insisted that his committee was open-minded and had not prejudged the issue. Ultimately, the committee's report in 2013 agreed with the argument of its first witness – namely Richard Branson – that Britain's drug war had failed and the country should follow the successful Portuguese model. On 6 June 2013, Vaz and Branson signed a letter to *The Times* declaring that the war on drugs was 'lost' and the government should change its policy. Branson's ideas were rejected outright by the government.

Rejection did not embarrass him, however. 'Virgin Dope', his critics believed, was a long-term punt, and for the time being his focus was on Virgin Care's struggle to earn profits. All his new ventures since Virgin Mobile's launch thirteen years earlier had been patchy and Virgin Care, his principal investment over the previous decade, was no better. But its losses were trivial compared to Virgin Galactic's.

15

Galactic – Delays

So much depended on Virgin Galactic – not just the brand and Virgin's finances but also Branson's credibility.

Originally, Branson had committed himself to starting commercial space flights in 2007, but since the fatal explosion there had been repeated delays. To mask the technical problems, he staged events to signal the imminence of take-off. Usually, he hosted a celebration. Most were successful, but his party on 7 December 2009 in California was peculiarly timed.

Gusts of cold wind were blowing across the dark Mojave desert into the faces of 400 people waiting to see WhiteKnightTwo trundle along the runway. To shelter from the howling winds, the guests squeezed into a silver marquee. The majority were journalists, but scattered among the crowd were prospective passengers. Standing at the front was Branson. Peering into the darkness, he wanted to share the first public glimpse of SpaceShipTwo – or the VSS *Enterprise*, as it was named – suspended beneath the catamaran-type plane. The ceremony was carefully choreographed. Purple lasers and the booming soundtrack from *Close Encounters of the Third Kind* flashed and rolled across the runway. Governor Arnold Schwarzenegger was standing beside Branson as the guest of honour. 'Chuck Yeager broke the sound barrier right here,' Schwarzenegger reminded his audience. Branson enjoyed the governor's allusion to *The Right Stuff* heroes. Thanking an 'astronaut' for a mock ray gun, he encouraged everyone to drink Vodka martinis at the Absolut ice bar – a free promotion organised by Virgin's publicists.

'Isn't that the sexiest spaceship ever?' Branson cried out, as the twin-fuselaged plane appeared, crawling towards the marquee. 'This', he told the journalists standing near an ice sculpture of an Apollo spaceman, 'will be the start of commercial space travel.' Smiling by his side, Schwarzenegger did not begrudge Branson's moment of glory. 'This is a truly momentous day,' continued Branson. 'The team has created not only a world first but also a work of art.'

Branson's magic conjured for his guests a grandiose vision. Within a decade, competing spaceship companies would be shuttling into space from spaceports dotted across the globe. With unhesitating certainty, he described rockets flying passengers in 2019 from Los Angeles to Australia and on to the Middle East. No fewer than 50,000 people, he promised, would be flown by Virgin during the first decade. Prices would be low and Virgin would be safer than NASA. Even his disclosure that his ninety-two-year-old father and eighty-five-year-old mother would accompany him on the first flight caused no surprise. He was the master of projecting total credibility. Branson was acutely sensitive about the effect of his words on his audience. Although he often mumbled and looked downwards, his eyes rose at appropriate moments to judge his performance. His hesitations were interpreted charitably. Despite the unusual secrecy imposed upon the venture, no one showed any doubts about the inevitable eventual triumph of his project, which so far had cost $400 million. 'There is this pent-up demand for access to space,' Will Whitehorn chipped in during one of his employer's pauses. 'We've had very rapid growth in the past months because people are seeing something coming to fruition and the breakthroughs coming in the next two years are going to game-change that.' Virgin had collected $42 million from about 300 people, he said, including $4 million within the last few months. Just weeks earlier, Virgin publicists had said that 430 aspiring astronauts had signed up. The numbers do not appear to have been independently verified, and none of the hand-picked guests embarrassed Whitehorn by countering that Virgin's income was insignificant compared to the billions of dollars NASA had offered other private operators for flights to the International Space Station. Any doubts were dispelled by Schwarzenegger's blessing: 'This is the stuff of science-fiction movies and now it has become a reality.' Hollywood's mythology made him an ideal choice to unveil the VSS *Enterprise*. 'It's really amazing. It opens up the space experience to ordinary people around the world.'

To seal Virgin's credibility, a publicist read the roll call of those who had signed up – by then a familiar list including Victoria Principal, the former *Dallas* star, Professor Stephen Hawking and James Lovelock, the ninety-year-old environmentalist who had been promised a ride on the inaugural flight. Although Lovelock preached a doom-laden warning that the world's growing population was creating excessive carbon dioxide, he had spoken emotionally five months earlier about his anticipation of gazing down on 'my first love Gaia, our blue planet, later this year'.

Lovelock had no reason to doubt Branson's timetable for take-off. At the beginning of 2009, Whitehorn had denied that Peter Siebold, the WhiteKnightTwo pilot, had any difficulty keeping the plane on the runway. On the contrary, Whitehorn told *Flight International*, 'We will begin testing SpaceShipTwo rocket planes in August and are optimistic that we will be flying into space with passengers by the end of the year.'

Months later, Whitehorn was unashamed that his confident prediction remained unfulfilled. He even repeated his unequivocal description: 'It's a trip of a lifetime. Reserve your place in space now. Travelling at over four times the speed of sound to a distance of around 360,000 feet above the Earth's surface, experience weightlessness and enjoy the breathtaking view.'

Whitehorn and Branson should have known that their confidence was misplaced.

Branson's guests could not imagine the problems troubling Virgin's designers: the risk of the expanded hybrid motor exploding had not been ruled out; the metal used to build the craft, designed to resist cracking during the rapid temperature changes, required constant retesting; and the safety of rubber burnt by nitrous oxide needed to be confirmed. Above all, firing the motor at full thrust for one minute had so far proved to be impossible. The uncertainty was dispelled by the combination of Branson's enthusiasm, Schwarzenegger's endorsement and the constant repetition about the dream.

Aspiration rather than certainty had attracted many invited to Mojave, including Governor Bill Richardson of New Mexico. Richardson's support added integrity to Branson's venture. The politician's trust in Branson had so far cost the state $203 million in building America's first spaceport. The justification, said Richardson, was the guaranteed $150 million income for New Mexico. Virgin's version disputed that certainty. Although the company had at the end of 2008 signed a twenty-year lease for using the spaceport, the terms allowed Branson to escape any commitment at the cost of a minuscule penalty. Those details were ignored when the politician and Branson agreed jointly to attend the dedication of the two-mile runway in October 2010. The concrete strip – to be completed within two years – would be called the 'Governor Bill Richardson Spaceway'.

Another guest at the party represented Aabar Investments of Abu Dhabi. Principally owned by the emirate's government and controlled by Sheikh Mansour bin Zayed Al Nahyan, Aabar owned stakes in major German and Swiss industries and Manchester City Football Club. Branson had visited the Gulf on many occasions to seek finance for Virgin's projects, and in 2008 had dispatched Stephen Murphy to elicit an investment in Virgin Galactic. Murphy pitched a scenario of Abu Dhabi enhanced by a spaceport, a facility to launch satellites, an Earth Observation Space Centre and a technical college. At the end of July 2009, Aabar bought a 32 per cent stake in Virgin Galactic for $280 million.

The agreement coincided with Branson's first flight in WhiteKnightTwo, the Virgin mother ship. 'This has been one of the most incredible experiences of my life,' said Branson, after the plane landed in Wisconsin. Five months later, WhiteKnightTwo, with VSS *Enterprise* suspended underneath, was rolling down the runway. 'When I saw it,' Branson beamed later, 'I was as near to being reduced to tears as is possible without actually crying.' Moved by that confession, one journalist would ascribe those words to 'Virgin's gleaming entrepreneur, Richard Branson'.

Branson's credibility was enhanced by the announcement that Virgin had ordered five SpaceShipTwos and three WhiteKnightTwo mother ships from Scaled Composites, which had recently been bought outright by Northrop Grumman, the giant aircraft manufacturer. 'Virgin Galactic is the world's first commercial spaceline,' Branson exclaimed.

'When will you do the first trip into space?' he was asked on Sky TV.

'2011,' he replied with certainty.

Virgin's publicists later quietly explained to the interviewer, 'Richard really meant 2012. That's more likely.'

The party in Mojave was abruptly halted – the storm was about to hit the airport. Everyone was ordered on to buses and headed back to Los Angeles. The evacuation was completed just as the storm hit. The marquee was uprooted and wrecked.

Three months later, Reuters headlined a dispatch from Los Angeles, 'Virgin Galactic Almost Ready for Space Tourists'. Shortly after, the news agency reported the 'first flight' of VSS

Enterprise, the 'spaceship'. The casual reader would have imagined that Virgin Galactic was on the verge of carrying passengers into space. In reality, WhiteKnightTwo had taken off for a three-hour flight around Mojave with the spaceship strapped underneath, and then returned to the spaceport. 'We're eighteen months away from taking people into space,' Branson told journalists six months later in Kuala Lumpur. Take-off in 2012, he ought to have realised, was impossible, but his brand depended on optimism.

On 10 October 2010, Branson returned to the desert to watch SpaceShipTwo glide back to the runway after being released at 45,000 feet from the mother ship. News of the successful ten-minute glide was intended to reassure any of his customers concerned by the escalating delays. One week later, he joined Governor Richardson, whose chances of a presidential appointment had been tarnished by a scandal over contributions to his re-election campaign – allegations he contested – at Las Cruces to celebrate the start of the 'spaceway's' construction. 'We'll be flying from here in nine to eighteen months,' Branson told his audience. Glancing around, no one could fail to notice the bare shell of what should have been the spaceships' hangars and the rough concrete foundations of the unbuilt spaceport terminal.

Outbursts of confidence had become necessary to balance the successes recorded by Branson's competitors. XCOR, the small neighbouring space-flight outfit in Mojave, had announced a $28 million contract with a South Korean company to take passengers and cargo into space. More importantly, SpaceX, owned by Elon Musk, the inventor of PayPal, had launched a Dragon spacecraft from a Falcon 9. After orbiting the globe, the rocket was recovered from the Pacific. SpaceX's safe return triggered Musk's negotiations with NASA for a $1.6 billion contract to shuttle twelve payloads to the International Space Station. In the future, he hoped to ferry astronauts to the orbiting station for $20 million a trip, compared to the $65 million charged by the

Russians. Unlike Virgin Galactic's sub-orbital tourism, Musk's venture was a serious orbital business replacing wasteful government spending. Even Branson understood the distinction between Musk and himself. 'Now I know what $1 billion looks like going up in smoke,' he had texted after watching the launch of a NASA rocket from Cape Kennedy. Virgin was not in Musk's league on several counts. Over 2,000 people were employed in SpaceX's Los Angeles factory to build a rocket that had already flown in space and returned.

To prove Virgin Galactic's commercial credibility, Branson needed NASA's imprimatur. Along with other private corporations, Virgin had bid for space contracts. In late 2010, NASA distributed about $270 million between Boeing, SpaceX, Sierra Nevada and Blue Origin – the four principal non-governmental space contractors. Virgin was not included. An emissary was dispatched to extract a morsel from NASA, and returned with a booking to fly a payload on SpaceShipTwo for $4.5 million. The gesture was announced by Virgin and embellished with legends about Branson's past.

Branson no longer regarded reminiscences to journalists about his remarkable career as a journey around his memory. Rather, his narrative had become a tool to project the brand. The businessman coloured his story to refashion his image and justify his investments, not least in Virgin Galactic.

'It's just like launching Virgin Atlantic,' he explained to a journalist comparing his journey into space with his love for new adventures. 'I had a record company and I went to my partner and said, "I'm fed up flying on those awful airlines," and listed the bad food, unsmiling crews, no entertainment and "horrible" lighting. I said, "I want to buy a second-hand 747 and start an airline."' His stories were rarely consistent. Myths were embellished with the anecdotes of an accomplished storyteller. The demeanour was hesitant, but his control never slipped.

A year later, he told another interviewer that Virgin Records 'wasn't focused on making money, but on an urge to do something new. I only tried to make money to pay bills.' In truth, Virgin Records was created by Branson, his cousin and a group of friends, and they did enrich themselves. As some of his friends and employees discovered to their cost, their contribution was ultimately ignored by Branson.

Warming to his theme, Branson presented another version of Virgin Atlantic's invention to a *Forbes* interviewer. 'The idea for Virgin Airways came when he got bumped from an American Airlines flight,' reported the magazine. 'He was already wealthy so he went back to the UK, called up Boeing, and told them he'd like to buy a 747.

'"What did you say your company's name was again?" he was asked.

'"Virgin," he repeated. There was a pause.

'"Well, with a name like that, we certainly hope you plan to have this new enterprise go all the way," the Boeing rep quipped.'

The pay-off line was: 'Today he runs 300 different companies and he says he employs 60,000 people.'

Branson's genius was his convincing performance. The story had gained something in the telling, as the idea for Virgin Atlantic was offered out of the blue to Branson by Randolph Fields, an American lawyer. Branson snapped up the idea, so long as Fields did much of the preparatory work, including organising the lease and finance for a second-hand Boeing 707 – not a 747. As an equal partner, Branson added important tweaks and organised a spectacular launch, including a vicious campaign against BA. His second offensive was against Fields, who, after being squeezed to accept a minority shareholding, accused Branson of double-crossing him to get total ownership of the airline. Branson repeatedly delayed signing a partnership agreement with Fields, who complained that Branson's aggressive negotiation tactics were overwhelming. Branson denied Fields's complaint, his manner simply disarming all but the most resilient complainants. In the aftermath, others accused him of being 'a dream thief'.

Performing as the genial English toff while promoting Virgin in America was a sturdy shield. Sceptics were appeased by Branson's self-deprecation, mumbled politeness, diligence and unostentatious clothing. If all else failed, he deflected his vulnerability by hosting meetings on his houseboat moored in central London. As a result, nothing critical was published in America, other than equating Virgin Galactic with a billionaire's *Boy's Own* folly. Meaningful challenges were brushed aside. And one occurred as Branson stood with Governor Richardson in Las Cruces.

It stemmed from a report published in *Geophysical Research Letters* describing the environmental damage caused by Virgin Galactic. For years Branson had asserted that space travel was 'very environmentally friendly. The carbon cost of us putting someone into space will be about 30 per cent less than flying to London and back on a commercial plane.' He added, 'By launching in air, you save a lot of carbon from the ground blast-off.' Martin Ross of the Aerospace Corporation described the opposite. Virgin Galactic's fuel, he wrote, caused more damage than conventional rockets. The rubber particles that flew out of the motor during the flight would remain in the atmosphere for ten years and cause the temperature of the Earth's surface to increase. By contrast, conventional rockets, burning hydrogen and oxygen, shed only debris on take-off, which fell to the Earth. Branson refused to admit the peril of bits of burnt rubber floating in the air. To dampen the dispute, Will Whitehorn described Virgin's fuel as 'a form of recycled nylon' with 'less impact on the atmosphere over ten years than one and a half shuttle launches'.

Whitehorn's skill was to suffocate any comments about damage and delays by orchestrating a stream of good news from Los Angeles. Virgin, his publicity team announced, would be

opening 'up to 25 hotels within seven years' in America's gate-
way cities; Robert Pattinson would be portraying Branson in a
Hollywood biopic; Branson was producing his own Hollywood
film about Christopher Columbus; and Virgin would beat James
Cameron in a record-breaking submarine dive to the bottom of
the Pacific Ocean.

Virgin Oceanic was an idea Branson inherited after the mys-
terious death of Steve Fossett, a rival ballooner. Fossett had
planned to dive in a special craft into the Mariana Trench, seven
miles (or 37,000 feet) below the surface of the Pacific Ocean.
Branson presented the expedition as a service to mankind: 'A
lot of scientists approached us saying they desperately needed a
research vehicle that can go to the bottom of the ocean. At the
moment only two submarines in the world can go to 18,000
feet. And that sounded like too big a challenge to resist.'

In fact, the approach to Branson came from Chris Welsh, who
was based in California and had been developing Fossett's submarine. After Fossett's death, Welsh was forced to search for
a new sponsor and telephoned Branson: 'I'm building Steve's
sub and wondered if you'd be interested in taking over?' Welsh
needed money and hoped that Virgin would encourage the
Scripps Institution of Oceanography and Google to co-sponsor
the $17 million venture. Branson agreed to co-finance it. The
eighteen-foot craft was designed to carry one person for twenty-
four hours along the bottom of the trench for a maximum of
fifteen miles. Branson was told by Welsh that the construction
of the craft's dome could not be completed for at least eighteen months and, once installed, the submarine would require
months of tests to prove it could withstand pressures of 16,000
lbs per square inch. Nevertheless, posing with Welsh for photographers beside Virgin Oceanic at a press conference on 4 April
2011 at Newport Beach, Branson firmly predicted that his submarine would complete five dives along the Trench the following

year and beat James Cameron's craft. Built by Triton Submarines of Vero Beach Florida, Cameron's submarine was built for two people to cruise along the seabed for a hundred hours. 'If I were to guarantee anything,' replied Cameron, 'I'd say we'll be the only ones to the bottom. I don't think Virgin Oceanic has a chance.' The certainty of defeat did not daunt Branson. All publicity was invaluable and six days later he posed for more.

On the morning of 11 April 2011, even Branson's critics were struck by a remarkable photograph. Against the backdrop of San Francisco's Golden Gate bridge, a Virgin America Airbus was flying alongside WhiteKnightTwo with VSS *Enterprise* strapped beneath. The beautiful image of invincible Virgin – in both business and exploration – zoomed around the globe. At midday, both aircraft were parked on the tarmac outside Terminal Two at San Francisco airport. Six hundred guests, led by Governor Arnold Schwarzenegger, were celebrating the opening of the refurbished building, which would be used by Virgin America. Among those mingling with the local celebrities were Virgin Galactic's pilots – and Buzz Aldrin, the second person to walk on the moon. Even in Branson's publicity lexicon, this was a moment to shine, as San Francisco's political establishment drank cocktails while surrounded by photographs showing Branson posing with Virgin Oceanic.

Relishing the spotlight, the maverick tycoon took the microphone. By the end of the following year, he announced, Virgin Oceanic would win the race to navigate the depths of the ocean, and Virgin Galactic would be flying in space. At that very moment, he continued, a giant hangar was being constructed in New Mexico for Virgin Galactic and, for the first time, SpaceShipTwo was about to be dropped from the mother ship at 51,500 feet and return to Mojave. The glide would be managed by releasing the 'feathers' on the twin tail section to smooth the re-entry into the atmosphere. Virgin, he said, was trailblazing in

space and as an airline. But just as important, Virgin was a leading campaigner for the environment. He was proud that together
with Governor Schwarzenegger, he had stipulated that Terminal
Two should be rebuilt to the highest environmental standards.
The crowd applauded. The bearded buccaneer had branded
Virgin as an environmentally successful business encompass-
ing an Airbus, a spaceship and a submarine. And Virgin also
cared for the poor. Virgin Unite and Galactic Unite, he said,
would encourage underprivileged Californian children, helped
by Virgin America pilots, to pursue careers in space exploration
and aviation. 'I hope eighteen months from now, we'll be sitting
in our spaceship and heading off into space.' Cheers and clap-
ping punctuated each statement.

Not mentioned by Branson was a serious mishap during
an unpowered flight by SpaceShipTwo in May. The rocket,
reported *Space Safety* magazine, had stalled and, according to
people watching from the ground, 'dropped like a rock and
went straight down' until the crew regained control. 'The tail
stall was a nail-biter,' said an eyewitnesses. Although George
Whitesides, Virgin Galactic's chief executive, dismissed the scare
as consistent with any new development, particularly in rocket
science, professional designers repeated their doubts about Burt
Rutan. Why, they wondered, had he not discovered the error
earlier during computer tests?

Four months later, in September 2011, just before flying
to New Mexico to celebrate the formal opening of the spaceport, Branson appeared on Piers Morgan's CNN TV show to
declare victory in the space race. Virgin's wish to be the leader
in space travel was helped by the destruction in flight of Blue
Origin, a rocket funded by Jeff Bezos, the Amazon billionaire. With Bezos's plan for manned flight in 2012 delayed, the
spotlight could be fixed on Virgin Galactic's countdown. Rick
Homans, the state secretary for economic development, exuded

confidence. 'In 2012, we will have our first commercial launches from Spaceport America,' said Homans, reading from Branson's script. 'We are ready to go operational in 2012.' Branson repeated his message to Piers Morgan. Virgin Galactic's first passengers, he said, would soon be passing through the Space Operations Center, a building designed by Norman Foster. 'The rocket tests are going extremely well,' Branson told Morgan, 'and so I think that we're now on track for a launch within twelve months of today.' He did not mention the reports from New Mexico claiming that the building was two years behind schedule, and the news from Mojave about further setbacks to the rocket motor's development. He was also told that even after SpaceShipTwo was successfully launched into space, the Federal Aviation Administration would require test flights before awarding a licence. 'We are now very close to making the dream of suborbital space a reality for thousands of people at a cost and level of safety unimaginable even in the recent past,' Branson told the TV audience. 'Virgin Galactic has shown in the past few years how private-sector investment and innovation can lead to a rapid transformation of stagnant technologies.' Branson was taken at his word, even though he had recently disclosed his worship of fantasy: 'Peter Pan is my favourite character, and I don't really want to grow up. I'm just ridiculously lucky and just love to live my dreams.'

From Morgan's studio, Branson headed to New Mexico. 'Are you ready, Bill?' he asked Bill Richardson as they flew towards the spaceport in Branson's jet.

'What for?' asked Richardson.

'We're all parachuting down to the spaceport.'

'Oh no,' said Richardson, white-faced.

'Absolutely,' insisted Branson.

Once the joke was over, Richardson appreciated why he had entrusted over $200 million to Branson's dream. The Briton was unique. There was creativity and spontaneity but at the same time hardcore discipline during their commercial negotiations. 'He goes to the edge but then comes back,' agreed Homans. However, Richardson would not negotiate the final contract. His term as governor had expired and he had been replaced by Susana Martinez, a Republican committed to cutting costs, especially at the spaceport.

Branson's Falcon was the first jet to land on the new runway. He emerged from his plane with his signature grin. In the sunshine, the party mood encouraged Branson to speak expansively. SpaceShipTwo, he told everyone, had completed a dozen test flights after being dropped mid-air from WhiteKnightTwo. There were cheers. No one appeared to understand that the real hurdle was not gliding down to Mojave but firing the rocket motor to go up into space.

Branson's publicists had arranged a stunt to entertain the 800 guests, some of whom owned tickets for the eventual ride, and to provide the media with a photograph: Branson would be abseiling down the side of Norman Foster's massive glass windows while swigging a bottle of champagne. The master of media spectaculars completed the drop without mishap, unlike three years earlier, when a similar bungee jump in Las Vegas had ended with Branson hanging injured in mid-air. After being guided through the concrete shells where the pre-flight facilities, the control room and the lounges would be built, the spectators continued to cheer Branson's promises. Flights, he confirmed, would start from Las Cruces the following year.

Governor Martinez beamed. 'We'll soon be handing over Spaceport America to you, Richard,' she said, concealing her misgivings. Richardson's original plan, she lamented privately, had been derailed. The expected 140,000 tourists had not materialised and the spaceport's $6 million annual costs had not been covered by charging mourners $1,500 to launch a canister of cremated remains into space. To limit the taxpayers' exposure to a white elephant, Martinez had told Christine Anderson, the new executive director of the spaceport, to halve spending and privatise it.

An unforeseen problem had arisen: other states had entered the spaceport business. Virginia and Texas were offering better terms for space tourists than New Mexico, and Florida was planning to open the Kennedy Space Center for private hire. Richardson's financial forecasts were looking dubious. Even Branson's annual $1.63 million rent was not payable until construction was completed. But Branson's euphoric speech glided over those doubts. In 2012, he said, two flights would taking off every day from the spaceport. One week later, David Mackay, Virgin Galactic's chief pilot, revealed that passenger flights would not start until 2013. And, he added, there would be one flight every week, not two per day. Branson's mistake was ignored.

The sliding deadline was smothered by Virgin's publicists. Stephen Attenborough, Virgin Galactic's commercial director, was presented to journalists in early 2012 to conjure confidently a vision of a two-and-a-half-hour suborbital, environmentally friendly transcontinental flight from Las Cruces or Abu Dhabi on VSS *Enterprise*. Videos of SpaceShipTwo in flight gave credibility to Attenborough's pronouncement of an imminent dash to Virgin's orbital space hotel. 'We are right at the edge of that final part of the test-flight process,' he said. Attenborough was, however, aware that the rocket motor had not yet been perfected and that Virgin's existing spaceship could only glide for four minutes in space. The company would need to spend billions of dollars on an entirely new rocket to fly between continents and to an 'orbital hotel'. Doubters among his audience were silenced by the latest roll call of Hollywood celebrities who had allegedly bought $200,000 tickets to fly: Tom Hanks, Brad Pitt, Demi Moore and, most recently, Ashton Kutcher.

The actor, said Branson, was Virgin Galactic's 500th customer since 2004.

Only one complaint was formally recorded. Bassim Haidar, a Lebanese tycoon, wrote that although he had paid his deposit six years earlier, his chance for a flight was receding: 'I can't get Branson to say when we will fly. I'm very disappointed in him. He's not the "can-do" businessman he likes to project to the media.' Instead of receiving details of his space flight, continued Haidar, Virgin sent him advertisements for other Virgin products – a game safari in South Africa, a hotel in Morocco and flights on Virgin Atlantic. To his disappointment, even the lunch arranged to meet Branson soon after he signed up was cancelled because, according to Haidar, Branson preferred to 'do his usual self-promoting antics at another show for the media'.

One disgruntled non-celebrity could be ignored, but Branson could no longer disregard his skewed timetable. To divert attention from the delays, he approved a conference in Palo Alto, California, on 26 February 2012 focusing on the 'Next Generation of Suborbital Researchers'. Virgin's publicists arranged for their test pilot, David Mackay, to be photographed with Neil Armstrong, the first man on the moon. Although their meeting was brief, Armstrong did curtly endorse Virgin Galactic. 'In the suborbital area,' he said, 'there are lots of things to be done.' Simultaneously, Virgin posted advertisements announcing the company's recruitment of pilots to fly WhiteKnightTwo and SpaceShipTwo. Finally, William Pomerantz, Virgin Galactic's vice president of special projects, appeared. First came the sugar: 'Across the globe, hundreds of Virgin Galactic future astronauts are preparing to turn their dreams into reality.' Then came the adjustment of expectations. Virgin Galactic, said Pomerantz, 'hopes' to perform the first rocket-powered test flight by the end of 2012, and 'commercial flights will begin one or two years later'. At best, Virgin Galactic was seven years late and, on its own account, was holding over $40 million of deposits without paying any interest. Branson's genius was to profit from unchallenged ambitions.

Six weeks later, a 'Global Aerospace' summit was held at the St Regis Hotel on Saadiyat island in Abu Dhabi. The star was George Whitesides, NASA's former chief of staff, who had replaced Will Whitehorn as Virgin Galactic's chief executive. Whitehorn had fallen out with Stephen Murphy and, despite their long association, Branson had apparently not insisted on Whitehorn remaining. After all, he had failed to deliver the rocket.

Whitesides, a self-confessed 'space geek', presented his host's tiny kingdom as 'the centre of technology research and international tourism of the region'. To confirm that anointment, Virgin appointed Steve Landeene as the chief adviser for Spaceport Abu Dhabi. Landeene's arrival, said Whitesides, foresaw the arrival in Abu Dhabi of passengers from New Mexico after a one-hour flight. The appointment, he continued, coincided with the 'move into the final stages of test flights prior to commercial operations at Spaceport America'. Landeene would also arrange attachments for students at Abu Dhabi's Zayed University to work as interns at Virgin Galactic's headquarters in London.

The applause was led by Mohamed Al Husseiny, the chief executive of Aabar Investments, who was sitting in the audience. In his reply, Al Husseiny praised Virgin for choosing Abu Dhabi as the centre of its space industry: 'It will help us realise the dream of Abu Dhabi as the regional hub for space tourists as well as space-based science research and education.' The self-congratulation revealed Al Husseiny as another disciple of Branson's genius. The tycoon had raised $280 million from Al Husseiny in 2009 and a further $200 million after Whitesides' promise of intercontinental travel.

Six days later, Branson arrived at the State Department in Washington to meet another believer. Hillary Clinton, the secretary of state, was hosting a conference on global investment. In her briefing notes, she was told about the help the department had given to Virgin Galactic. The government's restrictions on international space flights using American technology had been relaxed, and the Department for Transportation had also waived many safety regulations to allow Virgin Galactic's development. She was also briefed that take-off was imminent. 'I'm excited he's here,' said Clinton, looking at Branson, 'because many, many, many years ago I wanted to be an astronaut and I think he may be my last chance to live out that particular dream.' NASA, her guests were later told, had rejected Clinton's application because she was a girl. Branson smiled. Clinton's endorsement was, some thought, payback for Branson's collaboration with her husband's environmental campaign. Whatever cynics believed, no one could deny that the Briton was firmly placed at the centre of the American Establishment. However, no one at the State Department's reception was aware of his latest problems in Mojave.

Branson had ended his legal agreement with Burt Rutan during 2011. Despite appearances, Branson had never quite understood the politically incorrect maverick who doubted liberal causes, was sceptical about global warming and accused politicians of exaggerating the economic crisis. Rutan's ill health was given as the reason for his retirement, although another explanation may have been his failure to deliver a successful rocket motor. Branson became the sole owner of The Spaceship Company and contracted Scaled to develop the project. Doug Shane, Rutan's successor at Scaled, acknowledged his predecessor's mistaken optimism: no one had ever built such a big hybrid motor, nor was anyone else interested in overcoming the technical problems. In theory, the motor could be built, but the costs would outweigh any advantage. 'He's trying to jump from the Wright brothers to a DC3,' repeated Andrew Nelson, XCOR's chief operating officer and Branson's competitor. 'No one has ever done that.' Even Rutan acknowledged his own error. Before ending his partnership with Branson, he had started a new venture with Paul Allen, the co-founder of Microsoft, aimed at launching a Falcon 9 rocket into orbit from a 'Stratolaunch', a giant plane powered by six jumbo-jet engines. The Falcon's motor used conventional liquid fuel rather than a mixture of rubber and gas. Branson was stuck with his inheritance. Searching for salvation, he contracted the Sierra Nevada Corporation, independent experts based in California, to save his rocket. His costs were mounting.

Branson denied any embarrassment. Although his predictions were repeatedly wrong, his ego deflected any discomfort. Realistically, he should have been humbled on 21 May 2012, when, without fanfare, Elon Musk launched a SpaceX rocket into orbit with 1,148 lbs of cargo inside a Dragon capsule. After docking with the International Space Station above Australia, and once the cargo had been transferred, the rocket returned to Earth with 1,455 lbs of rubbish. NASA paid Musk less than $50 million for the trip, much less than they had previously been paying the Russians. Five months later, SpaceX delivered 882 lbs of supplies to the space station and returned with 1,673 lbs of damaged equipment and specimens of astronauts' urine and blood for analysis. Musk's $1.6 billion contract from NASA for twelve missions was confirmed.

Unlike Virgin Galactic, SpaceX was approved by the space agency, and this fact, alongside the successful completion of America's first commercial space flights and Musk's announcement that his rocket was being converted to carry seven passengers through space by 2017, should have shaken Branson. But he was not silenced. 'In this field,' Branson said, 'we don't have any competitors. Land-based take-off – they can never compete with us for people going into space. I may be being naive, and there may be somebody doing something very secretive which we don't know about, but my guess is that we are five or six years ahead of any competitor.'

He had held to this line for five years – ever since predicting Virgin Galactic would begin taking passengers into space in 2007 – until, passing through Warsaw in October 2012, he became rather more candid. Appearing before a group of students, he volunteered that he could no longer predict when Virgin's passengers would float in space. He was, he admitted, in the dark. He then resumed his management of expectations.

The following month, he flew to Mojave with his daughter, Holly. For the cameras, he glad-handed many of his 175 employees, featured in a group photograph and ended by signing autographs. But in the executives' offices he wanted answers about the troubled tests. On one occasion, a motor had burst into flames and fire-fighters had refused to quench the fire in the oxidiser tank, an incident which served as a reminder of the difficulties inherent in developing such a motor. Doug Shane's solution was to recruit engineers to build a completely new engine using liquid fuel. Branson replied that he needed something immediately. Shane reassured his boss that the rocket would make a powered flight during 2013. There would be spectacular flights in which Branson would feature as the star amid bursts of publicity. In private, they also agreed to develop an alternative motor powered by conventional fuel.

In his office alongside the Mojave runway, Stu Witt, the airport's chief executive, comforted by all his flying and hunting trophies hanging on the walls, uttered a tart truth: 'Things have not gone as planned for the past nine years.'

16

Slipping

Days after Elon Musk's success, Branson was nibbling a fresh crab sandwich in Vancouver. He was on familiar territory – regaling a journalist with his life story to grab publicity.

His arrival in western Canada in May 2012 followed a familiar pattern. Standing at the door of a Virgin Atlantic aircraft, he lifted a hostess into the air and grinned at the photographers. His routine was not as dramatic as jumping off a hotel roof wearing a tuxedo, but nonetheless he always appeared to enjoy the spotlight.

Watching from the foot of the aircraft steps was Christy Clark, the controversial premier of British Columbia. Although Virgin Atlantic would employ only twenty people at the airport, Clark could not resist the opportunity to stand beside the celebrity. 'You'll find that prices have come down since Virgin Atlantic announced it was coming on this route,' Branson told Clark. 'This is what happens whenever we start new routes.' His certainty silenced any contradiction. 'We've been practising new airline routes on the Africans,' he continued, hinting at the costly disasters of Virgin Nigeria and Virgin Atlantic's abrupt exit from Kenya, which had been blamed on high costs. Virgin's record in Canada was hardly any better. Virgin America and Virgin Megastores had come and gone, bearing huge losses. Virgin Mobile had been revived but was struggling. Even Virgin Atlantic had previously closed its routes to Canada due to their unprofitability. His airline's return, he said, would attract 40,000 passengers from his rivals in the first year. Branson's target was a risk, the ideal magnet for Vancouver's aspiring entrepreneurs, who were each willing to pay $400 to hear his wisdom on becoming rich in a speech for which Branson would receive his standard fee – about $250,000.

There were no empty seats at the Vancouver Convention Centre. One thousand four hundred people were there to seek inspiration from, in the organisers' description, a 'transformational leader in the international business community and someone who has turned incredible challenges into opportunities that have changed people's lives'. Helped by Virgin's publicists, the organisers explained that 'Branson claims to have established eight separate billion-dollar companies and oversees 400 Virgin companies in 30 countries. Across its companies, Virgin employs nearly 50,000 people in more than 30 countries and had global revenues of some $21 billion in 2011.'

The reality did not match the hyperbole. Equating products bearing Virgin's logo with Branson's direct management of Virgin companies was disingenuous. But the exaggerations did not harm his credibility. His audience welcomed the self-styled 'benevolent billionaire' offering a catchy homily: 'A business is simply you coming up with an idea to make a difference in other people's lives.' He also offered something more. The publication of *Screw Business as Usual* had become the platform for his sermon to inspire 'a better world'.

His focus was on entrepreneurs. Businessmen, he told his audience, should no longer chase profits but focus instead on ethical success. 'Doing good is good for business,' he said. Previously, he considered being 'a caring human being' required him to delegate 'good people to run each of Virgin's 300 companies worldwide'. But then he admitted: 'I hadn't even begun to scratch the surface of what was needed to be done to help ensure the survival of the planet. I was also very aware that there was too much poverty in the world. Those of us who have been fortunate enough to acquire wealth must play a role in looking how we use those means to make the world a far better place.' Virgin Unite, he said, would 'confront those global problems such as starvation and inequality'. To prove his commitment, he had visited two charities in the city – a youth centre and a housing group – and donated $51,000. Unite, he wrote in his book, 'doesn't believe in throwing money at problems'.

The audience applauded. His mistaken mention of 'Vancouvians', the misdescription of the 'province' as a 'state' and his reference to Christy Clark's 'Colombian government' were brushed aside by the audience as amusing errors. Nevertheless, over a lunch of shepherd's pie and treacle pudding, some expressed surprise at his poor oratory. The hall had not been energised. No one, however, questioned his sincerity.

'I never saw myself as a business person,' Branson explained to the journalist while he ate his crab sandwich and offered a revised autobiography. 'I just started off in the 1960s as somebody who wanted to create a magazine to help campaign against the Vietnam war. And then the business came along in order to pay the bills for the magazine, and ever since then I have created things often out of frustration. Virgin Atlantic was created because I hated the experience of flying other people's airlines . . . I've never been particularly interested in making money.'

Billionaires do not evolve by indifference to wealth, and Branson was no exception. Virgin Records was not created to pay for Branson's student magazine, because the magazine closed down just as the company was launched. Nor was the magazine created 'out of frustration', but rather from a schoolboy's burning ambition. As he admitted in 1986, when his memory about the history of his record business was more precise, 'People thought that because we were twenty-one or twenty-two and had long hair we were part of some grander ideal. But it was always 99.5 per cent business.' Since then, dozens of trusting people had been 'screwed' by Branson's tough demands for profits from their ideas and their work. Humiliated, they rarely challenged his own rebranding as an evangelist unmotivated by money. His self-portrayal as an altruist, ambitious to 'save the world' from an environmental catastrophe, was applauded. His suggestion that another airline – namely Virgin – might fly between London and Vancouver was, however, a questionable method of improving the atmosphere.

Over the following weeks, Branson energetically repeated his commitment to changing the world. 'Those that continue with "business as usual",' he said soon after his visit to Vancouver, 'and focus solely on profit maximisation, won't be around for long – and won't deserve to be.' Business, he told a newspaper, should consciously set out to 'do good' rather than chase profits. 'One of the most devastating theories of the Seventies was that – no matter what it took – the primary purpose of business was to maximise value for shareholders. This led to a variety of social ills where businesses polluted, discarded employees at the drop of a hat, or created unsustainable short-term gains.' No one dared to question the contradictions. His airlines were pollutants, Virgin ceaselessly sought profits from trains, airlines, health and banking, and the company's employees were dismissed when the profits disappeared. Those events sat uneasily with Branson's promotion of 'doing good'.

One year later, it became clear that Branson's gamble in Vancouver had flopped. Instead of flying 40,000 passengers to Heathrow, Virgin Atlantic carried under 9,000 of the 535,000 passengers in total. To limit his losses, the airline would fly only in the summer and not contract its employees during the winter.

The struggle for his airlines' survival reflected Branson's true values. With his approval, John Borghetti, the newly appointed chief executive of Virgin Blue in Australia, had slashed costs by 40 per cent by firing staff. Under pressure from Qantas, whose market share had recovered, Virgin Blue was unable to pay Branson a dividend and the share price fell towards 35 cents. The same purge was inflicted on Virgin America. Flying fifty-one jets between sixteen cities, the airline was still haemorrhaging around $100 million a year. His prediction of profits and a flotation in 2013 would not be fulfilled. To survive, he squeezed his costs, despite his employees' reaction.

In 2011, Virgin America's flight attendants sought to join the Transport Workers Union. In his submission to represent them, Frank McCann, the union's director, wrote that Virgin's attendants had discovered that 'work rules are inconsistently enforced, promises regarding rest, vacation and benefits are often broken, and discipline for minor violations can be unnecessarily harsh and inconsistently applied'. Branson did not address their complaints. Instead, he appeared in TV commercials urging Virgin America's staff not to join the trade union. Membership, said Branson, would take their 'independent spirit and uniqueness away'. He pleaded, 'Say "no" to the old way of flying and say "no" to the TWU.' In a tight battle, Branson narrowly won the ballot.

Similar disillusionment had arisen among Virgin Atlantic's staff. Branson enjoyed comparing BA's stuffy pilots in their stiff caps with Virgin Atlantic's cool airmen cosseted by glamorous blonde hostesses simpering over pop stars. In the past, Virgin employees had enjoyed sizzling toga parties in tropical locations and boozy parties in foreign hotels, especially if Branson was on board. Their proprietor always stayed in the same hotel as the airline's crews. But those heady days had become a fond memory. Virgin Atlantic was losing money, Branson usually flew on his Falcon and he was invisible at the company's headquarters in Crawley. In interviews, he boasted about delegating power, but his staff questioned his managers' skills and knew that no major decision was taken without his approval. A 2010 poll of Virgin

Atlantic's pilots organised by their union, BALPA, echoed their doubts about Steve Ridgway.

'There's no strategy,' a pilots' representative told Ridgway.

'That's for us to worry about,' Ridgway replied.

'You treat us like fodder,' countered the trade-union leader. 'Your headquarters are overstaffed and your car park is full – and all you've got are thirty-four aircraft. EasyJet's headquarters are smaller and they manage 220 aircraft. You're too small to survive.'

The trade unionist noted that the regulator's decision to award the profitable London to Moscow route to easyJet had humiliated Branson. 'We are very disappointed with the result,' Branson had said, 'which flies in the face of what the consumer wants and our economy demands.' He did not explain why travellers would choose Virgin's £400 return fare from Heathrow and reject easyJet's fares, which started at £125 from Gatwick. 'What can we do to fight that?' Branson asked Ridgway. 'Nothing,' was the answer.

Virgin Atlantic was drifting. Branson's advocacy of ethical business did not reassure his pilots, who feared that the airline might collapse. In that event, they would normally be re-employed by the next airline at the bottom of the pecking order and expect to lose half their income. Their misgivings were magnified by Branson's new mantra of deriding profits. Ryanair's and easyJet's profits were growing, while Virgin Atlantic lost money every year, but instead of dealing with his airline's managerial weakness, Branson remained intent on continuing with his environmental crusade.

Spending a few million had bought him considerable status among the Greens, but his laurels were fading. The Carbon War Room's new staff had not championed a fresh campaign. The Virgin Earth competition had become bogged down, with the suggestions submitted by the eleven finalists deemed to be uncommercial. Branson declared that the competition remained 'open', but Crispin Tickell and others involved at the outset became confused over whether the rules may have been changed to avoid awarding the first $5 million to a 'winner'. That possibility was denied by Branson's spokesman. Environmentalists also questioned how an airline owner could criticise polluters and at the same time pledge that 'Virgin will spend up to £5 billion to finance Heathrow's expansion.' Branson shrugged off the doubters. He believed that everything would be resolved – his airlines' survival, pollution and his fate – once renewable fuel became profitable.

Fuel prices, peak oil and the scarcity of energy had become his preoccupation. 'There will be an energy crisis within a decade,' he repeated. 'Energy, especially oil, is running short.' To prove his resolve, in 2011 Virgin's publicists released photographs of Branson hosting Jimmy Wales, the founder of Wikipedia, and Tony Blair in Necker. There was little surprise that the former prime minister had visited Necker in April 2010; he had holidayed with his wife and their son Leo in the Cliff Lodge suite at Ulusaba, Branson's private game reserve in South Africa. The standard rate for paying guests was £2,480 per person per night. Using his personal relationship with a politician to promote Virgin's financial interests was so natural that Branson's publicists automatically revealed that his discussions with Blair in Necker were about the 'energy crisis, the Carbon War Room and global warming'. United by their commercial relationship with Vinod Khosla, they were exploring options to generate 'green' profits. With his own money invested in 'green' ventures, Branson had good reason to barnstorm across the globe promoting his ideology. His political agenda enhanced his quest for profits.

Speaking to the converted in Manhattan, Branson appealed with unusual passion to the 'Green Generation' for 'a revolution in the way we think about the world and in the way we work together for the common interest. This revolution will reinvent our economic system to ensure sustainability of life on our planet by developing a world of prosperity for all in a low-carbon economy.' The more often his ideological message was repeated, the more reliant he became on Khosla.

Khosla had launched his first investment fund for the renewable-energy industry in 2009. He bullishly claimed that his second fund, started in 2011 and including his company Gevo, was oversubscribed. 'I challenge anybody to claim that clean tech done right is a disaster,' Khosla said. At their peak, each fund was worth over $1 billion.

Financing, Khosla knew, depended on good relations in Washington in order to obtain government grants. Since 1986, Khosla had declared donations of about $440,000 to the Democrats, including to President Obama for supporting alternative fuels. Branson was also helpful. 'I had the profile, the financial resources and the time to do more,' he said about his efforts to help Khosla. Having mastered government regulations to extract subsidies in Britain, he applied his expertise to working with officials and congressmen in Washington. He was knocking at an open door.

Strident members of Congress had given climate change traction on Capitol Hill. Politicians spoke about a '$500 billion green economy' employing over two million people in conservation, pollution control and other green jobs. Banks and businessmen were inventing funds to attract ethical investors in clean energy. Association with the environment had become the topic of big advertising campaigns among those hunting for green profits.

On 21 April 2010, Branson met Gary Locke, the commerce secretary, and Lisa Jackson, the director of the Environmental Protection Agency (EPA). Later that same day, he visited the White House. In both meetings, Branson urged the administration to support renewable fuels. Soon after, Lloyd Ritter of Green Capitol, Gevo's lobbyist, persuaded the US Navy to test Gevo's bio-jet fuel in its planes. The US Air Force followed, buying 11,000 gallons of alcohol-to-jet fuel costing $59 a gallon, compared to conventional aviation fuel at about $3 a gallon. Neither renewable fuel had yet been manufactured. The following year, Obama announced a $510 million purchase of biofuels for aviation. His target matched the Air Force's commitment to use biofuels for half their consumption in 2016. To manufacture the fuel, five million hectares of land would be converted to grow switch grass. Virgin's apparently astute investment was confirmed in the first court battle brought by Butamax against Gevo for allegedly infringing its patent. The judge accepted Gevo's argument that its own expertise was superior to Butamax's. The defeat was dismissed by Butamax as irrelevant because the judge was untrained in patent law and science, and the company appealed to a specialist court.*

Branson was thrilled. His personal relationship with Obama had helped, despite him asking the president during a visit to the White House 'if I could have a spliff, but they didn't have any'. Although Branson was accused by a newspaper columnist of being racist because he would not have asked George W. Bush for cannabis, and was criticised for boasting about the exchange afterwards to journalists, his proximity to Obama reconfirmed the fulfilment of his American ambitions.

Certain of success with biofuels, he next attached his reputation to LanzaTech of New Zealand. The company promised to produce fuel from the recycled carbon gases emitted during the production of steel. 'Recycling at its best,' said Branson. 'One day all planes could operate on this fuel.' Naturally, he predicted success: 'This new technology is scalable, sustainable and can

---

* At the time of writing, the case was still unresolved.

be produced at a cost comparable to conventional jet fuel.' His timetable was precise. A demonstration flight using LanzaTech's fuel was planned with Boeing, said Virgin's publicists, within twelve to eighteen months – during 2013. Virgin Atlantic, said Branson, would use the new fuel to fly from Heathrow to Shanghai and Delhi within two years of that test flight. 'Soon', he said, LanzaTech's process would be delivering fifteen billion gallons of jet fuel every year.

The company's prospects were hampered by a lack of finance. Virgin refused to invest, but Branson introduced Khosla. The venture capitalist bought a 51 per cent stake for an estimated $40 million, and with Khosla's help LanzaTech received a $3 million grant from the US government in 2011. Days later, Dr Jennifer Holmgren, LanzaTech's chief executive, announced in London, with Branson standing beside her, that the company would 'produce fuel for commercial use by 2014'. The publicity around the development of 'green' jet fuel was used by Virgin Green to rescue its second fund, which promoted especially the production of aviation fuel from algae. Emma Harvey, Virgin Atlantic's head of sustainability, told Tim Rice of ActionAid that Branson anticipated good results. The fund collected $220 million, slightly short of its $300 million target, but sufficient to reassure Branson in his conviction that green investments would realise a new fortune. Unmentioned in the splurge of good news was the decision by Virgin Trains and Virgin Atlantic to abandon Branson's plan to use butanol.

Then came more bad news. Ninety per cent of Branson's investment in Cilion, Khosla's first venture, was lost. Even worse, in 2011 Gevo's losses were £31 million on a turnover of £41.7 million. Range Fuels in Georgia, another Khosla venture that produced ethanol from woodchips, became insolvent, despite receiving a $76 million government grant. Local officials were accused of failing to conduct proper due diligence of Khosla's proposals and criticised for overruling those who opposed the grant. The argument escalated after Khosla bought the factory back from the administrator for $5.1 million. By 2012, his energy projects across America had accepted about $600 million of public money, yet none had produced sufficient quantities of renewable fuel. Riding with Khosla was proving to be bumpy.

Virgin Green's other loss-makers included Solyndra, a manufacturer of solar panels. The original attraction in 2008 had been its use of a substitute for silicon, whose price had rocketed. Twelve months later, silicon prices collapsed, and Chinese manufacturers were able to offer superior silicon panels costing $0.85 per watt of electricity compared to Solyndra's panels at $6.29 per watt. Despite President Obama's visit to the factory in May 2010 to promote the investment, Solyndra was declared bankrupt in September 2011. The government lost $535 million and private investors, including Virgin, more than $500 million.

Over the previous forty years, Branson had tilted the risk of investments in his favour. Virgin's Green Fund was the exception. Unusually, he had allowed Khosla to influence his commercial judgement. Travis Bradford, the former deputy director of the Carbon War Room, had become a critic: 'Khosla's in it for the buck and his stories are not impartial. He's not always successful.' Virgin's strategy, Bradford observed, 'is too traditional. It's all done badly. Venture capitalism doesn't work in these areas.' Khosla, meanwhile, was unrepentant about his losses. 'My willingness to fail is what gives me the ability to succeed,' he repeated, echoing Branson's excuse. Failure was paraded as success because genuine success was remaining elusive.

In April 2012, Khosla announced that Gevo's plant in Luverne, Minnesota, had been converted to produce butanol and would start production – ahead of Butamax. Gevo also announced talks with Coca-Cola to manufacture plastic bottles from butanol. Since Coca-Cola sold 1.7 billion drinks a day, Gevo's potential income was enormous. But the glory was short-lived. Five months later, Gevo's engineers abandoned the start of production and closed the Luverne plant, and the director of technology departed. Gevo's share price, reported analysts, was 'in the toilet'. *Bankruptcy Watch*, an investors' tip sheet, recommended, 'Sell Gevo Now'. Contrary to Branson's prediction of profits and glory, the company was burning cash to fight Butamax's legal action. By contrast, Butamax was on course to start producing butanol in America in 2014. Branson's reliance on Khosla had once again proved to be disappointing. By December 2012, Khosla's second investment fund had lost two-thirds of its peak value. 'In the end, success is never assured,' he wrote.

Khosla's prophecy about a scarcity of energy was also wrong. The rate at which new oil reserves were being discovered was rising, while demand for petrol in the States was falling. Fracking had slashed natural-gas prices, and US government subsidies for biofuels were threatened by a drought. Prices of food and crops were rising, and poultry and livestock farmers had become vocal critics of the government's policies. The profits of ethanol producers fell. Friends of the Earth also turned against Branson. 'Most aviation biofuels', their study asserted, 'contribute more to climate change than conventional jet fuel. Biofuels are causing land grabs, increased food prices, deforestation, biodiversity loss and human rights abuses . . . Biofuels are a false solution.' The aviation biofuels most condemned were those manufactured from palm oil and algae, both championed by Branson. Huge forests in Indonesia were being burned so that the land could be used for growing palms; paradoxically, in *Screw Business as Usual* Branson lamented the destruction of the Amazon rainforest and urged, 'This must be discouraged.' He hated admitting mistakes. He had relied on assurances that biofuels would be developed rapidly, but apparently had not understood the science or the costs.

'The numbers are not turning,' Branson was told about his green investments in 2012. 'There are no profits. Emissions are coming down because of the recession, not because of environmentalists.' Branson had invested his own money and lost, but he did not retreat from a movement which provided invitations to shine. In 2011, Bulova named him a 'brand ambassador' for its Accutron watch, with the citation: 'an entrepreneur, humanitarian and pioneer who reflects the spirit of innovation'. Recognition secured continuing membership of an elite club. Mixing with the world's power brokers, Branson was presented as a global star whose presence at any conference was valuable, albeit expensive.

Roberto Vámos, the Brazilian organiser of the Global Sustainability Forum, was one of many inviting Branson to speak about the environment. In May 2011, the forum was holding its second conference at the Hotel Tropical in Manaus, near Brazil's Amazon jungle, and Vámos invited Branson to join other star guests, including Bill Clinton, James Cameron and Arnold Schwarzenegger. Over 700 of Brazil's leading businessmen, politicians and power brokers had paid a notional $15,000 per person to hear Branson explain how business could profit by improving the environment. Vámos agreed the standard $250,000 fee for Branson's speech, which was entitled 'Entrepreneurial Strategies for Decarbonising the Economy'.

Branson arrived on his private jet, as seminars about reducing the consumption of materials, managing waste and using local food were under way. He followed Clinton and Schwarzenegger on to the same stage. Both had been rewarded with standing ovations for their excellent speeches, but as Vámos watched Branson approach the podium he became perplexed. Branson was not carrying any notes and, to Vámos's surprise, announced that he would not make a speech. 'I'll take questions,' he told his bewildered audience. Vámos was furious. 'Branson was a disappointment,' he said. 'He was vague and general and poor. He was not worth the large fee I paid him.' After muted applause, Branson headed back to the airport, refusing to stay for a ceremony in which the hall's lights would be turned off for one hour to draw attention to global warming. Feeling bruised by Branson's conduct was not unusual but, like others before him, Vámos did not protest because it reflected badly upon himself.

Branson had no difficulty receiving similarly large fees to address other conferences. He spoke around the world about his campaigns to save the cod and the tiger and about his recent venture with Bo Derek to protect polar bears – 'which could be extinct within thirty years' – in northern Ontario. He spoke about Virgin Atlantic's commitment to using renewable fuels in 'the near future' and about Virgin Oceanic's programme to protect the sea. He predicted Virgin Oceanic was certain to overtake and then beat James Cameron down to the Mariana Trench. 'We're not far behind,' Branson had told journalists, ignoring Chris Welsh's warning that 'We're years away from making the trip.' When Cameron finally won the race, Branson was as optimistic as ever and announced that he would dive to the Puerto Rico Trench, 30,000 feet under the Atlantic, 'this year' – meaning 2012. One year after his deadline, and with Virgin's continued support, Welsh was still waiting for the submarine's dome to be built so that he could start tests before heading for the seabed.

Those mistaken predictions and disappointing speeches never dented Branson's popularity. His celebrity erased any criticism, his magnetism corrected any deviation from his continuing upwards trajectory, and crowds waited to catch a glimpse of an icon. At a party in a Jamaican restaurant in New York, the guests – including Ben Cohen of Ben & Jerry's – waited one and a half hours for the star's arrival and voiced no irritation about his brief appearance before he flew back to Necker. Regardless of his empire's lacklustre financial performance, his popularity reinforced his sense of uniqueness, confirmed by his life on Necker and his accumulation of other sanctuaries across the globe.

In 2003, he had bought Makepeace, a twenty-five-acre island off Australia's eastern coast, for a reported A$5 million with Virgin Blue founder Brett Godfrey. First, he said it was for Virgin's staff; then, later, for eco-tourism. Eventually, it was advertised for hire at $8,000 a night. Next, he bought Mosquito Island, near Necker, in order to develop it immediately as 'a showcase for sustainability and eco-living'. Instead, Mosquito remained 'very much in the planning and development stages', as it was described by the Virgin Elite resort group. Then, he bought the Panchoran Retreat in Nyuh Kuning, Bali. Also known as the Linda Garland Estate, it comprised seven villas and a swimming pool over twenty-five acres. To add to the collection, he was 'delighted to announce' that he would be protecting one million wildebeest in Kenya by constructing Mahali Mzuri, 'a new safari camp that will help to protect the Great Migration'. Branson wrote that the Kenyan Tourism Federation had asked him to buy the land to prevent local farmers building fences for their cattle, which harmed the wildebeest. The farmers, said Branson, would be employed to work at Mahali Mzuri for higher rates: 'My solution is a win–win for everybody.' Not all the local Kenyans shared his enthusiasm. The farmers were nomads who, unlike Branson, would be unable to obtain a licence to build on a migration route through a protected national reserve.

In-between, he also bought the lease to a sprawling 491-acre estate in Peapack-Gladstone, New Jersey. Previously owned by King Hassan of Morocco, Natirar is a surreal mansion located on a steep hill that has been described as an 'epicurean oasis'. Together with Bob Wojtowicz, a local property developer, he opened a club which would offer guests a restaurant, a cooking school, a wine school, a spa and a farm. Membership cost

$37,500 and the annual fees were $4,800. In 2010, the hotel hosted a charity masked ball for the Susan G. Komen for the Cure Foundation. Branson was billed as the star attraction. On the evening, the hotel's rooms were almost empty and Branson was reported to be in Necker hosting a pre-Halloween party for a group of models. Three years later, the development was still uncompleted and Virgin was no longer associated with the project.

On the surface, the random collection of properties reflected a billionaire's eccentricity. Others interpreted the well-placed locations as a legitimate strategy to protect Branson from any government asserting that he was a resident liable to local taxes, even in the Virgin Islands. With a private plane to connect him to a string of remote locations, even a sophisticated tax inspector would find it difficult to ascertain the duration of his stay in any one residence. Legally avoiding corporation tax, capital-gains tax and income tax had become a preoccupation ever since he had been caught evading purchase taxes in 1971. He also avoided commenting about his status. Forty years later, as public anger over Amazon's and Google's tax-avoidance schemes rose, he expressed a benign opinion: 'If companies are trading in the UK, they definitely should be paying UK income tax. If they're trading overseas, then they'd be foolish to pay UK income tax. People should just play within the rules that are set up.' Ever since he had been arrested for his purchase-tax fraud, Branson played within the rules. His achievement was to deflect scrutiny while posing as the good citizen.

A gravy train of guests – mostly plucked from the music, media and art worlds – were regularly invited to Necker to reinforce his image. After enjoying a week's glorious holiday with twenty other guests in an idyllic playground, all of them returned to their homes to regale friends about Branson's generosity. All mentioned the fun, but the astute noted the distance their host maintained. Those attempting to forge a closer relationship were gently rebuffed, with Branson diverting any attempt to probe with, 'Right, let's see who can swim fastest around the island,' and other challenges. Most returned to London or Los Angeles flattered. A minority were bemused. Few were any wiser about the man behind the mask. They were aware, though, of his burning desire to secure political influence.

Having reached the age of sixty, Branson had become irritated with young politicians. While enjoying life in a succession of paradises, he doubted the politicians' ability to cure the world's economic crisis. He had particular disdain for David Cameron, criticising the prime minister, sixteen years younger than himself, for his abilities, not least in solving the plight of unemployed youth. Businessmen, he believed, were better placed to mentor the young, and finding platforms where he could advocate his solution was not difficult.

Two weeks after regaling his audience in Vancouver, Branson briefly visited London's East End. Dressed in a blouson leather jacket and jeans, sporting his Necker suntan and with grey streaks lining his fading blond hair, he delivered a philanthropist's solution to youth unemployment. 'This situation', he told his audience pointedly, 'cannot just be left to politicians and social workers.' Rather, it fell upon himself and other billionaires to bear the burden. 'With great wealth and power comes great responsibility,' he said. 'We want to encourage entrepreneurs worldwide to unite together to use our entrepreneurial skills to tackle some of the world's biggest problems.' Although he could not match Bill Gates's pledges to give away 95 per cent of his wealth to charity – and Gates had already given £17 billion – Branson did offer half his fortune, without quantifying the amount, and also offered his celebrity for the cause. That was too valuable to ignore.

In Britain, aspiring entrepreneurs still eagerly sought his endorsement. His support for StartUp Britain, a new campaign to 'celebrate, inspire and accelerate enterprise in Britain', thrilled the organisers. 'Our businesses need to be innovative, maintain a certain quality, be value for money and have a sense of fun,' he wrote. He described the importance of perseverance, overcoming early adversity and recruiting staff who 'you like, trust and who work hard'. At the Global Entrepreneurship Congress held in Liverpool, he advised young people to use student loans to set up businesses rather than going to university. In the midst of the recession, he urged the Conservative-led government to cut taxes, subsidise job sharing and educate schoolchildren in business studies. His advice mirrored his support for teaching aspiring businessmen at the Centre of Entrepreneurship in the Caribbean, although he was contradicting his earlier discourse: 'You can't teach people to be entrepreneurs except to learn from your mistakes.'

While Branson set himself up as an example of the perfect tycoon, there were some in London who were discovering the downside of his philosophy. A campaign had erupted on the internet criticising Virgin for its treatment of contractors who had supplied Virgin Vie, the clothing company; and Crispin Thomas, the creator of the Gadget Helpline, was perplexed by Virgin's bid to launch Virgin Digital, a similar service. 'We've taken our millionth call,' said Thomas, fearing Virgin might successfully copy his idea. Branson was also selling a majority of his shares in the chain of Virgin Active fitness clubs, the last of his big enterprises which he completely owned.

After the financial crash, Branson admitted, 'We were in survival mode.' To raise cash, Virgin tried to sell its fitness clubs in South Africa, Europe and Britain. But with too many rivals in a saturated market, Virgin Active's value had slumped and the planned flotation, which aimed to 'net over £1 billion', was cancelled. Instead, Matthew Bucknall, the co-founder, borrowed to buy indebted rivals and in 2010 tried again to sell the expanded chain of 254 clubs with 1.1 million members in five countries for £1 billion, including the debts. That plan was also abandoned. Finally, a 51 per cent stake was sold in 2011 to CVC Capital Partners, a London private-equity firm, for £450 million ($707 million). Branson was cashing in to fund his loss-making ventures, especially Virgin Atlantic and Virgin Galactic.

Commercially, he had reached a crossroads. He no longer owned any major business in its entirety. All were either jointly owned or merely branded offshoots. His reputation was intact – and still a lure for aspiring entrepreneurs. And yet, during over forty years of business, there had been many casualties in his quest for profits. To some of them, *Screw Business as Usual* might have appeared like an apology. After all, in his own words, he recognised the flaws of his conduct during the 1970s and later. So it was natural that a small group of decent professionals, attracted in 2012 to a new project financed by Virgin, should have allowed their instinctive concerns to be assuaged by promises made on Branson's behalf. For Branson, the small venture was inconsequential, but those who trusted Virgin were unprepared for the blowback of the company's terms of business. Whatever he wrote, Branson could not break the habit of a lifetime's profiteering. The Virgin model could crucify the unwary.

17

The Project

Branson's parties at his Oxfordshire farm were fun. He was a generous host and his enthusiasm was infectious. In 2010, he had, as usual, invited the winners of the *Sunday Times*' annual 'Fast Track' business competition to his home. The coveted prize for the aspiring entrepreneurs was an opportunity to meet the idol.

Among the guests was Sean King, the chief executive of Seven Squared, a digital-publishing group producing advertisements and content for retailers' magazines, including Waitrose and, later, Sainsbury's. Ranking thirty-seventh on the *Sunday Times* list, Seven had once successfully pitched to supply Virgin Atlantic's in-flight magazine, but the airline's losses had terminated the deal. The disappointment did not prevent Giovanni Donaldson, Virgin's development director, from approaching King at the party. Just as Alex Tai had introduced Branson to Formula One, Donaldson was an outrider competing for Branson's attention. Donaldson knew about Branson's irritation at having missed out on the internet revolution and his hankering to become a media mogul by owning a TV station or a Hollywood studio. Recently, Branson had created Virgin Produced to co-produce two films a year with Rogue Pictures in Los Angeles. 'The Rogue and Virgin brands seem an obvious fit for each other,' Branson had said. *Movie 43*, their first film, starring Kate Winslet, would be described as 'unremittingly awful', 'barrel-scraping sleaze' and 'the worst film ever'. There was a solution, Donaldson believed, and King was an ideal partner.

Apple had unveiled the revolutionary iPad in March, and Donaldson wanted to publish the first global magazine for the creative community as an app on the tablet computer. 'It'll be new and exciting,' he told King. 'It's where the new media is heading.' Virgin Galactic would be first in space, said Donaldson, and Virgin would publish the first iPad magazine.

Days after the party, Donaldson visited King with an offer. If Seven could assemble an editorial team and launch *The Project*, as he called it, their iPad magazine would be 'the start of a new era'. Ownership would be shared between Virgin and Seven. Virgin would invest £300,000 in cash, while Seven would invest more by employing the staff and paying for the production. The difference, Donaldson explained, was accounted for by Virgin's contribution of its brand.

Seven was not a risk-prone publisher, but Donaldson's proposition made the directors feel especially chosen. In common with most guests at the Oxfordshire party, they regarded Branson with awe. Donaldson's repeated mention of 'Richard thinks . . .' and his encouragement of Seven's participation in other Virgin ventures suppressed their doubts. The clincher was Donaldson's prediction that the magazine would attract advertisements from many of Virgin's 300 companies and be purchased by millions of its customers. To be certain, Seven's executives read Branson's book. 'I always wanted Virgin to be a strong model of social entrepreneurship,' he wrote. 'All my businesses have always focused on giving everyone a "fair go".' In print and in person Branson spoke with an honest-sounding voice and, with that testament, the directors clung to the magic. They decided to take the risk.

'We'd like to get Holly on board,' added Donaldson. 'It would be good to get her involved.' The directors of Seven did not object: Holly's participation would bring them closer to Branson. In Virgin's headquarters, Donaldson had spoken about 'giving

Holly an ambassadorial role, possibly as the publisher'. Her involvement, he hoped, would secure the support of her father, who would surely be enticed even further by Rupert Murdoch's announcement of *The Daily*, an iPad newspaper to be published in collaboration with Apple. Revenge for his fate over the ITV bid tilted the odds, and Branson approved Donaldson's proposal.

Anthony Noguera, an acclaimed former editor of *Zoo*, *FHM* and *Arena*, was appointed as the editor. His brief was to 'do something new and exciting in the digital space', focusing on entertainment, culture, design and travel. Since the iPad was not yet on sale in shops, no one was quite certain about the technology for a magazine's format. Donaldson's instruction to 'white-label something' hardly helped. Nevertheless, in May Donaldson approved Noguera's dummy of *Maverick*, the agreed name, and authorised the employment of twelve staff with an initial budget of about £500,000. Normally, a new glossy magazine targeting a large readership recruited around thirty editorial staff and would be given a launch budget of £5 million. *Maverick*'s limited funds restricted the advertising department to just one man, Charlie Parker, who was employed by Seven. Highly rated in the industry, Parker would usually have led a team of five salesman for a start-up. But since the budget was small and Parker expected Virgin's companies to advertise, no one complained. In anticipation of *Maverick*'s launch before Christmas, potential advertisers were introduced by Parker to a tablet offering unprecedented technology which allowed the publication of 'a monthly magazine that will change daily, hourly – minute by minute at all times'. *Maverick* would be promoted on Apple's app store as 'truly revolutionary' and sold at £1.79 an issue.

In August 2011, Donaldson summoned a meeting at the School House in Hammersmith to view Noguera's latest dummy. Even Apple's representative was excited by the links to the web, producing novel high-tech 3D content juxtaposing words, pictures and video clips with pop-up audio surprises. But Donaldson's excitement was tempered by disappointing news: Virgin's lawyers had discovered a music magazine called *Maverick*. The title had to be jettisoned and, bereft of other ideas, they reverted to *The Project*. Another dampener was Gordon McCallum's lack of enthusiasm. The chief executive was renowned for his grinding scrutiny of every business's financial viability, but he eventually approved *The Project* on Donaldson's assurance that Virgin's investment would, as usual, be minimal. With Richard and Holly Branson's support, Donaldson could brush McCallum's pessimism aside, disguising from the visiting journalists the fact that within Virgin he was a small fish swimming alone.

Any final misgivings during the meeting were suffocated by the euphoric tone of Catherine Salway, Virgin's marketing director. Salway spoke in 'super-positive words' about the 'amazing things that will happen' to promote, finance and sell *The Project*. As part of the Virgin family, she said, the magazine could expect 'a flood of advertisements'. Virgin took care of its partners. Like Donaldson, she ignored the industry's expectation of magazines being loss-makers during the first three years. Instead, to satisfy Branson's criteria, she forecast instant break even.

Light-headed, the editorial team left the building, exchanging smiles and high fives. But as they walked through Hammersmith, a Virgin employee unexpectedly appeared. 'None of those things will happen,' he whispered. 'It's all a lot of hot air.' None of the team believed his gloomy warning.

The honeymoon was brief. Eight weeks later, the initial budget had been spent and neither Virgin nor Seven was prepared to invest more money. Suddenly, *The Project* seemed likely to die. The lifebelt was thrown by Noguera. Committed irrevocably to the vision, he bought a stake in the company for about £30,000. Donaldson was thrilled: he needed a success to disprove McCallum's scepticism. The electronic magazine, featuring a video of the actor Jeff Bridges on the 'front cover', was launched on 30 November 2010 in New York.

In Branson's life, every minute was carefully programmed. His time was too valuable to waste. To those producing *The Project*, Branson was akin to the Pope, the figurehead of a vast, rich organisation. Until the launch, he had remained the invisible power. As the big day approached, they realised that the venture was of little importance to Virgin. The company's management was focused on the new bid for Northern Rock. Nevertheless, Branson's schedulers allotted four hours for him to personally promote the magazine across Manhattan. In their timetabled programme, Branson would meet journalists at a launch party and then perform colourful stunts to attract free publicity.

'Richard's on his way from Switzerland,' a Virgin publicist confided. 'He's been speaking to Kofi Annan, one of the Elders.' The image of Branson bidding goodbye to an international statesman and flying in his private jet to New York made one journalist swoon: '*The Project* is only a small part of his amazing life but he's coming.' He clutched the alluring profile provided by the publicist, which described Branson as the man who 'wants to revolutionize the consumer airline industry on multiple continents, take tourists into space and save the planet'. Branson's arrival with Holly was 'low key', one guest would say. Holly's presence, the editorial team agreed, aroused curiosity. They were meeting their publisher for the second time.

One hundred journalists and freeloaders turned up at the breakfast party at the Crosby Street Hotel to meet Branson and hear his comments about Murdoch's *The Daily* – also on the eve of its launch. The clash excited a frisson of interest among those enjoying the food, which had been provided, as usual, by sponsors in exchange for free publicity. Branson, the journalists knew, could never resist poking a Goliath with hype. 'I've read quite a bit in the last few days about a battle I've launched with a certain newspaperman,' said Branson to the crowded room. 'This is not a battle, it's not a war, it's the future of publishing.' Having secured his audience's attention, he continued, 'This was Holly's idea. She showed me the amazing, innovative editorial and advertising in *The Project* and then I got to know how groundbreaking digital publishing can be. To be frank, it blew me away. It's the future of publishing.' Branson looked at his daughter.

'It looks really cool,' Holly agreed. She was not heard to say anything more about the magazine. Ever.

Before arriving, Branson had been briefed on the facts. As he worked the room with encouraging words, he knew the answer to the question, 'How many downloads have had you so far?' But the second question – 'What's your capacity for downloads?', referring to the speed of the downloads and how many the site could handle – left him speechless. 'An awkward moment,' thought a Virgin aide. More troubling was his admission that 'If bloggers don't like it, we'll be dead very quickly.'

Despite the rain and cold, next he climbed into a dilapidated van. While driving uptown, he changed into a suit made of newspapers and pulled a mask over his face. At that moment, no one could doubt his commitment. At pre-selected spots – starting with Apple's flagship store – Branson sprang out of the back doors like a man possessed to surprise pedestrians who were invited to meet a celebrity. The waiting photographers recorded his pose beside a newsprint-covered mannequin. In Virgin-speak, the cheap promotion was part of their 'guerrilla' tactics.

Exactly four hours after arriving at the hotel, Branson bid everyone goodbye. He briefly reappeared in the evening at a reception for 300 people, but was not introduced to Charlie Parker and his guests from BMW and other big potential advertisers. Branson left, unaware of Parker's concern. 'It's a great opportunity,' Parker confessed to his employer, 'but Virgin's expectation of what it can earn without proper investment is ridiculous.' On the basis of the circulation which Virgin had predicted, Parker had obtained for the first issue the high rates the company demanded for advertisements, from BMW, Panasonic, Ford and Kronenbourg. Virgin's reputation, Parker acknowledged, had won the advertisers' trust.

Over the following days, Donaldson and King congratulated each other on the positive coverage for the first issue. Apple ranked *The Project* among the best apps. The absence of similar ones convinced Donaldson that the thousands buying iPads would automatically subscribe to the magazine, and he spoke optimistically about Virgin leading the revolution. At the company's headquarters, he was collating the real-time financial results. Gradually, his optimism faded. For a start, Catherine Salway had sold hardly any advertising, and Virgin's companies had declined to co-operate. Launching a magazine without a marketing budget was folly and, to Donaldson's surprise, Virgin's customers had not yet started to buy iPads. Contrary to the popular image that Virgin was for the hip and young, many of its customers were in fact quite old. Finally, Donaldson's requests to Apple to promote the magazine were ignored. Apple, he discovered, refused to create an accessible point-to-buy app to encourage sales. The corporation's enthusiasm for *The Project* had vanished after discovering that Virgin was unwilling to invest in the magazine or the marketing. Worst of all, no one had realised that most potential subscribers lacked the cable or wireless capacity to download the magazine's big file. At best, downloads took ten minutes, but repeated glitches disrupted the transfer. Donaldson's discomfort grew after Salway declared, two weeks after the launch, 'People think Holly shouldn't take any role and stay out of it.' Donaldson feared that his career was at stake, and instead of bracing himself to improve the magazine plunged into protecting his position. The editorial staff watched a confident executive metamorphose into a bit player uneasy in the spotlight. 'We've got to protect Virgin's reputation,' was his coded expression of fear.

'We need more money,' Basil Hassan, a Virgin accountant placed into the magazine's editorial office, regularly told Charlie Parker. 'How much are you getting? The sales aren't good enough.' The advertising executive was in a dilemma. Virgin wanted instant income from its paltry investment, but the advertisers wanted the first sales figures before making a further commitment. Since the circulation of the first edition was much lower than predicted, Parker could not sell new advertising. 'We need more money before we can invest,' Hassan told him. Without investing in marketing, replied Parker, the circulation would remain low and the advertisers would not commit. 'And Virgin wants too much for ads,' he exclaimed. Their disagreements became vicious, but *The Project* needed £1 million to survive.

'We want to carry on, but there's no more money from Virgin,' said Donaldson in the second month of the magazine's existence. In its own bid for survival, Virgin was not only refusing to invest more money but was issuing invoices to *The Project* for its management costs. Sean King was surprised that Virgin's financial support was less than expected. 'It's been sweat, blood and tears,' he told Noguera, 'and we've got to get out.' Seven was proud of its product but could not afford to spend more money.

Donaldson found a buyer for Seven's shares. Over a cup of coffee in Kingsway in April 2011, he introduced himself to Francis Malone, an aspiring publisher from Waterford in Ireland who would describe himself as 'one man and a dog'. With his brother Martin, Malone was the owner of Other Edition, a registered company selling *Interview*, an American magazine app which was also available on Apple's iPads.

'*The Project* is fantastic,' Donaldson told Malone. 'Apple are using it as a showcase. But we now need a new partner.' Donaldson proposed that the Malones buy Seven's shares. 'You can use the Virgin name to sell both apps,' he said, 'and with Virgin's help you'll be getting free publicity.'

Francis Malone had no money and little experience but, as he told his brother, 'It's not every day that Virgin calls me up and says, "We think you can help us."' Martin, a City trader, agreed to fund his brother's venture. The buy-in price, Donaldson said, was £500,000, plus 11 per cent of the gross revenue as a royalty for using the Virgin brand – plus a further £500,000 to cover Virgin's historic investment. To prove their interest, Martin Malone paid Virgin an unrecoverable deposit of £54,000.

'Have you checked out the Malones?' Donaldson was asked by Seven's executives and journalists.

'Yes,' he replied reassuringly. 'We've done the due diligence. They are OK.'

With Donaldson's encouragement, Seven transferred its shares to Virgin Digital Publishing, and Virgin's lawyers issued a 142-page agreement to the Malones. The brothers imagined the legal process would take two weeks and the fees would be £20,000. Instead, two months later their lawyers would charge over £100,000 and then complain that they were not paid. After the contracts were signed, Virgin and the Malones became partners in that company and in Virgin Interactive Publishing.

Convinced by Donaldson's assurances, Seven lent the Malones their Apple Macintosh computers worth about £50,000, and Noguera and his small team of journalists moved into the Malones' rented office in Park Lane. Charlie Parker refused to follow. 'I don't trust Francis Malone as far as I can throw him,' he said. 'And all Virgin wants is more money, more money, but they've got no interest in people.'

Unknown to the journalists and Seven, the relationship between

Virgin and the Malones had already fractured. Without Parker, the Malones could not sell advertising and thereafter pay Virgin.

'You sold us a pig,' Martin Malone told Donaldson. 'Virgin Digital Publishing is just a shell company. It hasn't got a single employee.'

'Francis knew what he was buying,' replied Donaldson.

'All you want is money,' Francis Malone spluttered. 'We're a backyard company without any money.' Malone felt sorry for himself and posed as the innocent wide-eyed country boy. 'We're poor Irish people,' he said. 'I believed Virgin would boost our credibility. Instead, everything was on their terms. They thought we should feel grateful. I got caught up in it.'

The journalists were unaware of the rupture. Their last salaries had been paid two months earlier but, trusting Donaldson's assurances – reinforced by the Malones' promises – they continued to produce the magazine. New editions were published as an Apple app, subscriptions were sold and revenue from advertising originally sold by Parker was banked, including $100,000 from BMW. Although Basil Hassan drew his salary and Virgin was paid its fees, the editorial team went unpaid. Over the following weeks, Francis Malone was repeatedly asked by the journalists for their salaries. 'The money's on the way,' he would reply. Trusting the Malones and Virgin, Noguera mortgaged his home to pay his staff. Neither Donaldson nor the Malones objected. His fears were placated by an assumption that 'Virgin will look after us.' After all, Hassan, an accountant, had been placed in the office by the company. 'I saw money was coming in,' Hassan said later, 'and Virgin did receive money from the Malones.' But he failed to persuade Virgin or the Malones to pay the journalists.

On the internet, complaints began appearing about the magazine. 'A complete rip-off,' wrote one subscriber. 'Not worth it,' agreed another after receiving only two issues for one year's subscription. 'You guys suck,' wrote a disgruntled blogger. 'How do we get our subscription money back?'

By November 2011, the editorial team was owed about £200,000. Donaldson insisted that under their agreement, the Malones were obliged to pay. The brothers made more excuses.

'You got us into this,' one of the writers told Donaldson.

'How do you think I feel?' Donaldson replied. 'I could lose my job over this.'

'Virgin don't give a shit about us,' shouted the writer. 'All you're interested is your own job and Virgin's reputation.'

'I just can't get into McCallum's head space,' retorted Donaldson. 'He's buying a bank for £700 million and this doesn't really matter.'

The journalist became particularly incensed by the simultaneous publication in the media of photographs showing Branson with his arms around a young businessman. 'What a bastard,' said one editor. 'Branson posing as the champion of young entrepreneurs.'

Re-reading Branson's philosophy about the new age of capitalism was revealing. 'The Age of People', he wrote, 'is all about shifting the focus to how businesses can and must deliver benefits to people and the planet – as well as shareholders.' Branson, the journalist thought, was playing with the emotions and ambitions of his awestruck believers. The journalist became doubly angry after reading a news post by Virgin's publicists stating that *The Project* had been nominated as Apple's 'App of the Year'. In the midst of its self-congratulation, Virgin ignored the unpaid editorial team. The reporter's anger was aggravated by Donaldson's lack of remorse. 'You said the Malones were reliable,' said the writer, who recalled one passage in particular from Branson's *Screw Business*: 'It is becoming more and more clear that there is no incompatibility between doing business in an ethical and transparent manner and achieving good financial results. This is the "false dilemma" which needs to be eliminated from business talk.'

Donaldson headed for the black-tie party at a hotel in Victoria, where the Malone brothers had booked a table to celebrate the nomination of *The Project* as 'App of the Year'. At the climax of an argument, he was ordered by the Malones to 'piss off'. He obeyed. Shortly after, *The Project* team walked out of their offices. They agreed to return only after they were paid. On their computers was sufficient material for three more issues.

The Malones relocated to London's East End to continue publishing the magazine but did not pay the journalists or Seven for the computers. When they failed to pay the rent, the landlord seized the Apple Macs. The crisis alarmed Donaldson's superiors. Virgin's reputation was threatened by Sean King's decision to take legal action in a bid to recover Seven's money. 'Like Anthony [Noguera],' King emailed Donaldson on 27 November, 'we had concerns with the Malones but were given comfort by Virgin's involvement. These guys have a plan and it seems like that it involves not paying us.'

In February 2012, Seven petitioned the High Court to recover its money. At a hearing in March, the Malones did not appear in court. On King's second petition, Virgin Digital Publishing was struck off the register at Companies House. Just before the next hearing on 23 July to wind up Virgin Interactive Publishing, Virgin changed the name to Project Interactive Publishing to avoid further damage to the Virgin brand. King's legal victories were pyrrhic. The Malones had no money, and Virgin was legally protected from any complaint.

'We've done the best we can,' said Branson.

'He knows he fails at some things, but at least he tries,' said his publicist.

The casualties at Seven and *The Project* won no plaudits and lost money. One journalist and his wife lost their life's savings, while others were unemployed for many months. But like most of Branson's injured partners and employees over the previous forty years, they remained silent. No one, they knew, had ever benefited by publicly complaining about Branson.

There was a piquancy in the sad saga. Several of those who had lost money had read one of Branson's homilies: 'Too many business leaders', he wrote in his book, 'are too quick to jump down people's throats, or rule by fear, which is foolish. You should lead by praise – you can't launch an idea if no one likes you.'

Virgin's values could be so confusing.

18

The Last Jewel

'Traders appear to think Virgin Media shares will sink,' reported the *Wall Street Journal* in September 2010. The gloomy speculation reflected the network's pre-tax losses, which had risen in the first half of the year from £186 million to £249 million. Buffeted by the recession, many customers were not renewing their contracts for a package of broadband, TV and telephone. Even Virgin Mobile was losing money because rates were subsidised to maintain a respectable number of subscribers.

Although Branson owned only 3 per cent of Virgin Media, his profile as a global player was enhanced by the public's perception of him having a considerably bigger shareholding. But like all his businesses, his options were declining. After a decade, Virgin Media had run its course. Branson had earned over £1 billion by backing a brilliant proposal, but the business was too short of money and too small to flourish independently. Ever since Virgin's defeat in the content war and his failed attempt to buy ITV, Virgin Media had been too feeble to rival Sky. The solution adopted by Neil Berkett, the company's chief executive, copied Branson's tried and tested strategy. Whenever his businesses were threatened, first, he sought protection from the government's regulators; next, he abused his competitors; finally, when all else failed, he looked for an exit.

Virgin Media needed TV programmes, especially sport. Sky's high charges for transmitting the Premier League and other events aggravated Virgin's losses, so in 2010 Virgin asked the OFT to order Sky to cut the price for showing the crown jewels of its output. Despite Sky's resistance to an uncommercial proposal, the OFT ordered the company to reduce its charges to Virgin by 23 per cent. The victory allowed Virgin to announce bargain prices. Sky's Premier League matches could be seen on Virgin for £15 per month, compared to Sky's price of £36 per month. Similarly, the rate charged by Virgin to watch Sky's cricket matches was slashed by a third. Sky appealed and won on the grounds that the OFT had 'misinterpreted' the evidence. 'This is simply not credible,' protested Virgin, once again outclassed by Rupert Murdoch. Berkett was resigned to the uneasy duopoly: Virgin had 4.2 million customers against Sky's 10.6 million.

In 2012, his company's fate was shaken. In a bidding war, BT bought the rights to thirty-eight live Premier League games and four seasons of rugby for £890 million. Overnight, Virgin was squeezed. Sky was available to every British home through its dishes, and BT's telephone network was universal, but Virgin's cable network was limited. Digging up roads to lay more cables risked bankruptcy. Faced with aggressive competitors, Virgin's share of the broadband market looked certain to decline unless it could repair a credibility gap.

The company's strength was the brand. For those who disliked BT and Sky, Virgin was an attractive alternative. With about a fifth of the market, Virgin could survive, but servicing the company's debt, now reduced to £5.7 billion, excluded any chance of serious profits for some time.

Speed was Virgin's virtue. Virgin promised faster broadband than Sky, and greater capacity and speed than BT's copper telephone wires or its replacement fibre optics. 'We will always be a leader in this space,' said Berkett, 'not by a neck but by a furlong.' In the near future, he said, Virgin would offer 100 MB broadband services, compared to BT's usual limit of 5 MB. Success depended on persuading the public of Virgin's superiority. Despite his reservations that Branson was 'overexposed within the Virgin group', Berkett recruited the master to present the advertising campaign 'Stop the Con'. The script was pure Bransonian: Virgin's rivals were accused of orchestrating 'the broadband con' by advertising exaggerated broadband speeds of up to 24 MB but delivering at best only 6.5 MB. Virgin, from Branson's mouth, was portrayed as saintly.

His presentation lacked resonance. In 2011, Ofcom reported that 22 per cent of Virgin Media's customers were dissatisfied and that Virgin trailed Sky and other rivals in all services, including broadband. One year later, the Advertising Standards Authority (ASA) criticised Virgin's claim to provide 'the UK's fastest broadband'. Comparisons by independent surveys showed that Virgin's 'Stop the Con' advertisements were misleading, and they were banned by the ASA. Weeks later, the ASA again criticised Virgin Media's targeting of households in particular streets to buy 'instant' connections. The streets, the ASA reported, were not linked to Virgin Media's network. Next, Virgin was criticised for misleading new subscribers by failing to mention the compulsory cost for a landline. The ASA also banned an advertisement to promote Virgin's Tivo recorder which featured David Tennant posing as Dr Who. 'Say bye-bye to buffering and hello to a superfast broadband,' was Virgin's slogan, which was judged by the ASA to be a misleading exaggeration. The BBC's complaint against Virgin's suggestion that the corporation endorsed Tivo was upheld, as was the accusation that Virgin had infringed the BBC's intellectual-property rights.

To escape the opprobrium, Berkett approved a new £53 million advertising campaign during the London Olympics. This was to feature Usain Bolt, the world's fastest runner. Fitted with a beard to impersonate Branson, the Olympic gold medallist promised TV viewers that 'Richard Branson is doubling your broadband speed.' In the next shot, Branson appeared alongside Bolt to confirm that all Virgin's speeds would double. Branson was congratulated for showing how Virgin 'likes to do things differently and with personality', whereas BT looked 'dull and corporate'. Rivals complained that Virgin's claim to double all speeds was misleading. Virgin replied that the advertisement was 'light-hearted' and the company was 'not making an absolute claim', but the ASA ordered that Virgin's advertisement be withdrawn. The succession of misleading advertisements created an unexpected impression of the company, much like the time when Virgin sued the owner of the Virgin Café, an unremarkable bar in the Australian outback, for infringing Branson's copyright.

BT lodged a more serious complaint. The corporation had paid a high fee to feature as the Olympics' official broadband provider, and BT accused Virgin of infringing those expensive endorsement rights. No one at Virgin's headquarters apologised. Bolt's campaign had attracted extra customers and, although the immediate additional profits were wiped out by the advertisements' costs, the company's image had been enhanced. Branson delighted in using what he called 'humour' to ridicule competitors, although he took great offence at any criticism of him or Virgin. BT's complaint was easily forgotten. The strategy had made a profitable exit easier.

In the aftermath of the Olympics, Neil Berkett no longer had the stomach to fight Sky. There had been constant conflict and repeated defeat. The company's fate was best sealed by a sale. For some years, Berkett had discussed Virgin's future with the managers of Liberty Global, the world's biggest cable company, founded and controlled by John Malone. Among Malone's trophies was beating Rupert Murdoch. He had accumulated 18 per cent of News Corp.'s shares before, to Murdoch's relief, agreeing to swap them in exchange for Murdoch's stake in DirecTV, America's biggest satellite TV business. Buying Virgin made sense for Malone: it would increase Liberty's total debt to $39 billion, and he favoured debt-burdened operators to minimise his own tax bill. Virgin also completed the jigsaw. Malone owned eleven cable networks across Europe, and buying Virgin Media could fulfil the goal that had eluded Branson: namely, challenging Sky's dominance from strength.

Berkett had made Virgin Media attractive to Malone, with the successful Bolt campaign coinciding with the company's first profits. Liberty's offer of £14.7 billion ($23 billion) was judged by some to be excessive. But Berkett knew he had a good deal. Branson received £205 million ($316 million) for his remaining stake, and he could expect to earn about £8.5 million annually from the branding licence. 'Branson's lucked out in the games of life,' commented an insider, noting that his ambition for more profits from Virgin Mobile was exhausted.

Posing as a sixties hippy, Branson had tried to relaunch the network in America by appealing to the Facebook generation and attacking his competitors, but Virgin's minuscule marketing budget was swamped by the billions of dollars spent by the major companies. Next, he again pledged to spend $300 million over five years to launch his network across Latin America. Chile and Colombia would be first in 2012, followed by Brazil, Argentina, Mexico and Peru. 'We focus on youth,' said Peter Macnee, Virgin's manager based in Miami. One year later, Virgin's tepid campaign had barely registered. Branson made a new announcement: he would raise $100 million to launch Virgin Mobile across Latin America, the Middle East, South Africa and central Europe, and thereafter in Russia. He spoke about already having eighteen million subscribers in nine countries, and expected $3 billion in revenue by 2020. The only certainty was the termination of Virgin Mobile in Qatar after a licence row. His model of a virtual network based on renting spare capacity was broken. Servers were providing a poor service for Virgin, and Branson could no longer undercut the established networks' prices. He had enjoyed a good run, but in the end Murdoch had come out on top.

That outcome was not unusual. Since his rout of Lord King, BA's chairman, during the original battle to establish Virgin Atlantic, Branson had not defeated another tycoon through outright commercial competition. His race had reached a new climax. Virgin, he decided, would withdraw from launching new businesses. To execute that transition, he appointed Josh Bayliss, a New Zealand lawyer, as Virgin's chief executive based in Geneva. Bayliss's task was to 'redefine the business as a family investment company growing the revenue stream from royalties' for the brand. To some, he appeared to be signalling Branson's retreat. Virgin was not aggressively searching for new business opportunities, and Branson had revised his plan for his daughter Holly to be his successor. His withdrawal was understandable. A sixty-three-year-old living in Necker was remote from the high-street buzz dictating global consumerism. One consequence of the brand's retreat was Branson's reduced wealth. Even if the Rich Lists' guesses about Branson's fortune, which over the previous decade were always about £3 billion, were accurate – and they were not – in real terms his fortunes had declined. Since his money-making hit its high point following the sales of Virgin Music and Virgin Mobile, he had coasted downwards. Despite the changes, however, his lifestyle would remain unaltered.

The survival of some of his businesses depended on government regulators. None were more important than the officials at the UK's Department for Transport. The image of Virgin Trains racing across Britain had become invaluable for the brand, and Virgin's franchise was at risk. New bids were invited in 2012 for the West Coast line, and Virgin's chances for renewal were uncertain. Branson was re-energised by the unusual prospect of possible defeat.

19

Resurrection

Tony Collins expected problems. Speaking regularly to officials at the Department for Transport, the Virgin Trains chief executive sensed Whitehall's cool attitude towards his company. Their misgivings, he knew, were sparked by his own success. Over the previous years, Collins's protracted negotiations with officials had usually ended with Virgin extracting an advantage. The bureaucrats' irritation was aggravated by Collins's exploitation of their own incompetence, illustrated by one episode in 2009.

Collins had arrived at the department to set out a proposition. 'Virgin', he said, 'will invest £100 million in additional carriages for the Pendolino trains if you extend the franchise by two years.' Collins's proposal was not a surprise. The media, briefed by Virgin's publicists, had already reported the company's plan to generate an additional £100 million in revenue every year if Whitehall granted its wishes. In Virgin-speak, the proposal was disguised as corporate generosity. By contrast, the department's officials regarded the suggestion as a ruse to grab more profits, on top of the £98.5 million Virgin Trains had earned the previous year. After all, the extra carriages that Virgin wanted would, as usual, be financed by government grants. The department's detailed scrutiny showed how, with the exception of '£5 million of improvements to a few waiting rooms', Virgin's £100 million 'investment' would be taxpayers' money. Even the £5 million could eventually be recovered by Virgin from Network Rail.

The officials intended to reject Collins's request, but as the discussions dragged on their resolution faded. In the end, they surrendered and extended the franchise by a few months. 'He's rubbing his hands,' griped an official about another Virgin victory.

The success came with a sting. Virgin had extracted government finance to add two carriages to each train. On the basis of Virgin's promises, 106 carriages were ordered, but soon after their delivery Virgin rejected them. 'We can't afford to use them', said Virgin's director, 'unless the franchise is further extended.' His request was refused, and the new carriages were parked in sidings as testament to Virgin's bullying of officials. They were also a tribute to Virgin's technique. The operator had pleaded for more carriages to relieve overcrowding on the West Coast line. In reality, the line was crowded only during peak hours, when Virgin charged its highest rates. The taxpayer's investment was wasted.

Branson's self-portrayal as the good guy risking his personal fortune to modernise Britain's railways was galling to officials who, since 2010, had cursed Virgin Trains for effectively negotiating a licence to print money. The combination of rebuilding the tracks, introducing Network Rail's new timetable allowing Virgin to run more trains in peak times at high fares, and the government's escalating subsidies had doubled the company's revenue. Improvements masterminded by the Department for Transport and financed by taxpayers had doubled the number of passengers using the West Coast line. 'He's got a gold mine,' said a senior official, reviewing Branson's accumulation of about £381.7 million of profits over the decade – although the figures were never clear. Branson would say that Virgin Trains' profits over fifteen years were £499 million but, according to the TUC, Virgin shared £519 million of profits with Stagecoach. The irrefutable truth was that after raising ticket prices by 9 per cent in 2012, Virgin's profits ranked among the highest of the nineteen train franchises and contributed to Britain's railways costing 40 per cent more to run than those in the rest of Europe.

The high profits reaped from an unpredictable business were an accolade to the directors of Virgin Trains. Over the years, they had mastered the matrix of managing disruption, dropped loss-making services to Shrewsbury and Blackpool, and reduced the number of trains travelling to the north of England and Scotland. Consequently, at peak times, business passengers could rarely avoid paying the standard £296 return fare from London to Manchester. Those waiting on Friday evening at Euston for Virgin's off-peak trains were held like cattle in pens near the platforms. Anyone mistakenly boarding a train with an underpriced ticket found themselves embarrassed by Virgin's staff. By maximising the opportunities provided by Network Rail, Virgin's profit in 2011 was £102.7 million, marginally down from a pre-tax profit of £105 million in 2009. Branson personally banked £17.8 million in dividends, and the company took an additional £40 million in government subsidies. Although in public Branson spoke about Virgin Trains paying the government '£100 million', he forgot to mention the subsidies and profits the Virgin Group received simultaneously from the taxpayer. The profits were not purely cash. The Virgin brand benefited from sleek trains decorated with the Virgin logo racing across the country. Abroad, Branson quoted Virgin Trains as proof of his importance. In America, he mentioned his train company as his qualification to build a $2.6 billion high-speed train line between Tampa and Orlando; and during a visit to India, he said that he would 'love to help' establish high-speed trains in the country: 'I have the experience to upgrade a crumbling network. In Britain we took over a dilapidated part of Britain's network fifteen years ago and transformed it.'

The guaranteed profits and the opportunity to pose on engines for photographers roused Branson to plan his tactics for the renewal of the West Coast franchise in 2013, following the extension from 2012. To tilt the odds in Virgin's favour, he visited Theresa Villiers, the new Tory transport minister. In the passengers' interest, he told Villiers, the government should grant a long franchise in order to benefit from Virgin's investment and experience. She should, he advised, ignore the impossibility of accurately predicting future revenues over the length of a thirteen-year contract, and also the certainty of disruption if construction started at Euston station for HS2, the high-speed train. Villiers accepted his argument.

In anticipation of his bid, in December 2011 he hosted a party on the concourse at Euston station. Virgin Trains, he told his staff and passengers, was Britain's most popular long-distance operator. In the National Passenger Survey, he said, the company had scored a 90 per cent satisfaction rate, partly thanks to his personal involvement. One particular advertisement featuring Branson had been praised by his publicists for generating an additional 1.8 million journeys. His guests applauded. Few realised that Network Rail's operational performance tables showed the opposite. Every year, Virgin ranked among the worst operators for punctuality and attracted the highest number of complaints. The company naturally disputed those statistics. Other surveys showed that when Virgin trains were late, many passengers blamed everyone except Virgin, but for identical breakdowns on other services passengers heaped the blame on the train operator. 'It's the Virgin halo effect,' moaned Branson's rivals.

Virgin, Branson told his guests at Euston, had introduced seventy new trains at a cost of £1.5 billion, and hundreds of millions of pounds would follow in his continued effort to please his customers. The guests cheered his self-congratulation for 'investing in innovation and quality'. No one mentioned that the billions of pounds were not Virgin's but taxpayers', and in turn Branson did not mention that his profits in 2012 would be £43 million, albeit slightly down on previous years because the Department for Transport was clawing back £160 million. Even though his income from trains was falling, he wanted the new franchise. He understood the difficulties. Virgin had lost the bid for the East Coast line in 2006, and there was no certainty that Tony Collins could accurately anticipate his rivals' bids. To calculate the winning sum, Collins hired Paul Furze-Waddock as development director. Furze-Waddock, a master of railway finance, would be expected not only to number-crunch but also to pick up clues inadvertently revealed by civil servants.

During their regular visits to the department's headquarters, Collins, Furze-Waddock and Patrick McCall, Virgin Trains' chairman, discussed the requirements for bidding. Their discoveries were revealing. To save money, the department had decided not to employ Grant Thornton or PricewaterhouseCoopers, the accountants, to scrutinise their own calculations. This was to be a fatal decision by the department. After years in the railways, Virgin's directors knew that the department's staff lacked the expertise to master the mathematical modelling. To cut overheads, the department had also reduced its staff. Among the departures was Mike Mitchell, the director of railways. Collins would not lament the retirement of his adversary: Mitchell was not only a shrewd operator but had been previously employed by FirstGroup, Virgin Trains' principal competitor. In Whitehall's games of musical chairs, Mitchell's job was divided between three people, with Peter Strachan the man now overseeing the bidding process. Known as 'a great guy in the pub', he had a reputation for chairing long, inconsequential meetings and had abruptly resigned from another rail company after Mitchell had become his boss. Mitchell had turned the operator's losses into profits. Among other departures were the department's most experienced commercial managers. Some were hired by Virgin to monitor how their replacements grappled with the complications introduced into the bidding process by Villiers.

One of the department's critical tasks would be to assess the risk of a bidder failing to fulfil the thirteen-year contract. The calculation would produce the financial guarantee – the so-called Subordinated Loan Facility (SLF) – which the operator would be expected to pay in event of failure.

In February 2012, Furze-Waddock was quietly told by an official that the mathematical model the department was using to calculate the SLF was flawed. Furze-Waddock made a note of that telephone conversation. Pertinently, none of Virgin's rivals heard the same information, and by chance the company found itself in a privileged position. In further conversations, Virgin obtained a special concession which was not discussed with rival bidders. The information involved the government's calculation of the income a train operator could expect to receive from passengers. The figures appear in the 'Passenger Demand Forecasting Handbook' (PDFH), but only Virgin reached an understanding that the revenue from fares would not be 'risk adjusted'. On that basis, Furze-Waddock recommended that Virgin could afford to submit a low bid and still win. Subsequently, he would claim that 'Virgin was pushing the boat out with a very risky bid, offering even more than FirstGroup in the first years.' Analysis of the bids would later cast doubt on that belief.

During more conversations in March, Virgin's directors heard that the rules about the PDFH calculation had been amended, and asked for clarification to solve the confusion. In reply, an official explained that the department would not release more information about the PDFH or about the SLF because the department's methods were 'very basic and open to challenge'. Leaks to Virgin about the deteriorating situation within the department's franchising group confirmed that the committee responsible for the process was in disarray. Strachan was providing questionable leadership.

That was no surprise to Patrick McCall. At Easter, he had received a letter from the department describing how a company's resilience would be judged by the operator's reaction to the PDFH. Soon after, during a visit to the department, McCall was told to disregard the letter. Then, minutes after leaving the building, he was telephoned and told the letter was accurate after all. Furze-Waddock made contemporaneous notes about those contradictory calls. None of Virgin's rival bidders, including FirstGroup, enjoyed similar access to the officials or became aware of the confusion across the department. Subsequently, the competing companies would complain about their perceived disadvantages.

On the eve of the department's critical meeting in March to begin the decision process, Furze-Waddock realised the officials' weakness. 'We're putting up issues they can't solve,' he reported. 'Our modelling is better than anyone else's, and the officials hate us because they can't answer my questions.' In anticipation of problems, Furze-Waddock and the Virgin directors warned the officials, 'You're doing it wrong' and their mistakes 'would lead to a protest'. At a meeting on 21 March, the same officials decided to ignore the possibility of the bidders challenging the department in court.

On 27 June, ten officials met to award the franchise. Inexplicably, Peter Strachan was not present at the Contract Award Committee, and the department was subsequently criticised for failing to give a satisfactory reason for his absence. The department's assessments had concluded that FirstGroup was the outright winner. FirstGroup had offered £5.5 billion for the thirteen-year franchise against Virgin's £4.8 billion and promised to invest more money to match bigger ambitions and produce more revenue for the taxpayer. With an agreed rate of inflation added over thirteen years, FirstGroup's offer was £13.3 billion against Virgin's £11 billion. Critically, both operators had predicted identical passenger revenues and growth in the first ten years. But in the last three years, Virgin forecast no further growth, while FirstGroup predicted a continued upward trend. Over the previous decade, the number of passengers on Virgin Trains had grown by about 10.2 per cent every year. FirstGroup assumed that the annual growth would continue at 10.4 per cent, the same figure used by the government to justify the construction of HS2.

To attract more passengers than Virgin, FirstGroup intended to reassign many first-class seats to cheaper fares; add extra carriages to popular trains; reduce fares; and reintroduce services to Blackpool, Shrewsbury and other towns that Virgin had abandoned. In summary, the company proposed to offer an additional 12,000 extra seats every day and eleven new trains, including the 106 new carriages unused by Virgin. To make the service more attractive, FirstGroup also proposed to enlarge the catering service. Virgin had bid conservatively in order to match the assurance Furze-Waddock received that the government was not expecting any operator to take risks. Accordingly, Virgin was outbid and FirstGroup was the winner. The remaining issue was the cash guarantee, or SLF, based on the forecasted revenue. FirstGroup's risk was calculated at £215 million, while Virgin's bid was so low that its SLF was assessed as zero.

During their discussions, the officials decided to change the SLFs. Anticipating that critics would suggest that Virgin could not have been awarded a £5.5 billion contract without any financial guarantee, the officials suggested that Virgin's SLF be set at an arbitrary £40 million. And to make FirstGroup's sum more reasonable, the officials decided to 'round down' the SLF to £200 million. 'Can we do that?' the chairwoman of the departmental committee asked their lawyer. Although changing the published guidelines for the bids was prohibited by law, the lawyer approved the 'rounding'. On that basis, FirstGroup was awarded the franchise, subject to the minister's approval. The decision was not announced publicly, but rumours leaked out describing 'a clear leading bid'.

After the meeting, the officials were warned by independent lawyers that the recalculation of the SLF could be challenged in court. The advice was ignored. Thereafter, the department's officials gave every minister and the external lawyers inaccurate information about their method of assessing the bids. The officials' behaviour was later criticised as a cover-up.

Virgin was told the result by the department on 20 July. 'There is clear blue water' between the two bids, said the civil servant. Branson was incandescent. He had been convinced by Virgin's directors that their bid was a winner. No one at Virgin had anticipated that FirstGroup would bid aggressively. 'I'm shocked by the size of FirstGroup's bid,' said Furze-Waddock.

Having miscalculated the bid, Branson looked for ways to challenge the result. The alternative would be incalculable damage to Virgin, both financial and reputational. Although some would say that he ignored 49 per cent shareholder Brian Souter's dismissal of protests as 'a waste of time', others mentioned that Martin Griffiths, Stagecoach's chief executive, was 'more enraged than most'. Unlike Stagecoach, Virgin could not afford to lose guaranteed profits, an interest-free cash mountain and free promotion of the brand via the railway; and just as seriously, Branson needed the taxpayers' money to balance the haemorrhaging of cash from Virgin Atlantic. In addition to the airline's £132 million losses in 2009/10 and £80.2 million in 2011, the 2012 losses would be a record £135 million. Losing the West Coast franchise would be a disaster for Virgin – and Branson.

Regardless of the merits of the case, Branson's default reaction to any loss was to attack the winner as wicked. BA, Camelot and Arriva had all been targets of his anger. FirstGroup now joined those enemies, and as usual Branson's aggression knew no bounds.

His first complaint was to David Cameron. Without flinching, he pushed the knife into his rival. FirstGroup, he wrote to the prime minister, had overbid. The company had won the franchise, he alleged, by offering to pay the government £9.6 billion, an amount Branson's advisers seemed to have plucked out of the air. Virgin's rival, continued Branson, was untrustworthy and guilty of offering unreliable financial predictions to grab a prize at the nation's expense.

Branson's accusations were inflammatory. In 2012/13, Virgin Trains paid the government a premium of £160 million out of revenues of £938 million. In its new bid, Virgin had offered to pay an average of £400 million a year over thirteen years, while FirstGroup's average annual payment would be £480 million. Both could be accused of overbidding by overestimating the extra number of passengers and Britain's economic growth, and FirstGroup was also guilty of committing itself to huge payments at the end of the contract. FirstGroup was only marginally more aggressive in its bid than Virgin, but by attacking first, loudly and in the public arena Branson portrayed his company as the victim of tricksters.

His letter to Cameron arguably breached the government's conditions for bidders. Under the terms governing 'confidentiality' and 'publicity', Virgin had undertaken not to lobby officials for information and assistance. On top of that the company had agreed not to challenge the process before the result had been announced. Branson was also bound not to reveal details about Virgin's bid. But, as ever, he was not deterred by rules and was delighted that FirstGroup's directors remained silent. Sensing that Cameron and the government officials were too intimidated to demand his silence, Branson's megaphone outrage dominated the confrontation he was engineering.

In alleging to the prime minister that FirstGroup had overbid, Branson was relying on Furze-Waddock's extrapolations rather than precise information. Although Virgin Trains had received privileged information from the department, the directors did not appear to have discovered the details of FirstGroup's bid. Despite that ignorance, Branson and Virgin's publicists uttered detailed descriptions of FirstGroup's bid with such authority that outsiders accepted their authenticity.

According to Branson, while Virgin predicted that passenger numbers would rise from thirty million to forty-nine million by 2026, FirstGroup was predicting sixty-six million passengers. 'You would have to pile people on the roof of a train like in India', scoffed Branson, 'to get anywhere near FirstGroup's numbers.' FirstGroup denied those numbers and, speaking to journalists off the record, even accused Branson of 'lying' but the company was ignored. 'He's just throwing spaghetti at the wall and hoping it will stick,' one FirstGroup executive complained.

Not mentioned was FirstGroup's own financial vulnerability. The company had failed to sell off expensive investments in America. To restore its balance sheet, it needed to win the franchise or else suffer a shortage of funds. Like all the train operators, FirstGroup's credit rating was poor. Virgin, with no rating at all, was battering a rival also fighting for survival.

On 23 July, Branson wrote to Theresa Villiers and sent a copy of his letter to David Cameron. He forecast an apocalypse. FirstGroup, he warned, would collapse just like National Express had in 2009, when it quit the East Coast line.

Branson had entered sensitive territory. National Express had won the East Coast franchise in 2006 after promising sizeable payments to the government. In the aftermath of the 2008 economic crash, however, the number of passengers fell on all train services. National Express could not fund the unanticipated losses and handed back the franchise. In Branson's terms, National Express had only won the franchise by deliberately overbidding, and that FirstGroup was committing an identical sin. The similarities appeared convincing. The officials at the Department for Transport had proven to be inept at assessing the applicants for the East Coast franchise, and National Express had certainly overbid. But Virgin Trains, the runner-up, had offered only marginally less. The unforeseen losses in 2008 would have forced Virgin to surrender the franchise too. That truth remained unspoken and Branson's version dominated the media.

On 30 July, Branson wrote again to David Cameron. FirstGroup, he alleged, could only make its bid work by 'drastically cutting the quality of its services'. He urged the prime minister not to confirm FirstGroup as the winner. In a continuing barrage of letters and telephone calls, Branson demanded that the government provide the documents showing how the department had decided to reject Virgin's superior bid. By then, Cameron was on holiday, but a Virgin director persuaded Ed Llewellyn, the prime minister's chief of staff, to disturb him. The prime minister, assured by his senior officials about the reliability of the process, angrily rejected Branson's protests.

Unknown to Cameron, the transport officials who had made the original decision were giving Downing Street wrong information based on an unreliable review of their decision-making process. Branson had an unusual advantage. Unlike the government, Virgin's executives had become aware of the truth. Furze-Waddock had extrapolated the audit trail and suggested that FirstGroup's SLF should have been at least £600 million rather than £200 million. He also decided that Virgin's SLF was too low. Pointedly, on 10 August Virgin requested sight of a new consultants' report commissioned by the department. After analysing the decision-making process, the consultants had identified the flawed calculations. Remarkably, at the same time, Theresa Villiers was told by her officials that the process had been faultless. Pertinently, if the department had levied a £600 million SLF on FirstGroup from the outset, Virgin would have been denied any reason to protest.

Branson rarely resisted attacking a competitor, even when his arguments were thin. On this occasion, some facts were irrefutable, and he added another. In his opinion, FirstGroup was vulnerable for handing back the Great Western rail franchise three years before the end of the ten-year period and avoiding a payment of £793 million to the government. That was proof, said Branson, that FirstGroup had overbid on that contract, lacked money and was unreliable.

Since abandoning the Great Western franchise, FirstGroup had indeed run the same service on a management contract. Branson attacked the operator's poor punctuality and dilapidated trains. His criticism, echoing the passengers' complaints, increased sympathy for Virgin against the government. Arguably, the facts were somewhat different.

The Labour government had awarded the franchise to FirstGroup in 2005, with an unusual option to end the agreement after seven years. By 2012, there were good reasons for FirstGroup to activate the break clause. The recession had reduced revenues and the tracks out of Paddington were due to be rebuilt and electrified, mirroring the same work on the West Coast line ten years earlier. Reading station, a key junction, was to be rebuilt, with inevitable disruption and a decrease in passenger numbers. Legal termination of the contract meant the taxpayer was protected from FirstGroup's claim for compensation. That was ignored by Branson. His purpose was served by portraying FirstGroup as financially risky, unlike Virgin Trains, an example of financial probity running a modern service. He ignored the poor infrastructure along the Great Western line from Paddington to the west of England, a problem that had faced the old West Coast line. Once the reconstruction of the Great Western line was completed and the new trains were introduced, the operation would be equal to Virgin's.

On 14 August, Branson wrote once again to Cameron. He complained that he was being ignored by the Cabinet secretary, who wielded supreme power over Whitehall and enjoyed constant access to the prime minister. The final decision, Branson suggested, should be delayed until an audit had been conducted. His protest was rejected, and on 15 August FirstGroup was officially awarded the franchise.

Branson's resolution intensified. 'I think under the current system you will be seeing the end of Virgin trains in the UK,' he said. Virgin, he explained, could not wait to bid again in thirteen years, apparently forgetting his advocacy of longer franchises. Emotionally, he attacked FirstGroup's victory as 'a big gamble' and 'insanity'. His warnings were supported by Bob Crowe, the militant leader of the RMT trade union. FirstGroup, said Crowe, planned to cut services and catering. Both accusations lacked substance.

Virgin's publicists found no difficulty in arranging for their employer to appear on radio and TV, urging David Cameron to intervene. Branson repeatedly offered to run what he called 'one of the best networks in the world' for no profit if the handover was delayed. Pertinently, a BBC interviewer refrained from linking three facts: Branson presented himself as the guardian of British taxpayers; Virgin passengers buying a ticket that morning would be charged £231 for a standard-class return on a crowded train to Liverpool which arrived late – and with smelly lavatories; and Branson was speaking from Necker, his tax shelter.

During subsequent interviews, Branson again criticised the award of franchises to operators who overbid 'on the East Coast and on Cross Country. We came runner-up twice and the successful companies ran into financial trouble.' That was not the case with Arriva. The new operator of Cross Country had won because passengers were dissatisfied with Virgin's service, and by 2013 Arriva was earning a reasonable profit. 'Branson's spooking the government,' a FirstGroup executive noted, fearing that the government would surrender. 'He's using his reputation to get heard.'

Branson's blitzkrieg took no prisoners. FirstGroup, he howled to journalists, would be earning 'outrageous' profits at the taxpayers' expense! His shock sounded genuine. 'We said we'd spend £800 million on new trains and improvements to the stations,' he continued. 'FirstGroup said they'd spend £300 million. That £500 million difference was not taken into account in the calculations. People should be encouraged to come up with innovative ideas to improve tracks and trains.' FirstGroup denounced Branson's figures as 'untrue'.

The distress among FirstGroup's executives was growing. Under the government's rules, the details of the bids were permanently secret, yet it appeared to them that Virgin's executives might have been receiving details about FirstGroup's confidential bid from officials in the Department for Transport. Virgin would deny receiving leaks, and there was no evidence that the company did improperly receive inside information, but details about FirstGroup's proposed improvements were published. Two weeks after Branson's tirade began, Tony Collins, Virgin Trains' managing director, proposed a practically identical list of 'improved services'. Among them was a commitment to start direct services from London to Shrewsbury and Blackpool, the same commitment Virgin had reneged on after 1997.

FirstGroup began fighting back, providing guidance to those interested in scrutinising Virgin's proposals. One argument deployed by FirstGroup was that in the calculations for its bid, Virgin Trains had failed to reduce its costs in the manner suggested by Roy McNulty in his report for the government. Nor had it increased the number of trains and destinations, and nor had it proposed to replace first-class carriages with more seats for standard-class passengers. Branson also omitted to explain that Virgin's additional services to Shrewsbury and Blackpool depended on the government agreeing to guarantee new subsidies. Swiftly, the media's sympathy for Virgin ebbed. Newspaper editorials criticised Branson as a bad loser who championed competition and then screamed 'I wuz robbed'. Tim O'Toole, FirstGroup's chief executive, joined the chorus. 'Sour grapes,' he said. 'FirstGroup will provide a better service for customers and a better return for the government.' His company was due to take over the service on 9 December, but he was up against a man who wanted the same as himself but who, to his surprise, happily dived for his opponent's jugular.

O'Toole, an experienced railway manager, suspected the Department for Transport's vulnerability. Although there was both an implied obligation on all the bidders not to challenge the process and, FirstGroup believed, an unofficial agreement with Virgin not to utter outlandish claims, the known facts had become too capricious for Branson to ignore. He cleverly diverted attention from the real issue – namely, the integrity of the department's process – to dispute the validity of FirstGroup's bid. And in terms of the cash the government would receive, FirstGroup's offer was superior to Virgin's. But O'Toole found himself impotent against such a wily campaigner.

Threatening a judicial review of an unwelcome decision by any government had long been Branson's natural reaction. Invariably, those threats had evaporated. But on this occasion, Branson approved the application. The government, announced Virgin, 'has acted unlawfully and irrationally'. Just before the contract with FirstGroup was signed at the end of August, the government received the notification of a court battle. Relying on her officials, Theresa Villiers responded that the government intended to 'defend robustly' its decision. Days later, Justine Greening, her successor, dismissed the legal challenge. 'Had Virgin won the bid they would have been perfectly happy,' she said, with her officials' encouragement. The following day, in an interview with the *Daily Mail*, Branson posed as the victim of a conspiracy. The department's officials, he said, had given privileged information to FirstGroup, and the newspaper reported that internal emails had circulated within the department which could be characterised as ABB – 'Anyone But Branson'. A subsequent investigation would find no evidence either of prejudice in favour of FirstGroup or of any departmental bias against Branson or Virgin.

The following day, an online petition mysteriously appeared, urging the government to award the franchise to Virgin. Overnight, the customer-relations screens at all Virgin stations broadcast appeals to passengers to sign the petition, supported by messages relayed on the tannoys and on Virgin's trains. Within a week, the petition had a list of over 120,000 names. The public had accepted Branson's version that the improved services owed everything to his personal financial investment. Compared to O'Toole, a low-key American, Branson was the champion of the public's interests, the buccaneering underdog. His few critics spoke about 'a manipulative force' – and were ignored.

On 10 September, Branson entered a House of Commons committee room. At his request, the MPs' transport committee had agreed to hold a hearing. The colour of his unkempt hair was fading, his beard was bedraggled and his jeans and jacket looked as if they had not been taken off for a few days, but the suntan shone. Although the meeting was at his request, his surliness suggested a distrust of politicians, a breed he dismissed as hostile. Kwasi Kwarteng, a Conservative MP, reinforced his suspicion. 'Some would say these are the heavy-artillery tactics,' said Kwarteng about Branson's legal challenge. Virgin's bid, said the politician, was 'too low' and, he continued, 'You are using your prestige and fame to try and force the government to change the decision.'

'I'm not in it for the money,' replied Branson, with passion. 'The profit motive is not that important to me. I am lucky. I can afford breakfast, lunch and dinner for the rest of my life.' Unlike the Tory MP, Branson implied, his social conscience matched the public interest and his employees' well-being. He had not flown from Necker to defend himself but to slay a devilish speculator. Awarding the franchise to FirstGroup, he continued, was 'completely ridiculous' because 'FirstGroup's bid is absolutely preposterous. It is taking the system for a ride.' The company, he said, was 'getting away with murder', which was 'bad for the country, bad for passengers'. His listless voice embroidered the venom against O'Toole. FirstGroup's submission, said Branson, was like 'renting out your house to the one who offers to pay twice the rent in ten years' time despite being burnt three times already'. Accusations of dishonesty came easily from a man who sued his critics for much less. With that, he stalked out, and O'Toole moved into the chair Branson had vacated. The tension in the committee room collapsed. In the anticlimax, the soft-spoken executive could not compete with a global star who had recently boasted about taking cocaine, ecstasy and Viagra. 'Those are histrionics by a self-publicist', said O'Toole in a quiet voice, 'who is peddling outrageous versions of history.' He made little impression.

Days before that appearance, Patrick McLoughlin had replaced Justine Greening as transport minister, the third secretary of state in just over two years. In the same week, the department's third permanent secretary since 2010 was appointed. The prime minister did not appreciate his own vulnerability. Virgin's publicists had restored their advantage, and the media were again describing FirstGroup's reckless bidding. An ingredient added by the publicists was the new minister's lack of awareness of his officials' cover-up. Innocently, McLoughlin ignored the accusations and announced, 'It is our intention to proceed with the bid that FirstGroup has made.'

Two weeks later, McLoughlin was poleaxed. Ernst & Young, the accountants, reported that his department's calculations suffered 'significant technical flaws'. No single person, the minister was told, had been in charge of a flawed process executed by inexperienced officials. A subsequent review by Sam Laidlaw, the remarkable chief executive of Centrica, would discover worse mistakes: officials had altered the minutes of departmental meetings and they had lied to ministers. The cover-up was exposed. Evidence of the fractured personal relationships within the department came with Peter Strachan's decision to publish unilaterally a ten-page version of events which exonerated himself and reprimanded FirstGroup. Pertinently, he complained about 'stark inconsistencies between the different accounts of about ten officials in attendance' at the meeting on 27 June to decide the winner, which he had missed. Soon after, Strachan resigned. Critically, Laidlaw had not questioned the financial aspect of FirstGroup's bid. The weakness he exposed was Whitehall's errors.

McLoughlin had a choice: he could award the franchise and allow his department's errors to be examined during a trial, or he could abort the process and escape embarrassing scrutiny. He decided to avoid a court battle. On 2 October, he first telephoned Tim O'Toole. FirstGroup, he said, had submitted the better bid, but the department had made some unacceptable errors. Then, at 11.30 p.m., the minister spoke to Branson, who was waiting for the call in a New York hotel. There had been 'deeply regrettable and unacceptable' mistakes in assessing the proposals,

McLoughlin told him, and the fault lay 'only and squarely with the Department for Transport'. After the call, Branson celebrated with two aides the success of their seven-week campaign. Virgin Trains had been resurrected. The media headlines, he was pleased to anticipate, would report Network Rail's 'biggest crisis', Virgin's vindication and Branson's justified vilification of FirstGroup. A measure of his victory was reflected by the *Financial Times*' somersault. Two months earlier, the newspaper had criticised Branson for refusing to accept the result. The day after McLoughlin's announcement, the newspaper criticised FirstGroup: 'It would be terribly unfair if the people who gamed the system by putting in this completely outlandish bid ended up achieving what they wanted to achieve.' Branson's campaign had shifted the blame entirely on to FirstGroup. But, contrary to Branson's allegations, FirstGroup's bid had not been 'outlandish'. The only transgression was the department's arbitrary fixing of the SLF.

The process was now paralysed. Branson predicted chaos if Virgin was forced to stop operating. The government's alternative was to transfer the West Coast line to Directly Operated Railways (DOR), the government's agency running the East Coast line. That solution, Branson warned, 'would be an absolute disaster. Without our team it would descend into absolute chaos.' Virgin's conduct after the loss of Cross Country to Arriva had demonstrated how a transfer could be frustrated. However, DOR had taken only four months to replace National Express on the East Coast line. No trains had been cancelled, no staff were fired and passengers had barely noticed the transition. But the obstacle to that choice was the public's support for Branson. Fearful of the idol, McLoughlin decided to extend Virgin's franchise for two years. Subsequently, it was extended until April 2017. None of the officials involved in the costly disaster was disciplined. Branson could feel triumphant. Drawing on decades of experience, the supreme operator had humbled his commercial rivals – and the British government.

Victory fuelled Branson's hyperbole. With the media eager to puff every assertion, he proclaimed that he was organising a series of fiftieth-anniversary concerts for the Rolling Stones. 'Rumour has it we've landed quite a good catch,' he told the *Financial Times* about what turned out to be a dream. His publicists also briefed the newspaper that he was considering repurchasing Virgin Records from Universal, twenty years after the original sale. 'Richard Branson and Virgin have been assessing how to get back into the recorded-music business for many years,' said the Virgin spokesman, securing a whole page of publicity. 'It would be a wonderful opportunity to recreate a dynamic independent label in the market.' The idea that he had the money or expertise to revive Virgin Records was a delusion confirmed by the recent collapse of V2, which had cost investors over £100 million.

Coyly, Branson refused to discuss the accuracy of Bloomberg's and *Forbes*'s estimates of his wealth at 'over $4 billion', and he had no comment about the absence of Virgin in the rankings of the world's top 100 brands collated by Interbrand and Millward Brown Optimor. Neither agency could value the Virgin label because Branson's earnings were low – less than £40 million from revenues newly estimated at £13 billion. In the fog Branson had created around his finances, the financial truth was impossible to discern.

So much depended on his self-portrayal. He offered himself as the wise guru. 'We are considered pioneers in many different industries based on our innovation,' he said in 2013, 'rather than the size of any of our companies.' Virgin, he said, is not about size, 'it's an attitude and a way of life'. The company, he added, 'embraces life and seeks to give the customers something new'.

Branson concealed his weaknesses by steering every interview towards LanzaTech and Virgin Galactic. He needed cheap fuel to make his airlines profitable and space travel because that was the last throw of his dice – 'the planet and the deep seas', as he said.

'I'd be very disappointed if we're not up and away by next year,' he said in July 2012. 'It's possible next year we might do both – go from the lowest part of the oceans into space.'

20

Journey into Space – Postponed

In April 2013, Branson was fizzing. The news from Mojave, he believed, was excellent, and his appearance at a conference in Las Vegas was the perfect occasion to unveil his success. Five thousand people in a giant auditorium witnessed Branson's excitement. 'Any day now,' he told them, 'it will be happening. A new era of space travel will begin.' SpaceShipTwo, he revealed, was about to make its first supersonic flight. 'In two months, SpaceShipTwo will be flying at 2,000 mph,' he predicted, 'and then it will be flying throughout the rest of 2013.' Having won the audience's rapt attention, he added that he would be travelling to space with his family in early 2014. And to spread the feel-good factor, he threw in, 'Most people in this room will go into space in their lifetime.'

Giving good news was a relief. Since the beginning of the year, the space programme's costs had risen. The construction of the spaceport terminals in New Mexico had been completed, and since 15 January Virgin was paying $1.63 million in annual rent. That payment was a pittance compared to the cost of developing a new motor for Virgin Galactic – a decision that had been taken reluctantly at the end of 2012.

Sticking to Burt Rutan's choice of the hybrid, Branson had been told, was a mistake. Burning rubber with nitrous oxide was too primitive for Virgin Galactic's big spaceship. It would be more sensible to power the craft with a conventional liquid-fuelled engine. Virgin could only regret their rejection of a partnership with Reaction Engines, the British rocket developer:

the company was about to receive a £60 million grant from the British government and sell its successful expertise for much more in America. By contrast, Virgin Galactic needed to start practically from scratch, and in January 2013 Scaled began recruiting propulsion-design engineers, not least to consider the replacement of the hybrid with a liquid-fuelled motor. Critics called the switch 'the spaghetti strategy' – keep throwing stuff at the wall and see what sticks. 'Virgin Galactic', read Scaled's advertisement, 'is on track to become the world's first privately funded commercial space line [and] a world leader in sub-orbital commercial space tourism.' Among the detailed specifications was Virgin's requirement for potential employees to 'check your ego at the door, be a self-starter and possess a sense of humility'.

Six days after his Las Vegas appearance, Branson was standing in the early-morning darkness on the tarmac at Mojave, ready for a new blast of publicity. Two hundred feet from the control tower, the man in charge of operations, Luke Colby, was supervising the pumping of 11,000 pounds of nitrous oxide into SpaceShipTwo, which was attached beneath WhiteKnightTwo.

At 7 a.m., the mother ship thundered down the runway and began climbing to 47,000 feet. Two small chaser jets were following, and after about forty-five minutes they recorded on video the rocket as it dropped from the fuselage. A gush of flames and soot shot out for sixteen seconds as the rocket disappeared up to 55,000 feet supersonically at Mach 1.2 – at 920 mph considerably slower than the 2,000 mph Branson had predicted in Las Vegas. Just after 8 a.m., WhiteKnightTwo and the rocket landed safely back at Mojave. Virgin's staff rushed on to the tarmac, cheering their heroes. Branson was ecstatic. George Whitesides praised 'the successful outcome of this test' and predicted 'a handful of similar powered tests' over the following months, to be followed by 'our first test flight to space'. His enthusiasm was matched by the chairman of Aabar, the Abu

Dhabi investor whose name was emblazoned on the rocket. Euphorically, Branson told Abu Dhabi radio, 'I will be going up on the first flight, which I hope will be December 25th of this year. So maybe I'll dress up as Father Christmas.'

The date was fixed. In eight months, Branson would personally fly into space on Virgin Galactic. His deadline was specific – Christmas Day 2013.

Branson's optimism disguised an unexpected hiccup. Four days after the flight, a group of rocket engineers led by Geoff Daly, the Briton with particular expertise in rocket motors, complained to Eric Berg, a director of California's Occupational Safety and Health Administration (OSHA), that he should investigate possible violations of safety orders on the tarmac before and after the flight. He was subsequently supported by Carolynne Campbell. 'Virgin's operating on the ragged edge,' said Campbell. Both feared that an accident would paralyse the private space industry.

Their complaint was based on Virgin's own video of the fuelling process. The staff clustered around SpaceShipTwo were not wearing special clothing, the fuelling was done in the open rather than in a bunker, and hundreds of spectators were standing unprotected just seventy feet away. 'One gallon of nitrous oxide', Daly wrote to Berg, 'has the explosive force of five sticks of dynamite.'

'I didn't realise that,' Berg told Daly in a subsequent conversation on Skype in which they discussed Daly's catalogue of violations. The project, Daly wrote, had not provided a fail-safe in case of an elementary error and there was no safety shut-off valve. If the 11,000 lbs of nitrous oxide had exploded, he continued, the devastation would have extended over a kilometre of terrain. The spectators would have been either injured or killed. Finally, wrote Daly, after the rocket's return safety procedures had been ignored by allowing employees to swarm on to the tarmac.

Notwithstanding what it had achieved, Virgin Galactic had been hoist by its own petard. The self-congratulatory video of the rocket's sixteen-second burn had been carefully scrutinised by Daly, Campbell and others. To the layman, the black flame discharged from the rocket seemed unexceptional, but the critics' interpretation raised issues of real concern. Frame-by-frame examination, they claimed, showed that the motor came close to experiencing a 'hard start', which could be followed by a split-second shutdown. The soot and haze indicated that Virgin was using an 'inconsistent' fuel which in extreme circumstances could explode but was more likely, in the event of a malfunction, to cause the engine to stop. In summary, some rocketeers believed that after a partial ignition, Virgin Galactic's motor had been vibrating. Virgin's experts dismissed those concerns as 'baseless', even though earlier ground tests by Scaled's engineers of the rocket's potential instability had been verified during the flight. Scaled could by then even rely on Al Cebriain's belief that the corporation had developed 'much more refined systems since the 2007 explosion'. But, Cebriain added, 'Scaled will still need to complete many safe firings on the ground, on at least five engines, to prove it's all safe for commercial flights.' Accordingly, on 7 May Scaled was required by Berg to respond to the dangers alleged by Daly.

Simultaneously, Geoff Daly wrote to the Federal Aviation Administration describing 'the considerable concern' expressed by the 'rocket motor/engine arena worldwide'. After describing 'a very serious situation' caused by Virgin's use of nitrous oxide in a hybrid, Daly concluded, 'This is another accident waiting to happen.' Among those concerned, he added, was the 'gentleman [who] had Glenn May die in his arms'. He was referring to the fatal accident in 2007 witnessed by a Scaled consultant. 'I still want to know', the eyewitness had emailed Daly, referring to May's death, 'if every one of those 500 prepaid passengers know about the fatal accident that left my friend dead with a blown open chest and exposed beating heart in the last seconds of his life?'

Confident in the advice he was receiving from his experts, Branson was unwilling to let a cluster of self-appointed critics derail his ambitions. Convinced that the anticipated $900 million investment was on the eve of success, he urged George Whitesides to push ahead as fast as possible. Ostensibly, he was on a roll. The company had taken $80 million in deposits from 610 people, and his publicists had just secured worldwide publicity by revealing that Justin Bieber had signed up as a passenger. To his delight, NBC, the American TV network, had agreed soon after to sign an exclusive agreement to film Branson, Holly and Sam on Virgin Galactic's first flight in 2014. The network hailed its coup as an exclusive which 'will go down in history as one of the most remarkable events on television'.

The ecstasy Branson generated was tempered by his finances. Despite spending about $900 million to employ over 145 engineers, some technical problems remained unresolved.

On 17 May, less than three weeks after the flight, Scaled was testing a hybrid motor less than one mile from the Mojave control tower. Seemingly unexpectedly, the engine exploded, sending the nozzle and casing beyond the perimeter fence. The devastation resembled the scene in 2007, except this time there were no casualties. Scaled described the explosion as an intentional test of the rocket's stability, but Daly was not persuaded. To stage destructive tests on the eve of commercial flights was unusually late. Given the apparent similarity with the May 2007 explosion and the fact that an explosion had happened so soon after their warning, Daly expected the FAA or the OSHA to conduct a full investigation and make a public ruling on these safety issues. Since the Wild West atmosphere at the airport did not encourage an independent investigation, Daly once again dispatched protests – to the State Department, the FAA, OSHA and to Grumman, Scaled's owners. The response, he considered, was encouraging. Daly believed that Grumman accepted that Virgin Galactic could not operate 'in its current design configuration as there is no real safety allowances [*sic*]'.

However, he was mistaken. On 9 July, the FAA had reissued an order 'in the public interest' to encourage the space industry, waiving the requirements on Scaled to comply with laws to shield people from hazards caused by the rocket. Scaled was safe from any criticism by the government in Washington. Similarly, safety orders issued by OSHA had been rescinded. Space tourism was an officially protected industry, the view having been taken that the development of space travel was inherently risky and did not merit the safety regulations imposed elsewhere in the field of aviation, and that what had happened at Mojave fell within accepted tolerances. Daly's complaint was therefore rejected.

In his search for allies, Daly turned to Professor Tommaso Sgobba, the president of the International Association for the Advancement of Space Safety. Previously employed by the European Space Agency, Sgobba had also been the safety manager for the Mir space station and the space shuttle. Based in Holland, he had become alarmed by Scaled's self-certified operation and its lack of any independent regulatory supervision. But Branson's boasts that the private space industry can 'do things much better than government' chilled Sgobba. Governments, in Sgobba's opinion, were best placed to ensure safety.

Sgobba was a nightmare for Branson. The softly spoken Italian had only one agenda – protecting the space industry by monitoring its safety. He disliked Branson's boastful description of Virgin Galactic as a trailblazer. 'He's not building new technologies but just copying very old ones,' Sgobba told Daly. 'No new principles of physics are involved. SpaceShipTwo is getting no higher than the high-altitude planes developed after 1945.' Branson's repeated mentions of 'record-breaking' were mere bluster. The big difference between Branson and the rest, continued Sgobba, was Scaled's record. 'The accident in 2007 was a true scandal. Every young engineer knows about pressure systems and how to prevent that accident.' The secrecy surrounding the work also caused Sgobba concern: his view was that all rockets, including SpaceShipTwo, required peer scrutiny to reduce the risk of a crash. 'I cannot rule out the possibility that an accident could happen,' he said. 'If people do die, any prosecutor might go through the designs and would want to decide whether the rocket had been safe.'

In Branson's cocooned world, he was only slowly becoming aware of the mounting criticism of Virgin Galactic's progress thus far. 'He's built the world's most expensive glider,' carped Carolynne Campbell. As Branson's deadline of firing into space on Christmas Day loomed – and its likelihood evaporated – he realised he was cornered. Not only was the deadline forever being extended but he would need to sell more assets to fund his troubled project. Some began to suspect that he refused to hear anything he didn't want to hear.

The smokescreen was his airline business. The sight of Virgin planes in every continent reinforced the public's conviction about the billionaire's global empire. Any doubts were swept aside by his choreographed appearances. Like a rock star, he excited anticipation among the crowds invited to witness his arrivals.

Eight days after Virgin Galactic's flight, Branson flew into Perth, Australia. The country had been a source of good profits since Virgin Blue's first flight in 2000, although the experience had been a roller coaster. Australia was a tough market and Virgin's competitors had successfully fought back. As part of his contribution to Virgin Galactic's development costs, Branson had gradually sold his stake in Virgin Blue and its successor, Virgin Australia. Taking profits to fund new developments was normal for him. His most recent sale had come a week earlier, when he sold a 13 per cent stake to Singapore Airlines for A$123 million. And he refused to rule out selling his last 10 per cent as Virgin repositioned itself as a branding rather than investment business. Pertinently, John Borghetti had not used Branson to promote Virgin Australia since 2011. In his bid to recategorise the airline as an upmarket carrier, the chief executive had described Branson's image as a hindrance, but in his latest battle for profits he changed his mind. In reality, he had little choice. The airline was about to announce an annual loss of £56.5 million, and he needed help. Branson had accepted a speaking engagement in Perth and would be addressing 1,700 people who had paid $250 for a 'business breakfast ticket' to hear about *Screw Business as Usual* and Virgin Galactic's recent glory.

Although Branson had arrived in the city at 2 a.m., nine hours later he was leaning out of the cockpit window of a Virgin plane and waving at journalists as if he had just landed. Borghetti was grateful for the enormous interest Branson generated, and as he faced his large audience in a marquee, Branson was glad to repeat the mantra about Virgin Galactic. 'We had an incredibly historic trip last week with Virgin Galactic breaking the sound barrier,' he said, 'and by the end of this year Virgin Galactic will be up, up and away into space. It's literally the start of commercial space travel.' In a short time, he said, 'Virgin Galactic could put 3,200 satellites into space per month.'

None of the audience knew of any facts to challenge Branson's exuberance, and there were no controversies concerning Virgin's tiny business in Australia to dent his reputation. Similar appearances in Britain had become rare. He had last flown with thirty British journalists to Mumbai in October 2012 to relaunch Virgin's flights to India. Shepherded to various vantage points, they would witness his flower-strewn drive through the city, with Branson dressed as an Indian groom on the roof of a black and yellow taxi and surrounded by Bollywood dancers. His destination was the British High Commission, where 300 guests waited to see the celebrity, accompanied by four glamorous Virgin stewardesses, make a grand entrance. 'Welcome to the party,' said Branson. 'There's great food and lots of pretty women.' During the journey in the taxi, he had wondered out loud what he could announce to get a new headline. 'I'll say we are planning routes to Hyderabad, Goa and Bangalore,' he told his staff. He faced the difficulty that Virgin Atlantic had no slots at Heathrow, nor the money to finance the routes in the near future, but Virgin got the desired headlines. His flamboyance once again smothered the sceptics.

His charmed life even silenced potential critics when Virgin Atlantic entered into a formal alliance with Delta in December 2012. The American airline paid £224 million ($360 million) for the 49 per cent stake owned by Singapore Airlines, who had paid £630 million ($965 million) for the same stake in 1999. Together, Delta and Virgin would have a 25 per cent share of the transatlantic market from Heathrow, compared to BA's 60 per cent. 'Consumers', said Branson without embarrassment, 'will benefit from the alliance.'

This was nearly the last throw of the dice. For the fourth year in succession, Virgin Atlantic had lost money – this time £128 million. Branson's wealth could not continue to fund repeated losses. He finally bid farewell to his long-standing managing director, Steve Ridgway, and recruited Craig Kreeger from American Airlines, the very man who had arranged AA's alliance with BA. The appointment was a blow to the internal candidates. Kreeger immediately announced redundancies, cuts and a pay freeze, contrary once again to Branson's homilies in *Screw Business as Usual*. Branson was unembarrassed.

BA boss Willie Walsh could not resist predicting that Virgin Atlantic would disappear within five years. Branson's attempts to persuade Holly and Sam to become joint captains of his conglomerate had come to nothing. Now in his sixties, Branson's own public performance was deteriorating, and yet his presence held Virgin together. With alacrity, he bet Walsh £1 million that Virgin

Atlantic would survive. Walsh replied, 'I don't think £1 million would hurt him but I don't have £1 million. Maybe we should make a bet that would be as painful to him as to me. Maybe a knee in the groin.' He added, 'I don't know Richard Branson very well, but on the limited occasions I've met him I haven't seen anything that would make me want to meet him again.'

On 5 September, Virgin Galactic executed a second powered flight. Visually, it looked better after flying for twenty seconds at Mach 1.43 – or 1,100 mph – than on the previous test, but to send six passengers into space the rocket would need to fly at 2,500 mph within seventy seconds. Branson's critics doubted that the gap could be closed in time for him to fulfil his prediction and fly on Christmas Day.

Branson refused to appear daunted. On 25 September, he welcomed 600 guests, including many ticket-holders, to a newly built hangar in Mojave. His text was Virgin Galactic's future. Although it was exactly nine years since he firmly predicted taking tourists into space by 2007 – as long as NASA's original moon programme – his ambitions remained unfulfilled. Instead of showing any embarrassment that Virgin Galactic had not yet achieved its objective of gliding for just four minutes in space, Branson told his audience that Virgin would soon offer an 'unprecedented range of new, smart technologies'. His spaceship, he said, would be capable of launching a hundred satellites every day! Plus, Virgin would offer the world space-based solar power, asteroid mining and 'giant mirrors to reduce solar radiation on Earth, offsetting the effects of global warming'. And on top of that, Virgin's new two-man spaceships based at the company's space hotels would be programmed to fly guests on an excursion to just 'a couple of hundred feet above the moon's surface'. Thereafter, Virgin would be flying 'to Mars and beyond'. And all that courtesy of a man and his corporation who had so far only managed to fire a primitive rocket for twenty seconds in the Earth's atmosphere. Nevertheless, the applause was loud, especially from those ticket-holders who had enjoyed holidays on Necker. They believed in Branson. His ability to appear untroubled by another missed target had been an essential ingredient in his survival. In mid-November, he finally conceded that he would not be heading for space, dressed as Father Christmas, in 2013. His next target was autumn 2014. The timetable for his biggest personal investment had slipped yet again. Regardless of his failures and faults, he expected that in 2014 he would, as ever, inspire the ambitious and the perennially optimistic by posing as the people's champion.

The reward for his celebrity is influence among believers. It is to his advantage that, in a world short of larger-than-life heroes, his admirers have confused stardom with enduring greatness. Even his limited admission in October 2013 that he was a tax exile drew few criticisms. The reason, he explained from his newly rebuilt home in Necker, which was available to rent for £37,600 a night, was 'to look after my health'. Most Britons believed his explanation that he would not have left his homeland for 'tax reasons'. In any event, he added, he was not liable to British taxes since nearly all his time was spent earning money for charity, on which he would not pay tax. He did not mention the unquantified millions of pounds his companies based in tax-free offshore sanctuaries still earned every year to sustain his lifestyle. The impression following his reluctant admission that he no longer actively managed his empire was of an ageing sun lizard.

Without Branson, can Virgin survive like Apple continues to without Steve Jobs? It's a question he deflects adroitly. His silence poses another riddle: does his remarkable success as a businessman justify his continuing status as a unique trailblazer?

A decade ago, his ownership of global music, media and airline businesses ranked him alongside the Silicon Valley billionaires as an inspirational star. But since then, his empire has shrunk and his relative wealth has diminished. He no longer owns any of the principal Virgin businesses, and the company has ceased to innovate. In December 2013, Virgin revealed that it was even withdrawing from the management of trains, surrendering 90 per cent ownership of Virgin Trains to Stagecoach, its partner. In normal circumstances, a fading idol is of little consequence. But Branson is special. For a new generation of aspiring entrepreneurs, the master still maintains his mystique. He remains in the spotlight as the iconic model of a super wealth-creator whom many yearn to copy. No doubt he has created prosperity for himself and for a handful of others, but any enhancement of Britain's economy and society by the nation's most famous businessman has been limited. Virgin is proving to be a brand without a legacy. The inventor has enjoyed an amazing ride, but his new followers will draw the wrong lessons from his glory. As the curtain begins to fall, his swansong appears to be protecting the money stashed away offshore. Financing innovation, with the exception of the risky investment in Virgin Galactic, features only in Virgin's history. Over forty-five years, the deal-maker has hit gold, but then, like his rocket, his trajectory has faltered. Refusing to succumb to age is understandable, but to disguise his flaws within a book called *Screw Business as Usual* provokes the question: what is the reality behind the mask? The answer is important for his disciples.

Acknowledgements

This book is not a revised version of the biography I completed fifteen years ago. Rather, it focuses on the quest over the last decade of Britain's most popular businessman as he sought to become a global star. Even Sir Richard's uncritical admirers will find the result revealing.

Branson and Virgin did not give me any help. On the contrary, some employees who had originally agreed to speak to me suddenly became unavailable. Virgin's spokesman wrote that the company would not assist me but would be prepared to read and correct my manuscript. I did not take up the offer.

In writing the book, I relied on many people. Most asked for their contributions to remain anonymous. Of the others, I would like to thank the following:

Solomon Hughes, who undertook critical research, was immensely helpful, finding information which would otherwise have been overlooked. He was more of a partner than he realised.

I am grateful to Carolynne Campbell and Geoff Daly, whose steadfast research into Virgin Galactic's fate was invaluable.

Of the others who I can publicly thank, I am grateful to Kathy Gyngell and Dave Raynes for their information about drugs; Chris Green and Gerald Corbett about Virgin Trains; and Graeme Lowdon, Darryl Eales, Nick Fry and Nick Wirth about Virgin Racing; and to so many others who, for understandable reasons, prefer not to be mentioned.

I am grateful to Joseph Busuttil at Merrill, who organised and provided the transcripts to the trial of the BA executives.

As always, I owe a lot to the publishers. Angus Cargill, Ian Bahrami and Will Atkinson at Faber and Faber are loyal supporters. David Hooper, my libel lawyer, has been as enormously helpful as usual. Jonathan Lloyd, my agent at Curtis Brown, never misses an opportunity to voice encouragement. Thanks are also due to Doug Messier of Parabolic Arc and Susan Watt for editorial advice.

The rock remains Veronica, forever crushing the demons and keeping the flame alight.

Notes and Sources

The sources listed below are in the public domain. I have not named any of the numerous people I interviewed. The vast majority did not want to be acknowledged and, on lawyers' advice, it was considered best not to name the others. Where only a date is given for newspaper articles, that is because the relevant material is an amalgamation of several press sources published on that date.

INTRODUCTION

p. xii 'In his breathless quest for publicity . . .' Agence France-Presse, 28 June 2008.

p. xiii 'While business has been a great . . .' Richard Branson, *Screw Business as Usual* (Virgin Books, 2011), p. x.

p. xiv 'We must change the way we . . .' ibid., p. 50.

p. xv 'Among Virgin's strengths, Branson wrote . . .' ibid., pp. 17, 19.

p. xv '"Our vision", he wrote, "is a world where business . . ."' Virgin Unite accounts, 15 February 2013.

CHAPTER 1

p. 4 '"My gut feeling", he explained, "was that we . . ."' *Australian Financial Review*, 18 December 2004.

p. 6 'By adapting proven technology . . .' *Wall Street Journal*, 2 January 2008.

p. 6 '"several years before I met Rutan . . ."' *Wall Street Journal*, 17 December 2011.

p. 11 'His commitment to spend $110 million . . .' Dow Jones, 22 October 2004; *Chicago Sun-Times*, 9 October 2011.

CHAPTER 2

p. 14 'Not mentioned was the fact that seven . . .' *New York Times*, 30 April 2002.

p. 15 'In particular, he described his plan . . .' Ben Berkowitz, Reuters, 18 October 2002.

p. 15 '"He plucks what he wants out . . ."' Tom Bower, *Branson* (HarperCollins), p. 16.

p. 16 'Flush with money deposited in . . .' ibid., p. 30.

p. 16 '"You don't have to be a complete shit . . ."' ibid., p. 54.

p. 16 'They noticed that by the late 1970s . . .' ibid., p. 67.

p. 16 'In 1992, he became one of Britain's richest businessmen . . .' ibid., p. 141.

p. 16 '"For the first time in my life I had enough . . ."' ibid., p. 144.

p. 17 'The halo had slipped . . .' ibid., p. 293.

p. 18 '"always racing to one-up his rivals . . ."' *New York Times*, 15 April 2004.

p. 18 'The winner would receive a $1 million prize . . .' Dow Jones, 2 April 2004.

p. 19 '"If *Rebel Billionaire* is a success . . ."' *New York Times*, 9 November 2004.

p. 19 'His message to the *Los Angeles Times* was similar . . .' *LA Times*, 9 November 2004.

p. 20 '"The show", praised one newspaper . . .' *Atlanta Journal*, 7 November 2004.

p. 20 '"We are building five spacecraft . . ."' *New York Times*, 7 November 2004; *Atlanta Journal*, 7 November 2004.

p. 20 '"Trump may already know . . ."' *Chicago Daily Herald*, 9 November 2004.

p. 20 '*Rebel Billionaire*, wrote a *Washington Post* reviewer . . .' *Washington Post*, 9 November 2004.

p. 21 'Others reported that Branson's show "flopped" . . .' *LA Times*, 15 November 2004.

p. 21 'while "contestants leap over a 350-foot gorge . . ."' *Dallas Morning News*, 16 November 2004.

p. 21 'While Branson's audience fell below four million . . .' Reuters, 25 November 2004.

p. 22 'He even wrote to Branson, saying . . .' *New York Times*, 22 November 2004.

p. 22 '"I don't know the guy . . ."' *Chicago Tribune*, 12 November 2004.

p. 22 '"Your article about Richard Branson . . ."' *New York Times*, 28 November 2004.

p. 23 'Coincidentally, Branson appeared at a fashion . . .' *New York Times*, 13 September 2005.

p. 23 '"My aeronautical engineers", chirruped Branson . . .' ibid.

p. 24 'If Virgin Galactic moved to New Mexico . . .' Based on study by Futron.

p. 25 'The New Mexican government, Homans revealed . . .' *Wall Street Journal*, 16 December 2005.

p. 25 'And no one questioned the exaggerated statistics . . .' *New York Times*, 14 December 2005.

p. 27 '"We'll have a cargo service from . . ."' *Cincinnati Post*, 15 December 2005.

p. 28 '"A number of companies around the world . . ."' Reuters, 29 March 2006.

p. 28 '"Personally," said Branson, "I think there's . . ."' *Sunday Business*, 2 April 2006.

p. 29 '"Stephen Hawking plans to hop a flight . . ."' *LA Times*, 3 March 2007.

p. 29 '"This is your classic Old West story . . ."' 26 November 2006.

CHAPTER 3

p. 30 '"I've got a plan for you."' *Daily Telegraph*, 26 June 2009.

p. 31 'Many supported taxation . . .' *Wall Street Journal*, 12 December 2005.

p. 33 'Like many other dotcom billionaires . . .' Dow Jones, 12 June 2006.

p. 33 '"We need to declare war on oil . . ."' *New York Times*, 30 November 2012.

p. 33 'Together, the "ethanolites" were promoting . . .' The friends' good fortune was a law passed by Congress in 2005 encouraging ethanol production. Oil corporations were given a subsidy of 51 cents per gallon for mixing petrol and ethanol, and motorists received a tax incentive to use cars powered by biofuel. Under the law, America was compelled to produce and use about 7.5 billion gallons of ethanol a year by 2012. To protect American producers, the government imposed tariffs to prevent cheaper imports from Brazil.

p. 33 'For Branson, focused on money . . .' Tom Bower, *Branson* (HarperCollins), p. 20.

p. 34 'His success echoed that of Bill Gates . . .' Russell Hasan, 'Ethanol Investment Claims Bio-ethanol Will Not Be Profitable', *Alternative Energy News*.

p. 35 'The company by then held a majority stake . . .' Almuth Ernsting, *Biofuel Watch*, January 2008.

p. 35 'The project, Jerry Wilhelm of the Greater Rochester Enterprise group . . .' *New York Times*, 14 June 2006.

p. 35 'In June, he won approval from . . .' Dow Jones, 25 June 2006.

p. 35 'A month later, he said that Virgin's investment . . .' *Business 2.0* magazine, July 2006.

p. 36 '"In a few years it will be a major field . . ."' *Sunday Times*, 10 September 2006.

p. 36 'The IMF estimated that the increase in ethanol . . .' *The Spectator*, 18 August 2012.

p. 38 'The majority of Virgin America's shares . . .' *Wall Street Journal*, 2 February 2007.

p. 40 'Senator Hillary Clinton would also be attending . . .' *New York Times*, 28 February 2008.

p. 43 '"Sir Richard usually owns a big chunk . . ."' *New York Times*, 22 September 2006; *Washington Post*, 22 September 2006.

p. 43 '"If you're hoping to stand . . ."' *Wall Street Journal*, 22 September 2006.

p. 44 'The *Wall Street Journal* concluded after hearing . . .' *Wall Street Journal*, 22 and 25 September 2006.

p. 44 'Speaking three weeks later at a celebrity dinner . . .' 17 October 2006.

p. 45 'A fortune would be earned . . .' *Sydney Herald*, 26 April 2013.

p. 45 'He was guilty, wrote one analyst . . .' Peter Lilley, 'What's Wrong with Stern?' 31 August 2012, Global Warning Policy Foundation.

p. 45 '"Man created the problem . . ."' Reuters, 9 February 2007.

p. 46 '"If I ground my fleet . . ."' Associated Press, 25 June 2008.

p. 46 '"Thank God it's happened . . ."' *Boston Globe*, 19 August 2007.

p. 46 'The fund's authenticity was . . .' *Financial Times*, 20 February 2007.

p. 47 'In America, the fertilisers used . . .' Almuth Ernsting, *Biofuel Watch*, 26 April 2013.

p. 47 'Governor Schwarzenegger offered $15 million . . .' 21 December 2003.

CHAPTER 4

p. 50 'Critically, Randy Chase was similarly reassured after . . .' 'Federal Aviation Administration, August 10, 2004, Nitrous Oxide', *Federal Register*, vol. 69, no. 153, p. 48,549.

p. 52 'Friction causes heat, and that heat . . .' For those interested in a fuller explanation: it is well known that the vapour or gas phase in many compounds ignites first, with the least amount of energy, well before the liquid phase. Although ignition in this configuration and scale has not been demonstrated as proof, it is apparent that vapours from the top of the tank entered the liquid stream. This could have been through a leak at the connection or in the body of the newly installed submerged drain pipe. Fluids flowing at sufficient velocity through small openings, as a vapour will, create friction and heat. Ignition occurred both at the top of the composite vessel and in the metal pressure vessel.

p. 55 'Virgin's flawless publicity machine . . .' *Space*, 23 January 2008.

p. 55 'Take-off, he said with certainty . . .' *Guardian*, 25 January 2008.

p. 56 'but a *Washington Post* writer had described . . .' *Washington Post*, 29 July 2008.

p. 56 'Just as Burt Rutan was about to speak . . .' *Guardian*, 25 January 2008.

p. 57 '"Richard lives a certain lifestyle . . ."' *News Anchor*, 21 August 2008.

p. 58 '"We've already had a number of inquiries . . ."' ibid.

p. 59 'Unlike Branson's fascination for space tourism . . .' *Wall Street Journal*, 27 March 2008.

p. 59 '"The signal that we wanted to get across . . ."' *Aeronews*, 30 July 2008.

CHAPTER 5

p. 64 '"Ridgway did reveal to Sir Richard Branson . . ."' *R* v. *George and others*, Ref. T20080944, day 7, para 104.

p. 64 'That allegation would be repeated by a defence lawyer . . .' ibid., William Boyce QC, representing Burnett, day 9, p. 89.

p. 64 'Or as another defence lawyer alleged, "Sir Richard . . ."' ibid., day 10, p. 82.

p. 65 'If Virgin's executives, with Branson's agreement . . .' ibid., day 7, p. 35, line 17.

p. 66 'To conceal Virgin's financial reality . . .' *Wall Street Journal*, 18 May 2004; Reuters, 30 August 2002.

p. 66 'Yet Branson, despite his financial problems . . .' 8 May 2003.

p. 67 'Branson, as the champion of competition . . .' *Wall Street Journal*, 4 March 2003.

p. 67 'He railed against BA's new bid . . .' *Sunday Business*, 27 November 2005.

p. 67 'Few ever quite understood his undisguised fears . . .' *R* v. *George and others*, Ref. T20080944, day 7, pp. 51, 81.

p. 68 'Soon after the decision was taken . . .' ibid., day 9, p. 89.

p. 68 'Moore reported to Branson that BA was briefing . . .' ibid., day 11, pp. 13ff; day 7, p. 104.

p. 68 'Branson, it was alleged, did not want Virgin . . .' ibid., day 9, p. 89.

p. 69 'The two men did, however, agree about . . .' ibid., day 7, p. 98.

p. 69 'Moore told them, "You won't believe the call . . ."' ibid., day 7, p. 99.

p. 69 'Virgin's two executives decided that the airline should . . .' ibid., day 7, p. 99.

p. 70 'Weeks after the £6 surcharge was announced . . .' ibid., day 7, p. 105.

p. 70 'Boulter reported his agreement with Burnett . . .' ibid., day 7, pp. 104/5.

p. 70 'Acting as messengers, they agreed . . .' ibid., day 7, pp. 108/17.

p. 70 'On 24 June, after more discussions . . .' ibid., day 8, p. 3.

p. 71 'On the same day, Branson appeared on TV . . .' ibid., day 9, p. 12.

p. 71 'Branson had discussed imposing a higher . . .' ibid., day 9, p. 24.

p. 71 'Initially, Boulter explained, he was "reluctant" to . . .' ibid., day 8, p. 25.

p. 72 In an email sent to Virgin Atlantic staff . . .' ibid., day 9, p. 21.

p. 72 'Pertinently, the prosecution would decide not to mention . . .' ibid., day 15, p. 25.

p. 72 'Moore, for example, while implicating Branson . . .' ibid., day 15, p. 33.

p. 73 'In his early statements, he always . . .' ibid., day 15, p. 31.

p. 75 'One indignant executive even ordered . . .' 3 April 2005.

CHAPTER 6

p. 80 '"Since our launch in November 1999 . . ."' Reuters, 2 February 2002.

p. 81 'Many customers modified their handsets . . .' Reuters, 1 October 2004.

p. 81 'There, Virgin Mobile was reported to have been . . .' Dow Jones, 6 May 2002.

p. 82 '"There are no plans to change . . ."' Reuters, 16 July 2004.

p. 83 'At the end of a tense trial . . .' 30 April 2013.

p. 83 'The company was valued at £502 million . . .' 22 July 2004.

p. 84 'Virgin Mobile's position deteriorated . . .' Reuters, 28 September 2004.

p. 84 'Virgin had been shunned and few . . .' 6 April 2006.

p. 86 'Virgin would receive 0.25 per cent . . .' *Wall Street Journal*, 5 April 2006.

p. 87 '"BSkyB is dominant . . ."' *Guardian*, 28 April 2006.

p. 88 'Speaking from Necker, he described . . .' Tom Bower, *Branson* (HarperCollins 2008), p. 374.

p. 89 'British broadcasting, he said . . .' Dow Jones, 30 November 2006.

p. 89 '"A businessman's job", Branson admitted . . .' *Daily Telegraph*, 22 November 2006.

p. 90 'Virgin Mobile in Canada would attract . . .' Reuters, 13 March 2007.

p. 91 'While in the past Branson had aggressively attacked . . .' *Virgin Mobile* v. *Orange*, March 2001.

p. 91 '"He never bothered to return . . ."' *Guardian*, 5 March 2007.

p. 92 'The government, he said . . .' Dow Jones, 5 March 2007.

p. 92 'Another 64,300 subscribers had been lost . . .' Reuters, 2 March 2007.

p. 92 'His solution was for Virgin . . .' Dow Jones, 21 August 2007; 11 November 2008.

p. 92 'He gambled that if the shares . . .' *The Times/Financial Times*, 7 June 2007.

p. 93 'Next, he borrowed a further $80 million . . .' *Guardian*, 15 May 2009; *Financial Times*, 12 September 2009.

p. 93 'During the preparations, he approved . . .' Tom Bower, *Branson* (HarperCollins), p. 389.

p. 94 'Five months later, the share price . . .' *The Times*, 14 March 2008.

p. 94 'Within a year of the flotation . . .' *Kansas City Star*, 14 August 2008.

p. 94 'By the end of the year, Virgin Media's shares . . .' *Daily Telegraph*, 1 November 2008.

p. 94 'At the same time, Branson also withdrew . . .' *Daily Telegraph*, 28 July 2009.

p. 94 'He had finally found a partner . . .' Reuters, 14 April 2011.

p. 95 'In its potted description of the chairman . . .' *Guardian* interview, 20 September 2007.

p. 95 '"Like Virgin Trains," he said . . .' 9 May 2007.

CHAPTER 7

p. 97 'In its first year, Eurostar carried . . .' Tom Bower, *Branson* (HarperCollins), p. 199.

p. 100 'Instead, he relied on a consultants' report . . .' *Guardian*, 1 April 2004.

p. 105 'The pugnacious politician had already condemned . . .' Tom Bower, *Branson* (HarperCollins), p. 292.

p. 108 'With skill, Virgin's executives . . .' 21 March 2007.

CHAPTER 8

p. 113 '"Richard broke my back," he recorded . . .' Tom Bower, *Branson* (HarperCollins), p. 270.

p. 114 'Despite Branson's denunciation of those who . . .' ibid., p. 206.

p. 114 'Virgin's annual management fees . . .' *Daily Telegraph*, 19 June 2009.

p. 115 'His philosophy had become famous . . .' Tom Bower, *Branson* (HarperCollins), p. 204.

p. 118 'Branson was furious about AMP's decision . . .' Reuters, 4 December 2002.

p. 118 'In *Screw Business as Usual*, Branson described Virgin Money . . .' Richard Branson, *Screw Business as Usual* (Virgin Books, 2011), p. 131.

p. 119 'His best idea was to launch a Virgin credit card . . .' 12 May 2003.

p. 119 'Unlike AMP, Westpac refused . . .' *Sydney Morning Herald*, 28 July 2010.

p. 119 'Branson had taken a punt . . .' *The Australian*, 12 January 2006.

p. 119 'Four months later, before he had actually . . .' Reuters, 18 March 2004; *Australian Financial Review*, 12 August and 18 October 2004.

p. 120 'The joint venture to provide insurance . . .' Dow Jones, 26 June 2006.

p. 121 'Over the next five years, he added . . .' *Wall Street Journal*, 15 October 2007.

p. 121 'The government's loan to the bank . . .' Alistair Darling, *Back from the Brink* (Atlantic, 2011), p. 26.

p. 124 'Days later, the prime minister announced . . .' Dow Jones, 26 November 2007.

p. 124 '"We have made it clear . . ."' *Guardian*, 30 November 2007.

p. 125 'Just before leaving from London . . .' Dow Jones, 17 January 2008.

p. 126 'Cable returned to the attack. He described Branson's bid . . .' *Financial Times*, 13 December 2007.

p. 127 '"There are serious public-interest grounds . . ."' *Daily Mail*, 9 February 2008.

p. 127 'Virgin's bid, advised the government's bankers . . .' 21 February 2008.

p. 127 'Branson cursed that Brown . . .' Agence France-Presse, 15 September 2008.

p. 128 'Two days later, a huge wave . . .' *Wall Street Journal*, 23 October 2008.

CHAPTER 9

p. 129 'He added, unsmilingly, "We're ready . . ."' Reuters, 27 and 29 July 2009.

p. 130 'Alitalia, he added, should also . . .' *Daily Telegraph*, 16 September 2008.

p. 130 'Virgin America's unusual comfort . . .' *New York Times*, 17 July 2007; Reuters, 8 July 2007.

p. 130 'Just ten months after the inaugural flight . . .' *Guardian*, 18 June 2008; Associated Press, 10 September 2010.

p. 131 '"The bank's demands", Branson retorted . . .' Reuters, 30 August 2002.

p. 131 'His litigation against the government . . .' 6 December 2007

p. 132 '"I always travel with a bar . . ."' interview, *Daily Mail*, 2 March 2009.

p. 133 'The apology from Virgin's customer-relations department . . .' *Daily Telegraph*, 26 January 2009.

p. 133 'The company's flights to Mumbai were among . . .' 12 March 2009.

p. 134 'Branson agreed that Nigerian businessmen . . .' Reuters, 8 April 2005.

p. 134 '"The Nigerian government ignored . . ."' *The Times*, 31 August 2008.

p. 135 'His appeal to President YarAdua . . .' *Financial Times*, 20 August 2008.

p. 135 '"I think Branson needed to understand . . ."' Reuters, 2 June 2010.

p. 135 'At the end of 2008, the airline's . . .' 27 August 2009.

p. 135 'In a financial crisis, Branson's characteristics . . .' *The Times*, 17 December 2009.

p. 135 '"At least if you've got a job . . ."' *Daily Telegraph*, 9 February 2009.

p. 136 '"For some of you," Branson wrote . . .' *The Times*, 1 January 2008.

p. 137 'Although Julie Southern, Virgin Atlantic's commercial manager . . .' 10 April 2012.

p. 137 '"It'll be the end of Branson . . ."' Reuters, 13 September 2008.

p. 138 'In private, he admitted . . .' Bloomberg, 14 August 2009.

p. 138 'In his letter to a man whom . . .' *Wealth*, winter 2009.

p. 138 'Other statistics showed . . .' *Daily Telegraph*, 13 August 2009.

p. 138 'But as Branson's campaign developed . . .' *Daily Telegraph*, 15 August 2008; *The Times*, 31 August 2008.

p. 138 'Branson, said Walsh, "should wake . . ."' *Daily Telegraph*, 8 August 2009.

p. 138 '"Airlines", he said, "risked alienating . . ."' *New York Times*, 16 October 2009.

p. 138 'Branson's condemnation was odd . . .' 29 March 2009.

p. 139 'For years he had single-mindedly focused . . .' *Independent*, 16 September 2002.

p. 139 '"I am absolutely delighted", he exclaimed . . .' Dow Jones, 10 July 2002.

p. 140 'Even Branson admitted that if HBOS had crashed . . .' Fox News interview, 20 October 2008.

p. 140 'In July 2009, after Bishop activated . . .' *The Economist*, 4 July 2009

p. 141 '"We would relish the chance to buy Gatwick . . ."' 2 September 2008; 14 November 2008.

CHAPTER 10

p. 142 '"Oil is too precious to burn in cars . . ."' *Business Day*, 1 August 2010.

p. 142 'Although global aviation was allegedly responsible . . .' Friends of the Earth, 15 April 2013.

p. 143 'Over the following three days, he continued to jet . . .' *Toronto Star*, 14 February 2008.

p. 144 'Friends of the Earth challenged . . .' Friends of the Earth, 15 April 2013.

p. 144 '"Boeing has done five flights using biofuels"' *Guardian*, 27 August 2009.

p. 144 '"Up to now," he said, perplexingly . . .' *Daily Telegraph*, 26 June 2009.

p. 145 'The manager of the fund, Shai Weiss . . .' *Independent*, 11 August 2009.

p. 145 'Khosla sermonised about "the green-technology revolution" . . .' *Sunday Times*, 29 March 2009.

p. 145 'including Tony Blair, who in 2010 agreed to join Khosla . . .' *Guardian*, 25 May 2010.

p. 146 'The federal government advanced a $535 million loan . . .' *LA Times*, 28 September 2011.

p. 147 'Despite receiving this money . . .' *Atlanta Journal-Constitution*, 2 September 2012.

p. 148 '"Richard has been in touch with Jim Lovelock . . ."' 27 September 2007.

p. 149 '"I want to give something back," he said . . .' Richard Branson, *Screw Business as Usual* (Virgin Books, 2011), p. 233.

p. 151 'With a smile acknowledging the applause . . .' *New York Times*, 12 October 2009; Joel Kirkland, 'Climate Wire', *New York Times*, 22 April 2010.

p. 152 'He was baffled when Branson subsequently wrote . . .' Richard Branson, *Screw Business as Usual* (Virgin Books, 2011), p. 291.

p. 152 'He even joined those demanding that carbon trading . . .' 16 December 2009.

p. 153 'In his reliance on Will Whitehorn, Virgin's . . .' *Daily Telegraph*, 22 May 2008; Tom Bower, *The Squeeze: Oil, Money and Greed in the 21st Century* (HarperCollins, 2009), p. xx.

p. 153 '"I think a real collapse of oil prices . . ."' *Daily Telegraph*, 16 September 2008.

p. 153 'Investing in a new refinery . . .' *Edinburgh Evening News*, 11 May 2008; 31 May 2007.

p. 153 'On the same day in September 2009 that Branson . . .' 22 September 2009; 24 September 2009

p. 154 'Its income from the trustees had fallen from $5.5 million . . .' Carbon War Room accounts, 2011.

p. 154 'In another report, he now predicted . . .' *Guardian*, 7 February 2010.

p. 154 'King pronounced in 2010 that the world's oil . . .' 22 March 2010.

p. 154 'Helped by Virgin publicists to appear on . . .' 26 April 2010.

p. 155 'Unusually emotional, he told his audience that oil prices . . .' 6 December and 14 December 2010.

p. 155 '"Because we've been believers that . . ."' *Financial Times*, 10 August 2009.

p. 156 '"We've also been investing", continued Whitehorn . . .' *Business Day*, 1 August 2010.

p. 156 'The Department of Energy, he complained . . .' *Financial Times*, 10 August 2009.

p. 156 'On the contrary, the proof gathered in America . . .' 18 June 2011.

p. 157 'Branson himself had invested in Solazyme . . .' *Australian*, 9 September 2008.

p. 157 'Under the banner of Virgin Unite, he cast business . . .' Richard Branson, *Screw Business as Usual* (Virgin Books, 2011), p. xx.

p. 158 'The charity's principal bequests were £209,000 . . .' Virgin Unity Accounts, p. 31.

p. 158 'The accounts did not clarify all the bequests . . .' ibid., p. 27.

p. 158 'The charity claimed to have generated . . .' ibid., p. 41.

p. 159 'The competition began to attract criticism . . .' *Sydney Morning Herald*, 26 April 2013.

p. 160 'His carbon-capture schemes were described . . .' ibid.

CHAPTER 11

p. 161 'Across the globe, his image as an intrepid buccaneer . . .' 23 April 2009.

p. 161 'An attempt to launch Virgin Radio in Dubai . . .' *Guardian*, 1 September 2007.

p. 161 'Branson blamed supermarkets for selling CDs too cheaply . . .' *Daily Telegraph*, 19 November 2006 and 18 March 2009.

p. 162 'In Britain, after transferring twenty-two Megastores . . .' Agence France-Presse, 17 September 2007; Dow Jones, 24 December 2008; *Financial Times*, 5 December 2009; *Observer*, 6 April 2008.

p. 162 'In New York, an attempt to launch Virgin Comics . . .' *The Times*, 7 January 2006; Reuters, 27 November 2007; *New York Times*, 27 August 2008.

p. 162 'Virgin Vine, a new wine label . . .' 15 January 2008.

p. 162 '. . . and Virgin abandoned the music business.' Sold to Sheridan Square Entertainment of New York.

p. 162 'Within the first months, the £1,500 ($2,940) charge . . .' *Seattle Times*/Merlin Biosciences, 2 February 2007.

p. 162 'In Miami, he told local journalists that Virgin . . .' *Miami Herald*, 20 November 2005.

p. 163 'Once Ho realised that Branson . . .' Dow Jones, 25 January 2007.

p. 163 'Virgin's substitute was a virtual casino . . .' 29 August 2010.

p. 163 'Casting around for other opportunities, Branson envied . . .' *Daily Telegraph*, 31 January 2008; Reuters, 15 May 2008.

p. 164 'Ignoring his promise not to make a third attempt . . .' Reuters, 2 April 2008; other sources 27 March 2005, 27 September 2009, 8 November 2009, 22 November 2009, 23 February 2010.

p. 164 'Pertinently, after the death of Steve Jobs . . .' *Daily Telegraph*, 6 October 2011.

p. 165 'The mocked-up images of the tycoon flying . . .' *Time*, 5 September 2010.

p. 165 'Branson's hope, said Peter Norris . . .' Mark Kleinman, Sky News, 4 November 2010.

p. 167 '"Formula One must tidy itself up . . ."' *Daily Mirror*, 8 February 2009.

p. 169 'But after Button described the incident to Piers Morgan . . .' *Daily Mail*, 7 July 2009.

p. 169 'He offered to help Ecclestone reduce costs . . .' Agence France-Presse, 31 March 2009.

p. 170 '"Everyone is just frozen in the headlights . . ."' *New York Times*, 5 April 2009.

p. 172 '"The prospects of healthy profits . . ."' *Financial Times*, 11 November 2010.

p. 174 '"They've certainly got me addicted"' *Motorsport*, 22 June 2009.

p. 175 '"We're the new car on the block . . ."' Reuters, 15 December 2009.

p. 178 'Converted to Branson's credo, Booth exaggerated . . .' Crash.net, 8 January and 17 March 2010.

p. 178 'Formula One, he complained . . .' 23 December 2009.

p. 178 'Without spending the same as Ferrari . . .' 16 December 2009.

p. 179 'Eales was unaware of a recent admission . . .' *Sydney Morning Herald*, 7 May 2011.

p. 179 '"Virgin cars will limp to . . ."' Crash.net, 3 March 2010.

p. 181 'Formula One, he added, could only prosper . . .' Crash.net, 17 March 2010.

p. 181 '"We're still hoping to be the best of the new teams . . ."' 6 April 2010.

p. 182 'At that moment, a computer glitch . . .' 27 September 2010.

p. 182 '"This cements our place on the Formula One grid," said Branson . . .' *New York Post*, 17 November 2010.

p. 183 'Soon after this latest setback, Branson posted . . .' virgin.com/richard-branson/blog.

p. 183 'Days after leaving Abu Dhabi, Media Control . . .' 26 November 2010.

CHAPTER 12

p. 184 '"Kate Middleton turns to Sir Richard Branson . . ."' 2 August 2009.

p. 184 '"It's a fantastic halo" effect . . .' *Independent*, 10 December 2012.

p. 184 'Together, they had launched Global Zero . . .' *New York Times*, 10 December 2008.

p. 185 'Angered that his group of self-appointed . . .' Reuters, 8 May 2009.

p. 185 '"The Elders", he said, "are in . . ."' *Wealth*, winter 2009.

p. 185 'Israel, urged Carter, should negotiate . . .' *Washington Times*, 28 January 2009.

p. 185 'The resentment towards him . . .' Richard Branson, *Screw Business as Usual* (Virgin Books, 2011), p. 252.

p. 185 'Eric Bost, the American ambassador in Pretoria . . .' *Independent*, 14 October 2011.

p. 185 'Branson denied Bost's report . . .' *Observer*, 27 January 2008.

p. 185 'Ever since 1969, when he had . . .' Tom Bower, *Branson* (HarperCollins), pp. 23, 26/31, 44.

p. 186 'Without the benefit of BA's disasters . . .' 30 July 2010.

p. 186 'He had lied about his purchase-tax fraud . . .' Tom Bower, *Branson* (HarperCollins), p. xx.

p. 187 'In *Screw Business as Usual* he had written . . .' Richard Branson, *Screw Business as Usual* (Virgin Books, 2011), p. 57.

p. 187 'Although he denied having "direct contact" . . .' *Daily Telegraph*, 14 July 2009.

p. 187 'Richard Latham QC, the British prosecutor, intended . . .' *The Times*, 29 April 2010.

p. 188 '"A staggering omission by the OFT," a defence lawyer . . .' *R v. George and others*, Ref. T20080944, day 11, pp. 90/93.

p. 188 'Yet throughout that period, the two airlines were furiously . . .' ibid., day 11, p. 26.

p. 188 'Every lawyer in the courtroom noted . . .' ibid., day 14, pp. 23, 38.

p. 189 'From the outset, the four accused . . .' ibid., day 10, p. 13.

p. 189 'According to the defence's claims, Virgin was refusing . . .' ibid., day 10, p. 42.

p. 190 'Virgin's executives, claimed a defence lawyer, "thought it was . . ."' ibid., day 10, p. 41.

p. 190 'In other words, the OFT relied . . .' ibid., day 15, p. 15.

p. 190 'Herbert Smith's letter to Moore asking . . .' ibid., day 14, p. 39.

p. 190 'Just before the trial started, Virgin agreed to show . . .' ibid., day 7, p. 54.

p. 190 'Herbert Smith, however, declined to disclose . . .' ibid., day 14, p. 26.

p. 191 '"This is deeply disquieting," said the judge . . .' ibid., day 11, pp. 112, 115.

p. 191 'Just before the lawyers ended that day's arguments . . .' ibid., day 11, p. 34.

p. 192 '"That sounds good to me," said Moore . . .' ibid., day 7, p. 115.

p. 192 'At exactly 1.56 p.m., ten minutes . . .' ibid., day 10, p. 39.

p. 193 'In its defence, Virgin claimed that Knowles' message . . .' ibid., day 12, p. 27.

p. 193 'Nevertheless, the disclosure . . .' ibid., day 15, p. 14.

p. 193 'The defence had been denied access . . .' ibid., day 12, p. 26.

p. 193 'Virgin was now accused by the defence . . .' ibid., day 13, p. 19; day 12, p. 35.

p. 193 'Herbert Smith found themselves criticised . . .' ibid., day 12, p. 33; day 13, p. 22; day 14, pp. 25, 33.

p. 193 '"My feelings are of grave . . ."' ibid., day 13, pp. 19, 24, 30.

p. 194 'Moore added, "I might ring Iain Burns at British Airways . . ."' ibid., day 7, p. 97; day 11, p. 46.

p. 194 'Moore then called again and heard that BA . . .' ibid., day 9, p. 90; day 11, p. 39.

p. 194 'The prosecutor revealed to the judge . . .' ibid., day 14, p. 14; day 15, p. 10.

p. 195 'After his client's acquittal, Ben Emmerson QC . . .' ibid., day 15, p. 37.

p. 196 'The OFT's last gasp was an announcement . . .' *Guardian*, 23 April 2010; Reuters, 10 May and 22 April 2010.

p. 196 'Virgin Atlantic set aside £35.4 million . . .' Virgin Atlantic Accounts 2013, note 6, p. 19.

p. 196 'He dismissed a further 600 employees . . .' Bloomberg, 14 August 2009.

p. 196 '"I wouldn't forgive anybody . . ."' *Daily Telegraph*, 18 January 2012.

p. 197 'The masquerade of the underdog . . .' *Time*, 5 September 2010.

p. 197 '"The preliminary decision beggars belief . . ."' *Independent*, 15 February 2010.

p. 197 'Over the following weeks, he fumed that the alliance . . .' *Financial Times*, 13 April 2010.

p. 197 '"I've long argued . . ."' *Time*, 5 September 2010.

p. 198 'Amusing quips and his description . . .' ibid.

p. 198 'Asked, "Is Virgin Atlantic going to be around . . ."' *USA Today*, 4 August 2011.

p. 198 '"Anyone can make an offer . . ."' Reuters, 6 June 2011.

p. 198 'Although the airline, which had 11 per cent of . . .' Associated Press, 10 December 2009.

p. 198 'criticised the decision not to open one . . .' BBC, 16 March 2012.

p. 199 'The Germans were equally bewildered . . .' *City A.M.*, 9 September 2010.

p. 199 '"It is vital", Branson protested immediately . . .' Dow Jones, 15 April 2012.

p. 199 'They had secretly been pleased . . .' *Independent*, 7 April 2012.

p. 199 'Those critics applauded Walsh for adding . . .' *Daily Telegraph*, 18 January 2012.

p. 200 '"The only reason that British Airways . . ."' *Sunday Telegraph*, 11 March 2012.

p. 200 '"We will challenge every aspect of this process . . ."' Dow Jones, 15 April 2012.

p. 200 'He demanded that government regulators . . .' 12 December 2011.

p. 200 '"The decision is a travesty . . ."' Bloomberg, 4 April 2012.

p. 201 '"Whatever he says", replied Walsh . . .' *Guardian*, 30 March 2012.

p. 201 'Isolated, he was now compelled to search for an alliance . . .' *Daily Telegraph*, 21 February 2011.

p. 201 'In May 2011, he admitted . . .' *Evening Standard*, 20 May 2011.

p. 202 'His potential partners were Air France . . ." 27 May 2011.

p. 202 'His contemplation of the sale of his own . . .' Bloomberg, 26 May 2011.

CHAPTER 13

p. 203 '"This can happen quickly and smoothly . . ."' *Financial Times*, 26 May 2011.

p. 203 'Two years later, the regulators ordered . . .' 27 May 2011.

p. 203 'After Virgin Money invested £37.3 million . . .' *Financial Times*, 30 January 2010.

p. 204 'After the FSA, the government regulator . . .' 7 April 2010.

p. 204 'Branson offered less than £400 million . . .' 6 May 2010.

p. 204 'RBS rejected his bid . . .' Bloomberg, 7 May and 4 August 2010.

p. 204 'Buying the Lloyds branches was . . .' Reuters, 25 July 2011.

p. 205 '"We've come to Australia . . ."' *The Age*, 30 July 2010; *Sydney Morning Herald*, 30 July 2010.

p. 205 'The business was later reported . . .' *Australian Financial Review*, 2 February 2009.

p. 205 'The lure was promises of lower interest rates . . .' *Sydney*

Morning Herald, 28 July 2010; other source: 23 September 2010.

p. 205 'Despite his repeated claims of success . . .' 10 April 2013.

p. 205 'The remaining prize was Northern Rock . . .' *Financial Times*, 5 January 2013.

p. 205 'Unconcerned by Gordon Brown's distress . . .' *Guardian*, 16 February 2010.

p. 206 '"It would be dangerous . . ."' *Evening Standard*, 16 February 2010.

p. 206 'In 2009/10, Virgin Group Holdings had paid . . .' 29 July 2011.

p. 206 'For the same reason, his second . . .' Richard Branson, *Screw Business as Usual* (Virgin Books), p. 87.

p. 207 'Bids were invited for the bank's . . .' *Guardian*, 25 December 2010.

p. 207 'The government's price of about . . .' National Audit Office report, 18 May 2012.

p. 208 'With no other bidder . . .' *Daily Mail*, 20 November 2011.

p. 209 'Baxby praised "a very charismatic founder . . ."' *The Australian*, 24 December 2011.

p. 210 '"That isn't the way it should . . ."' Showbiznews, 27 September 2012.

p. 210 'In New York, he told his audience about . . .' Reuters, 1 December 2011; *Wall Street Journal*, 7 December 2011.

p. 210 'Branson's purchase of Northern Rock would . . .' Richard Branson, *Screw Business as Usual* (Virgin Books), p. 129.

p. 210 'Back in the UK and dressed in . . .' *Northern Echo*, 10 January 2012.

p. 210 '"Our customers", he said . . .' *Financial Times*, 10 January 2012; *Independent*, 10 December 2012.

p. 211 'Virgin Money announced charges on current accounts . . .' 13 December 2012.

p. 211 'In *Screw Business*, he had criticised . . .' Richard Branson, *Screw Business as Usual* (Virgin Books), p. 131.

p. 211 'Together they amounted to over . . .' *Guardian*, 23 November 2011.

p. 212 '"This is of course complete garbage . . ."' 23 November 2011.

p. 212 'Other than pledging to offer . . .' 27 June 2013.

p. 213 'Within hours of the announcement . . .' *Sunday Times*, 14 October 2012.

p. 213 'Previously, Branson had offered . . .' *The Times*, 27 June 2013.

CHAPTER 14

p. 214 'The report, "Customer Service in the NHS" . . .' http://socialinvestigations.blogspot.co.uk/2013/01/labour-used-virgin-restricted-report-to.html.

p. 216 'Slightly more helpful was Virgin Active . . .' 7 February 2011.

p. 217 'After studying medicine for five years, Branson's . . .' 28 July 2008.

p. 217 'Branson wanted his daughter . . .' *Financial Times*, 21 October 2012.

p. 217 'Fearing the erosion of the brand's . . .' *New Zealand Herald*, 22 October 2012.

p. 218 'By the end, about 200 doctors . . .' *Guardian*, 9 April 2008.

p. 221 'Virgin, said Branson, would be . . .' 4 March 2010.

p. 221 'In *Screw Business as Usual* he wrote that health . . .' Richard Branson, *Screw Business as Usual* (Virgin Books), p. 179.

p. 221 'Biopsies of suspected skin cancers . . .' 25 March 2011.

p. 221 'patients discovered that Virgin was employing . . .' 'Skin Complaints', *Private Eye*, April 2011.

p. 222 'Based on Assura's network . . .' *Guardian*, 7 January 2013.

p. 222 'The budget was £500 million.' 7 April 2012.

p. 222 'An objection by the mother . . .' *Guardian*, 8 October 2012.

p. 223 'GPs would continue to provide . . .' 25 October 2012.

p. 223 'The only profiteers were . . .' *The Times*, 5 December 2012.

p. 223 '"Global drug strategy should . . ."' *Globe and Mail*, 26 April 2012.

p. 223 'After all, in the past he had admitted . . .' *Daily Mail*, 25 January 2012.

p. 224 'Since the use of cannabis for medicinal purposes . . .' BBC, 31 May 2013.

p. 224 'Against the backdrop of the ferocious drugs war . . .' *Guardian*, 4 June 2011

p. 224 '"Stop criminal penalties for people who use drugs . . ."' *Globe and Mail*, 26 April 2012

p. 225 'In Portugal, they replied, decriminalisation had caused . . .' The Portuguese Institute for Drugs and Drug Addiction found cocaine use increased from 0.9 per cent to 1.9 per cent between 2001 and 2007.

p. 225 'The actual United Nations Office on Drugs and Crime . . .' Kathy Gyngell, 19 September 2011. 4.8 per cent of the population take drugs once a year and just 0.6 per cent of the population, or 210 million people, are permanent abusers.

p. 225 'On one interpretation, the UN's report . . .' Kathy Gyngell, 19 April 2013.

p. 225 'They accused him of wishful thinking.' Kathy Gyngell, 4 July 2013.

p. 225 'The fall in consumption in Britain . . .' *The Times*, 17 June 2013.

p. 226 'In January 2012, Branson was quoted . . .' *Daily Mail*, 25 January 2012.

p. 226 'In a letter to Kathy Gyngell . . .' Letter to Kathy Gyngell, 6 December 2011.

p. 226 'Ultimately, the committee's report in 2013 . . .' 10 December 2012; 21 January 2012.

CHAPTER 15

p. 229 'With unhesitating certainty, he described . . .' *Wall Street Journal*, 8 December 2009.

p. 229 'No fewer than 50,000 people . . .' *New York Times*, 27 May 2009.

p. 229 '"We've had very rapid growth . . ."' 3 December 2009.

p. 230 'Although Lovelock preached . . .' *LA Times*, 6 July 2009.

p. 230 'On the contrary, Whitehorn told *Flight International* . . .' *Daily Telegraph*, 8 January 2009.

p. 230 'He even repeated his unequivocal description . . .' *New York Times*, 27 May 2009.

p. 231 'The justification, said Richardson . . .' *Wall Street Journal*, 4 January 2009.

p. 232 'Murphy pitched a scenario of Abu Dhabi . . .' 26 December 2009.

p. 232 'At the end of July 2009 . . .' *Independent*, 1 August 2009.

p. 232 '"This has been one of the most incredible . . ."' ibid.

p. 232 '"When will you do the first trip . . ."' Sky News, 8 December 2009.

p. 232 'Three months later, Reuters headlined a dispatch . . .' Reuters, 4 March 2010.

p. 232 'Shortly after, the news agency reported . . .' 23 March 2010.

p. 233 '"We're eighteen months away . . ."' Dow Jones, 27 September 2010.

p. 233 'News of the ten-minute glide . . .' 11 October 2010.

p. 233 '"We'll be flying from here in nine to . . ."' Associated Press, 23 October 2010.

p. 233 'XCOR, the small neighbouring . . .' 31 January 2010.

p. 234 '"It's just like launching Virgin Atlantic . . ."' 27 April 2011.

p. 235 'A year later, he told another interviewer . . .' *Forbes*, 19 September 2012.

p. 236 'In the aftermath, others accused him . . .' Tom Bower, *Branson* (HarperCollins), pp. 56, 63.

p. 236 'For years Branson had asserted . . .' *New York Times*, 27 May 2009.

p. 236 'To dampen the dispute . . .' 23 November 2010.

p. 237 'Branson presented the expedition . . .' *LA Times*, 5 April 2011.

p. 237 'Nevertheless, posing with Welsh . . .' 5 April 2011.

p. 238 '"If I were to guarantee anything . . ."' Fox TV, 28 April 2011.

p. 238 'The glide would be managed . . .' 4 May 2011.

p. 239 'Virgin Unite and Galactic Unite, he said . . .' *Seattle Times*, 15 October 2011.

p. 239 '"The tail stall was a nail-biter . . ."' *Space Safety*, 3 October 2011.

p. 240 '"In 2012, we will have our first commercial . . ."' Space.com, 29 December 2010.

p. 240 '"The rocket tests are going extremely well . . ."' Agence France-Presse, 14 September 2011.

p. 240 '"We are now very close to making . . ."' Space.com, 29 December 2010.

p. 240 '"Peter Pan is my favourite character . . ."' 27 April 2011.

p. 241 'Branson's publicists had arranged a stunt . . .' *LA Times*, 18 October 2011; BBC, 18 October 2011.

p. 241 'The expected 140,000 tourists . . .' *Wall Street Journal*, 2 September 2011.

p. 242 'To limit the taxpayers' exposure . . .' 23 February 2011.

p. 242 'One week later, David Mackay . . .' *Wall Street Journal*, 26 October 2011.

p. 242 'The company would need to spend billions . . .' 21 April 2012.

p. 243 'The actor, said Branson . . .' Associated Press, 21 March 2012.

p. 243 'Bassim Haidar, a Lebanese tycoon, wrote that . . .' *Daily Express*, 10 May 2012.

p. 243 '"In the suborbital area . . ."' *Daily Record*, 1 March 2012.

p. 243 'Virgin Galactic, said Pomerantz . . .' April 2011.

p. 244 'Six weeks later, a "Global Aerospace" summit . . .' 18 April 2012.

p. 245 '"I'm excited he's here," said Clinton . . .' Bloomberg, 26 April 2012.

p. 246 'Before ending his partnership with Branson . . .' *Seattle Times*, 14 December 2011.

p. 246 'NASA paid Musk less than $50 million . . .' *St Louis Dispatch*, 26 May 2012.

p. 246 'Musk's $1.6 billion contract from NASA . . .' *LA Times*, 29 October 2012.

p. 246 '"In this field," Branson said . . .' *Wired*, March 2013.

p. 247 'The following month, he flew to Mojave . . .' 19 November 2012.

p. 247 'On one occasion, a motor had burst into flames . . .' parabolicarc.com, 23 January 2013.

CHAPTER 16

p. 248 '"You'll find that prices have come down . . ."' 16 May 2012.

p. 249 'Helped by Virgin's publicists, the organisers explained . . .' *Vancouver Sun*, 2 May 2011.

p. 250 'Unite, he wrote in his book . . .' Richard Branson, *Screw Business as Usual* (Virgin Books), p. 69.

p. 250 '"I never saw myself as a business person . . ."' interview with Denise Ryan, *Vancouver Sun*, 26 May 2012.

p. 250 'Virgin Records was not created to pay for . . .' Tom Bower, *Branson* (HarperCollins), p. 2.

p. 250 'As he admitted in 1986, when his memory . . .' ibid., p. 20.

p. 251 '"Those that continue with 'business as usual' . . ."' interviewed with Jack Preston, *Daily Telegraph*, 23 November 2011; repeated by Geoff Lean, *Daily Telegraph*, 10 February 2012.

p. 251 '"One of the most devastating theories . . ."' Richard Branson, *Screw Business as Usual* (Virgin Books), p. 96.

p. 252 'To survive, he squeezed his costs . . .' 2 March 2010.

p. 253 'He did not explain why travellers . . .' *Guardian*, 25 October 2012.

p. 254 '"There will be an energy crisis . . ."' *New York Times*, 22 April 2010.

p. 254 'The standard rate for paying guests . . .' 12 April 2010.

p. 254 'United by their commercial relationship . . .' *New York Times*, 20 September 2011.

p. 254 'Speaking to the converted in Manhattan . . .' *New York Times*, 21 November 2010.

p. 255 'Financing, Khosla knew, depended on good relations . . .' *Atlanta Journal-Constitution*, 15 January 2012.

p. 255 '"I had the profile, the financial resources . . ."' *Wealth*, winter 2009.

p. 255 'Later that same day, he visited the White House.' *New York Times*, 22 April 2010.

p. 256 'The US Air Force followed . . .' Reuters, 16 July 2012.

p. 256 'His personal relationship with Obama . . .' *The Atlantic*, 17 March 2012.

p. 256 '"Recycling at its best," said Branson . . .' *Sydney Morning Herald*, 15 May 2013.

p. 257 '"Soon", he said, LanzaTech's process . . .' *Irish Times*, 28 October 2011.

p. 257 'Days later, Dr Jennifer Holmgren, LanzaTech's . . .' PR LanzaTech announcement, 11 October 2011; *Sydney Morning Herald*, 23 April 2013.

p. 258 'The government lost $535 million . . .' *LA Times*, 28 September 2011.

p. 258 'Since Coca-Cola sold 1.7 billion drinks . . .' 5 April 2012.

p. 259 'By December 2012, Khosla's second investment . . .' *Wall Street Journal*, February 2011; quoted in *Atlanta Journal-Constitution*, 15 January 2012.

p. 259 'The rate at which new oil reserves were . . .' *Gulf News*, 31 May 2012; *Financial Times*, 17 November 2012; other sources: 18 February 2010.

p. 259 'Huge forests in Indonesia were being burned . . .' Friends of the Earth, 15 April 2013.

p. 259 'paradoxically, in *Screw Business as Usual* Branson . . .' Richard Branson, *Screw Business as Usual* (Virgin Books), p. 238.

p. 260 'In 2011, Bulova named him . . .' 25 March 2011.

p. 261 'After muted applause, Branson headed . . .' 28 May 2012.

p. 261 'When Cameron finally won the race . . .' Agence France-Presse, 26 March 2012.

p. 261 'At a party in a Jamaican restaurant . . .' *Wall Street Journal*, 3 December 2011.

p. 262 'First, he said it was for Virgin's . . .' Reuters, 16 May 2003.

p. 262 'Eventually, it was advertised for hire . . .' *News Ltd*, 11 January 2013.

p. 262 'Instead, Mosquito remained "very much in . . ."' 9 January 2009.

p. 262 'To add to the collection, he was "delighted . . ."' *The Star* (Nairobi), 2 April 2012.

p. 262 'Membership cost $37,500 and . . .' *Guardian*, 23 November 2009.

p. 263 'On the evening, the hotel's rooms were empty . . .' *Wall Street Journal*, 1 November 2010.

p. 263 '"If companies are trading in the UK . . ."' *Daily Mail*, 1 November 2012.

p. 264 'Businessmen, he believed, were better placed . . .' *Wall Street Journal*, 28 May 2012.

p. 264 '"This situation", he told his audience pointedly . . .' *Sunday Times*, 20 May 2012.

p. 264 'His support for StartUp Britain . . .' *Daily Telegraph*, 28 March 2011.

p. 265 'His advice mirrored his support . . .' *The Times*, 7 February 1998.

p. 265 'But with too many rivals . . .' *Financial Times*, 30 December 2012. The group was comprised of 187 clubs with 920,000 members. It was 76 per cent owned by Virgin Group; the remainder by Permira and Bridgepoint Capital.

p. 266 'Finally, a 51 per cent stake was sold . . .' 14 October 2011.

CHAPTER 17

p. 267 '"The Rogue and Virgin brands seem . . ."' *Daily Mail*, 31 January 2013.

p. 268 '"I always wanted Virgin to be a strong model . . ."' Richard Branson, *Screw Business as Usual* (Virgin Books), pp. 16, 24.

p. 274 'Their disagreements became vicious . . .' In its first year it had a turnover of £159,000 and lost £322,000.

p. 277 '"The Age of People", he wrote . . .' Richard Branson, *Screw Business as Usual* (Virgin Books), p. 255.

p. 279 '"Too many business leaders", he wrote in his book . . .' ibid., p. 4; Showbiznews, 27 September 2012.

CHAPTER 18

p. 280 '"Traders appear to think Virgin Media shares . . ."' *Wall Street Journal*, 8 September 2010.

p. 280 'The gloomy speculation reflected . . .' *Daily Telegraph*, 29 July 2010.

p. 281 'Similarly, the rate charged by Virgin . . .' *Daily Telegraph*, 16 January 2010.

p. 281 '"This is simply not credible," protested Virgin . . .' *Guardian*, 9 August 2012.

p. 281 'In a bidding war, BT bought . . .' *The Times*, November 2012.

p. 281 '"We will always be a leader in this space . . ."' *Daily Telegraph*, 19 January 2009.

p. 282 'The script was pure Bransonian . . .' 18 November 2010.

p. 282 'In 2011, Ofcom reported that 22 per cent . . .' *Daily Mail*, 27 November 2011.

p. 282 'The streets, the ASA reported . . .' 31 October 2012.

p. 282 'Next, Virgin was criticised for misleading . . .' Press Association, 9 May 2012.

p. 284 'Posing as a sixties hippy . . .' *New York Times*, 6 March 2012.

p. 284 'Next, he again pledged to spend $300 million . . .' 15 February 2012.

p. 284 'Branson made a new announcement . . .' *Financial Times*, 15 October 2012.

p. 285 'To execute that transition . . .' *Aviation News*, 18 May 2013.

CHAPTER 19

p. 286 'The media, briefed by Virgin's publicists . . .' Reuters, 19 May 2009.

p. 287 'Branson would say that Virgin Trains' profits . . .' *Guardian*, 21 June 2013; 'The Great Train Robbery', TUC report, 10 June 2013, p. 51 (http://www.tuc.org.uk/greattrainrobbery).

p. 287 'The irrefutable truth was that after raising ticket prices . . .' Roy McNulty, 'Realising the Value of GB Rail'. According to the report, Virgin's profits rose after 2008 from 6.6 per cent to 10 per cent. In 2010, Virgin's profit per employee was £23,185. The following year, Virgin's premium payment increased according to the contract by £107 million and its subsidy was reduced by one-third, yet the company's profit per employee was still £19,132.

p. 288 'Branson personally banked £17.8 million . . .' *Sunday Times*, 3 July 2011.

p. 288 'Although in public Branson spoke about Virgin Trains . . .' 'The Great Train Robbery', TUC report, 10 June 2013, p. 30 (http://www.tuc.org.uk/greattrainrobbery).

p. 288 'In America, he mentioned his train company . . .' 17 November 2010.

p. 288 'and during a visit to India, he said that . . .' *India Times*, 26 October 2012.

p. 289 'One particular advertisement featuring Branson . . .' *Guardian*, 6 May 2009.

p. 289 'Virgin, Branson told his guests at Euston . . .' 7 December 2011.

p. 290 '. . . Branson did not mention that his profits . . .' *The Times*, 3 August 2012.

p. 290 'Some were hired by Virgin to monitor . . .' Laidlaw Report into Lessons Learned from the West Coast Competition, House of Commons HC809, 6 December 2012, 7.17.2, 7.17.3.

p. 291 'In February 2012, Furze-Waddock was quietly . . .' ibid., 3.2 and 4.12.

p. 291 'During more conversations in March . . .' ibid., 4.25 and
4.23.

p. 291 'In reply, an official explained . . .' ibid., 4.107.

p. 291 'Leaks to Virgin about the deteriorating situation . . .' ibid.,
5.17.

p. 292 'Then, minutes after leaving the building . . .' *Sunday Times*, 7
October 2012.

p. 292 'None of Virgin's rival bidders . . .' Laidlaw Report into
Lessons Learned from the West Coast Competition, House of
Commons HC809, 6 December 2012, 3.12, 7.26.5.

p. 293 'Virgin had bid conservatively . . .' *Guardian*, 18 August 2012.

p. 294 'After the meeting, the officials were warned . . .' Laidlaw
Report into Lessons Learned from the West Coast Competition,
House of Commons HC809, 6 December 2012, 4.73, 4.27 and
4.55, 4.64.4.

p. 294 'Thereafter, the department's officials . . .' ibid., 4.80.

p. 294 'The officials' behaviour was later criticised . . .' ibid., 4.82
and 7.14.

p. 294 '"There is clear blue water" between . . .' ibid., 4.75.

p. 297 'In a continuing barrage of letters and telephone calls . . .'
ibid., 4.105.

p. 297 'Unknown to Cameron, the transport officials . . .' ibid., 4.95.

p. 298 'Remarkably, at the same time, Theresa Villiers . . .' ibid.,
4.106 and 4.110.

p. 299 'The final decision, Branson suggested, should . . .' ibid.,
4.114.

p. 300 'FirstGroup, he howled to journalists . . .' *Daily Telegraph*, 25
August 2012.

p. 300 '"We said we'd spend £800 million on new trains . . ."' *Daily
Mirror*, 1 November 2012.

p. 300 'Among them was a commitment to start direct services . . .' 4
September 2012.

p. 302 '"Had Virgin won the bid . . ."' 28 August 2012.

p. 302 'The department's officials, he said, had given privileged
information . . .' *Daily Mail*, 5 October 2012.

p. 302 'A subsequent investigation would find no evidence . . .'
Laidlaw Report into Lessons Learned from the West Coast
Competition, House of Commons HC809, 6 December 2012, 2.6.

p. 303 '. . . could not compete with a global star who had recently
boasted . . .' *GQ*, October 2010.

p. 304 'Innocently, McLoughlin ignored the accusations . . .' 12
September 2012.

p. 304 'Evidence of the fractured personal relationships . . .' *Daily Telegraph*, 26 November 2012.

p. 305 'A measure of his victory was reflected . . .' *Financial Times*, 14 October 2012.

p. 305 'Fearful of the idol, McLoughlin decided . . .' 6 December 2012.

p. 306 '"Rumour has it we've landed quite . . ."' *Financial Times*, 14 October 2012.

p. 306 '"Richard Branson and Virgin have been . . ."' *Guardian*, 18 July 2012.

p. 306 'The idea that he had the money or expertise . . .' *New York Post*, 17 May 2006, 10 August 2007

p. 306 'Neither agency could value the Virgin label because . . .' *Guardian*, 18 July 2012.

p. 306 '"We are considered pioneers . . ."' *Business News*, 9 May 2013.

p. 307 '"I'd be very disappointed if we're not up and away . . ."' *Guardian*, 18 July 2012.

CHAPTER 20

p. 309 'Among the detailed specifications was Virgin's . . .' parabolicarc.com, 4 January 2013.

p. 310 'Euphorically, Branson told Abu Dhabi radio . . .' KRQE Albuquerque, quoting interview on Abu Dhabi radio.

p. 311 'Virgin's experts dismissed those concerns . . .' Occupational Safety and Health Administration, 7 May 2013.

p. 312 'Scaled described the explosion as an intentional . . .' 20 May 2013.

p. 313 'On 9 July, the FAA had reissued an order . . .' *Federal Register*, 18 July 2013, vol. 78, no. 138, p. 42,994.

p. 313 'But Branson's boasts that the private space industry . . .' RB at Global Financial Leadership conference at the Ritz-Carlton in Naples Beach, 13 November 2012.

p. 315 'The airline was about to announce an annual loss . . .' *The Times*, 31 August 2013.

p. 316 '"Consumers", said Branson without embarrassment . . .' *The Times*, 12 December 2012.

p. 316 'The appointment was a blow to the internal candidates . . .' *Sunday Telegraph*, 13 January 2013; *Guardian*, 17 May 2013.

p. 317 'Walsh replied, "I don't think £1 million . . ."' *Guardian*, 12 December 2012.

p. 319 'In December 2013, Virgin revealed . . .' *Guardian*, 12 December 2013.

Index

Index